PLANNING THEORIES AND TECHNIQUES IN INDIA

About the Author

SHRI BHAGWAN DAHIYA (*b.* 1954) is currently on the faculty of the Department of Economics at Maharishi Dayanand University, Rohtak. He obtained his M.A. and Ph.D. from Kurukshetra University. During 1987, he has been a Visiting Fellow on a Commonwealth Staff Academic Fellowship at the Institute of Development Studies, University of Sussex, England. Earlier, he was also awarded a Research Fellowship by the University Grants Commission.

Dr. Dahiya is the Chief Editor of the International Journal of Development Planning Literature. He has published several research papers in Indian and foreign professional journals.

PLANNING THEORIES AND TECHNIQUES IN INDIA

A Critique

SHRI BHAGWAN DAHIYA

Foreword by
JAN TINBERGEN
Nobel Laureate

ICSSR Consultant
YOGINDER K. ALAGH
Member, Planning Commission

CONCEPT PUBLISHING COMPANY PVT. LTD.
NEW DELHI-110059

The Indian Council of Social Science Research gave the financial support towards the publication of this work. However, the responsibility for the contents of the book- facts, opinions, conclusions, etc, - is entirely that of the author and not of the ICSSR.

ISBN: 978-81-7022-234-7

First Published 1989

Published and Printed by

Concept
Since 1974

Concept Publishing Company Pvt. Ltd.
A/15-16, Commercial Block, Mohan Garden,
New Delhi-110059 (India)
T : 91-11-41101460
E : publishing@conceptpub.com, *W*: www.conceptpub.com

TO THE LOVING MEMORY
OF MY DEAR DAUGHTER
SUVARCHA "GULLU"
(27-12-1981 to 16-8-1988)

Foreword

In this book Dr. Bhagwan Dahiya discusses the models that have served as the theoretical basis to India's successive Five-Year Plans. By so doing he illustrates the progress made by development economics over the period covered especially by the aspects relevant to India and as seen by mathematically-oriented economists. This scientific development is due both to Indian economists and to foreign economists. India at an early era was impressed by Soviet planning but simultaneously maintained free exchange of ideas with Western economists.

The most important techniques are discussed, such as static and dynamic, few-sector and many-sector models, for fixed periods as well as "rolling forward" periods.

The author shows an amazing knowledge of the literature on his subject and related issues. After having set out the development of planning models used by the Indian Planning Commission he offers, in Chapter IX, a multi-regional multi-sectoral optimizing planning model; that is the mathematical structure such a model could have. This may be considered as a huge research programme, whose realization would imply the estimation of a large number of coefficients such a model is in need of.

Many mathematical economists involved in whatever compartment of the planning operation will profit from this book for a general orientation about the area of their responsibility.

J. TINBERGEN

Preface

Planning Theories and Techniques in India provides comprehensive survey of those development planning models which have been followed or have been proposed to be followed in India. This study discusses the problem of the choice of planning techniques in the planning process, i.e., the permanent plan technique, the fixed plan technique, the sequential plan technique, the semi-rolling plan technique, the technique of semi-continual planning revision, and the technique of continual planning revision. A comparative-dynamic optimising planning model is also developed to compare the relative efficiency of the various plan techniques. A multi-regional, multi-sectoral optimising planning model is also developed to show the mathematical structure such a model can have. A special feature of this model is the integration of human resource planning with economic planning through a general equilibrium approach. This study also suggests certain elements of reality in the context of Indian economy which must be introduced in the formulation of planning models in future.

Planning Theories and Techniques in India is a revised and updated version of my Ph. D. thesis submitted to Kurukshetra University in March 1981. I am highly grateful to Prof. Prakash Chander of the Indian Statistical Institute, New Delhi, for kindly initiating me into this study. I am also thankful to Dr. B. K. Vashist for his valuable comments and guidance. I am also thankful to the University Grants Commission for awarding me a research fellowship for this study.

I am particularly grateful to Prof. P. R. Brahmananda and Prof. Dilip S. Swamy for their kind suggestions, comments, and recommendations for the publication of my Ph. D. thesis in their capacity as my Ph. D. examiners. My gratitudes are also due to Dr. Yoginder K. Alagh for his kind suggestions, comments and recommendations for the publication of this thesis to the Indian Council of Social Science Research for necessary financial grant. I owe an intellectual debt to Prof. Jan Tinbergen for his kind comments and suggestions and for writing the foreward to this study.

Throughout the drafting I have profited from the comments and criticism of a number of colleagues. In particular, I would like to thank T. R. Kundu, V. S. Kundu and Kavita who read the entire draft and made valuable suggestions. I am very much indebted to Professors Irma Adelman, Ifzal Ali, J. Bergsman, L. S. Bhat, Charles R. Blitzer, Ronald G. Bodkin, H. Cetin, Hollis B. Chenery, Giancarlo Gandolfo, Steven M. Goldman, Wafik Grais, Michael D. Intriligator, Leif Johansen, J. Kornai, Arie Kuyvenhoven, L. Lefeber, K. C. Majumdar, Alan S. Manne, Andre Martens, Ashok Mathur, Jaime de Melo, Gerald M. Meier, Takashi Negishi, Robert Pindyck, G. Pyatt, Sherman Robinson, Jeffery I. Round, H.W. Singer, Lance Taylor, Clem A. Tisdell and Thomas E. Weisskopf for their continuing stimulus, encouragement, suggestions and supply of the material. The present study has greatly benefitted from their works.

In the end, I wish to place on record my thankful appreciations for the co-operation extended to me by my wife Suprabha, late daughter Suvarcha and son Sidhartha for cheerfully suffering my involvement in this work.

SHRI BHAGWAN DAHIYA

Contents

ONE

Introduction

1.1 MACRO-STATISTICAL MODELS AND DEVELOPMENT POLICY

Policy makers in developing countries have long been concerned with issues of growth and structural change in the medium to long-run. They have recognised that growth models have serious deficiencies as a basis for development policy. Of course, these models focus on the savings investment relationship and on the possibilities of substitution between capital and labour. But they exclude certain important questions of concern to policy makers, such as the changing structure of demand, the redistribution of income, the allocation of resources, the role of foreign trade, and so on. In this way, formal growth theory does not clarify the relationship among the several instruments of development policy, which must be one of its major functions. As a result, in many of the developing countries much of the policy debate is concerned with issues related to the choice of an appropriate development strategy and of the proper mix of supporting policies. The long-run policy focus is largely on issues of economic structure such as the evolving relationship between industry and agriculture, the allocation of resources between export promotion and import substitution activities, the role of foreign trade and foreign investment, the balance of production between investment goods and consumer goods, and the redistribution of income. In the post-war period, the debate about the desirability of different development strategies has also become steadily more sophisticated as our understanding of the structural transformations in economies undergoing modern economic growth has deepened. The works of Clark (1940), Kuznets (1966), Chenery (1979), Chenery and Syrquin (1975), and their many disciples have provided both the quantitative and the theoretical appreciation of the process of economic development and of the different feasible paths that can be followed. They have pointed out that the process of transformation of a developing economy to a developed economy involves large and systematic shifts in the structure of production, demand, employment, investment and trade. The systematic nature of this transformation implies that sectors cannot be considered in isolation from one another. Bottlenecks arise, and it is necessary to view the economy at a sufficiently disaggregated level to reflect important differences in production, demand, employment, investment, income distribution and trade structures.

Alongwith increased knowledge about the development process there has been an evolution in the nature of the policy tools that have been used to support different development strategies. There have also been parallel developments in the analytic tools to support policy analysis. In understanding and managing structural change as per requirements of the development policy, macro-statistical models have provided the most useful framework. Professor Jan Tinbergen did the classic work in this field. His pioneering work on economic policy was published in 1956 in which he has taught us that a policy model should contain variables reflecting the economic goals of the society and the main instruments of government policy, and that it should specify the more important structural relations connecting them.

Macro-statistical models have been constructed for a number of different objectives: among others, first, for describing the structure and the functioning of a given economy and for explaining its development, and second, for searching means of influencing its development in the desired direction. *Macro-econometric models* of the Tinbergen-Klein type belong to the first category and the *development planning models* to the second.

Macro-econometric Models

Econometric models are generally, but not exclusively, short-term in nature. They provide ingredients, especially in the initial stages, or realism and consistency check. They contribute to development policy in several ways: for example, to test hypotheses and estimate past economic relationship; to test and refine many basic assumptions about the effects of changes in income and prices on consumer demand, and so on. These results can then replace general deductions from economic theory as a basis for designing policy measures. They also provide components of more comprehensive models of the whole economy. During the course of the implementation of a plan, they may supplement the long-term predictions of the planning models with their short-term forecasts on a continuing basis, permitting the planners and the policy makers to take informed decisions on adapting the on-going planned programmes to the revised circumstances. In this way, they serve as a useful intellectual appendage to the development planning models and provide a secondary support system for the implementation of general planning programmes. In other words, concern with medium and long-term development strategies and their impact on growth, structural change, and income distribution requires a quite different set of tools for theoretical and policy analysis than a concern with short-term issues. Thus, the econometric models and the planning models can be complementary and are certainly not independent, but they are nonetheless distinct.

By most accounts, macro-econometric modelling began with the publication of Tinbergen's (1939) classic work. Goodwin (1948) and Koopmans (1950) put forward the idea of formulating econometric models in continuous time. Thiel (1958) dealt with the three basic issues in econometric model building : The *first* is that of the predictive quality of such model; the *second* is that of the relationship between decision making and the econometric model which is used in order to formulate predictive statements; and the *third* is that of the estimation of systems of simultaneous equations. By mid 1960s when Nerlove (1966) conducted a survey of macro-econometric models, over twenty-five major models were already available in the published form. Since the mid-1960s, input-output analysis and conventional macro-econometric modelling have been combined in a number of large scale econometric models, e.g. Preston (1972) and Bodkin (1976). Since inter-industry flow system is an important component of any planning model, in this trend we find a degree of convergence in planning and econometric models. Intriligator (1978, Chapter 12) has conducted an excellent survey of twenty-one major econometric models of the U.S. economy: this overview takes one to the mid-1970s. The contemporary debate on three main issues, namely, size of the model, the purpose of forecasting and assessment of its accuracy, and evaluation and comparison of models, is dealt with in the excellent edited work of Kmenta and Ramsey (1981). In one of the most important and significant work, Gandolfo (1981) emphasised continuous time dynamic models. In fact, during the past about forty-five years of its history, macro-econometric model building has grown almost exponentially. These models are virtually available for any large or small economy and several hundred would have to be included today in any systematic survey. These models had a number of antecedents. The three outstanding antecedents are:

1. The various models of competitive general equilibrium sketched first by Walras and later by Pareto which have been an important source of inspiration to econometric model building;

2. the German Historical School approach to economics; and

3. the most important stimulus to macro econometric model building has been the operational heritage of Keynesian economics in general and the publication of Keynes' (1936) 'General Theory' in particular.

India has perhaps been the first among developing countries for which economy-wide econometric models were estimated. Most of these models, however, have been the outgrowth of Ph.D. dissertations under the guidance of either Professor Jan Tinbergen or Professor L.R. Klein. Desai (1973), Bhaduri (1982), and Sinha (1986) have conducted excellent critical surveys of these models.

Macro-econometric model-building in India is presently passing through the third generation of the model-building art. As nicely pointed out by Krishnamurty and Pandit (1984), the major focus in different models of the first generation includes such as price behaviour (Marwah, 1963 and 1972; Chakravarty, 1977), investment behaviour and endogenous population growth (Krishnamurty, 1964), the role of foodgrain output in growth and price stability (Pandit,

1973), interaction between monetary and real variables in the monetized component of the economy (Bhattacharya, 1975), the structure of monetary and financial markets (Gupta, 1973; Mammen, 1973), external trade (Choudhary, 1963; Dutta, 1964), and growth in a dualistic economy (Agarwala, 1971). The model by Aggarwala (1971) is in some ways Lewisian. All the rest are more or less Keynesian. The models of Pani (1977), Ahluwalia (1979), Bhattacharya (1982), Pandit (1982) and Srivastava (1981) belong to the second generation. These models have their emphasis on policy analysis. Most other features of these models follow from this objective. They are more disaggregated and therefore much larger. In these models there is an explicit recognition of the mixed nature and some other institutional characteristics of Indian economy. The third generation models include models by Ghosh, Lahiri, Mathur and Ray (1983), Pani and Seshan (RBI, 1983), Bhattacharya (forthcoming), Sarkar and Rao (NCAER, 1983), Krishnamurty (1984) and Pandit (1984). These models explicitly deal with the problems of macroeconomic adjustment and venture to address themselves to issues that have not until recently been discussed in formal quantitative terms.

Development Planning Models

During the last thirty years or so, there have been some of the most exciting advances in planning theories and techniques through the formulations and applications of planning models. Recent extensions of the work by Ramsey (1928) into the field of optimal economic growth have addressed themselves to describe a theoretical basis for economic planning. Economists have identified major problems of development and have tried out various intuitive forms of planning. As is apparent from the works of Manne (1974), Blitzer et al. (1975), Dahiya (1982), and Dervis et al. (1982), the field is still open and attempts are being made to formulate more comprehensive analysis of future development possibilities which bring out the direct and indirect effects and interactions of government policies differing in nature. These attempts derive their theoretical background from Tinbergen's (1956) classic formulation of the nature of economic policy which was later on extended by Theil (1958, 1964) and Fox et al. (1966). These developments in the theory of quantitative economic policy provided a bridge between economic theory and operations research.

As is well known, development planning models draw on the results of theoretical growth models but differ from them in that they contain empirical estimates and are solved with numerical methods; are usually disaggregated into many sectors; and involve more complex specifications of development processes and specific policy constraints. The net effect of these differences is to make theoretical models more useful for studying the general character of growth in an abstract setting and to make the planning models more useful for studying more disaggregated and complex systems which include instruments and constraints of development policy. These models have by now gained a universal acceptance as useful tools for the analysis and design of development policy. Perhaps all the formal development plans, both in developed and developing economies, are formulated with some reliance upon a planning model of varying theoretical and technical sophistication. Since it is operationally impossible to include all the relevant economic activities in a single analysis, models are specialised according to sectors, regions, time periods, objective functions etc.

As with other models, development planning models are also abstractions of reality, capturing the objectives and efforts involved in planned development. These models have considerably bridged the gap between the highly esoteric theoretical and technical developments and the practical needs and possibilities of the policy planners.

As is nicely explained by Gupta (1986, p. 29), the usefulness of these models "lies in making the analysis and understanding of the highly complicated economic relations comparatively easier and in helping the policy-makers and the planners to devise ways and means by which the economy can be given the desired direction. In this context, it is well appreciated that there are many behavioural responses of the economy and institutional factors which cannot be captured in a rigorous model frame. Therefore, formal models have to be used with due caution and care. But the absence of any formal model structure in a highly interrelated economic system may result in a lopsided emphasis in priorities and allocation processes in the plans' investments and production programmes. Formal modelling is regarded as a very useful way of disciplining the thought processes of the policy makers and users."

In fact, these models are used for a variety of purposes. They are used to establish relationship between social objectives and the instruments of policy. They can be used to work out the values required for instrumental variables, once the objectives of the plan are given and the structure of the economy is estimated. On the one extreme, more abstract formulations are designed to explore general economic phenomena and/or to test the application of certain analytical techniques. At the other extreme, detailed models are designed to produce specific policy recommendations for a given sector. The empirical content of these models is limited to the specification of realistic orders of magnitude for the main structural relationship. In fact, the major usefulness of these models is not in their particular empirical results, which may quickly become outdated, but in the fact that they enable policy makers to analyse the implications of policy choices within a consistent, analytical and informative framework. These models are helpful in focussing on and harmonising many areas of complementarity and of conflicts. Although these models originated as numerical procedures for solving specific problems of resource allocation, they are increasingly being used as a means of theorizing about development phenomena, i.e., the numerical analysis of the properties of these models under alternative empirical assumptions provides a method of exploring theoretical phenomena which can otherwise be described only in general terms.

The formulation of development planning models usually involves three sets of considerations. Firstly, there is the *empirical part* which refers to the collection and processing of data pertaining to the particular economy one is interested in. Secondly, there is the *theoretical part* which tells us what the appropriate design of a model is and the nature of the relevant economic considerations. This choice of a theoretical framework is dictated largely by the available data and the computational methods available for solving planning models. Finally, there is the *computational part* of working out actual numerical solutions in the light of the first two considerations.

Development planning models have been growing larger on an

average over the past two decades, at a rate of growth that surely exceeds those of the economies being modelled. This is mainly because of the five broad interrelated trends: the revolution in computer technology; the implementation of a team approach to modelling; the development of an institutional framework largely independent of the model's originator; detailed and large scale modelling; and increasing theoretical sophistication. It is a characteristic of these models that different empirical specifications require different numerical methods of computation. The development of their methodology requires an investigation of the type of consistency and/or optimization that is best suited to each empirical formulation. In fact, it involves the interplay of new theoretical formulations with empirical perceptions of problems of resource allocation. On the technical side, progress has consisted in developing increasingly powerful methods of solving constrained optimization problems. On the empirical side, a more realistic description of the structural constraints within which the economy operates has affected the basic formulation of the planners' problems.

The core around which all planning models are built is the input-output framework pioneered by Leontief and its extensions. The essence of input-output analysis is that it captures the crucial element of the interrelatedness of production arising through the flow of intermediate goods among sectors.[1] This framework has provided the starting point for virtually all planning models focussed to analyse policy issues concerning the structure of production, trade and resource allocation, and their impact on economic policy under different development strategies. Historically, these models have focussed on the real sphere of the economy. Such models have been widely used in developing economies because they provide a consistent framework for considering changes that affect a number of productive sectors in an interdependent economy. Different models focus on different kinds of economy-wide consistency. Malinvaud (1977) explains it nicely: "The type of consistency that is assumed to exist between individual decisions is specific to each equilibrium theory. For the study of (Keynesian) employment it can be short-run consistency which will be quite different from the long-run consistency that one would want to consider when studying, for instance, industrial structure". And a multisector general equilibrium model need not always conform to Walrasian theory. Although the equilibrium described may not be Walrasian, neo-classical resource allocation theory remains the fundamental framework of analysis.

The first extension of Leontief's traditional input-output method was made by Tinbergen (1966a, 1966b) by formulating the semi-input-output method.[2] Its special character derives from the distinction between international and national sectors.[3] This method attempts to solve the closely related problems of efficiency in production and international trade through the right choice of sectors and projects to be developed. This method is particularly suitable for developing countries with open economies as it explicitly emphasises the role of a country's comparative advantages in the investment decisions. Through appropriate shadow pricing, the international competitiveness of new activities is brought into the planning process from the very beginning.

Another extension of input-output framework was made by the U.N. (1968) through a more complete 'System of National Accounts' which integrates the input-output and 'national income and product accounts' into a single general framework.

The most interesting and recent extension of input-output method has been made to deal with distributional issues through organisation and analysis of national accounts data in terms of a 'Social Accounting Matrix' (SAM). A 'SAM' can be designed to accommodate the distribution of income in its several forms (functional as well as institutional); to provide some answer to the question of 'who gets what out of the national product', and to organise macro-economic data in ways which might prove more useful in monitoring the process of development.[4]

All these accounting techniques provide a complete and consistent picture of the 'circular flow' in an economy. These techniques focus on the interrelationships among different 'actors' in the economy and impose the requirements that all real and nominal flows must be consistent. Thus, these accounting frameworks provide useful tools of analysis even in the absence of a fully specified formal planning model. The 'consistency check' in these techniques often reveals problems both with the data and with the economic assumptions underlying policy analysis.

1.2 NATURE AND SCOPE OF THE PRESENT STUDY

Both because of the particularly pressing problems of growth in low income economies of the world, and because of widespread belief that the market mechanism tends to be less effective in relatively underdeveloped economies[5], many of the planning models in the literature have been formulated and tested with data from developing economies. India, in particular, has been favoured in this respect: India's long standing commitment to economic planning, as well as a relatively plentiful supply of statistical data, have made her especially attractive for model builders.

In India there has been a steady evolution of economic thinking on questions relating to planning theories and techniques.[6] The availability of new methods and adequate data have enabled us to formulate and try models of more complex nature. Thus, the planning models in India include examples of the best economic techniques available for development planning. The techniques employed in these models offer a progression from the most aggregative forms of planning to the most disaggregative; from various feasibility and consistency analysis to optimising approach; and from comparative static approach to intertemporal analysis. With all these developments, we find the methodology of Indian plan models to be rightly regarded as being among the most sophisticated of the developing economies. This methodology has been evolving itself, on all counts, to higher levels of methodological sophistication both in the conceptual and operational fields.

These development planning models have been and are being formulated to help the planners in their attempts to hasten and harmonize the pace of India's economic development. They explain the medium to long-term trends and structural responses to changes in development policy, focussing on the problems of growth, structural change, trade strategy and income distribution. They reflect various attempts to narrow down the gap between theoretical analysis and its practical applications in the planned development of the Indian economy. They also clarify the very basic nature of development planning models, their relationship to theoretical reasoning and their usefulness to model builders, the theorists and practical policy makers. They contain certain theoretical novelties, a number of practical conclusions and formulate operational ways of thinking about development problems. They illustrate and point out the possibilities of fruitful interaction between theoretical and empirical approaches to development planning and the need to strike a balance between them. They also analyse the direct and indirect effects of specified combinations of policy instruments and constraints on several important aspects of economic behaviour. In the earlier exercises the model builders engaged themselves to explore the implications for growth and structural change of alternative policies with respect to international trade and domestic resource allocation. But in the later exercises, there has been a growing concern about the impact of alternative development strategies on the distribution of income and especially on the alleviation of poverty[7].

The present study is primarily concerned with the theoretical part of such model-building work and with a systematic discussion of the theoretical basis of economy-wide planning models in the context of Indian economy.[8] Thus, in this study we conduct a survey on the question of Indian planning theories and techniques which have been followed or have been proposed to be followed, that is to say, to point out the limitations and potentialities of the Indian planning theories and techniques so that it can be helpful to bridge the gap between the theoretical and practical approaches to development problems and to indicate to both groups the most promising directions for future research. Specifically, the purposes of this study are:

i) to conduct a survey of the methodology of Indian planning models; i.e., (a) to present an analysis of the main planning problems relating to India; (b) to discuss the nature of the work that has been done so far; and (c) to suggest possible areas where more research needs to be done;

ii) to make an attempt to solve theoretically the problem of the choice of planning techniques in the planning process and then to make an analysis in the context of Indian economy;

iii) to formulate the theoretical structure of a comparative dynamic planning model so that the changes in initial conditions, and/or the changes in exogenous forces, and/or the changes in internal parameters may be dealt with. The comparative dynamic model is also used to show the operational implications of the various planning techniques; and

iv) to formulate the theoretical structure of a multi-sectoral multi-regional optimising planning model which integrates human resource planning with economic planning through a general equilibrium approach.

Thus, in the present study, we make an attempt to have a connected, analytical and critical account of all the planning models that have been put together for the Indian economy. In this discussion references have also been made to a large number of models relating to other countries.[9]

At the very outset, we may also point out that three types of planning models may be distinguished, depending upon the degree of aggregation involved, namely, aggregative models, multi-sector models and decentralized models. For a comprehensive planning all the three types are indispensable and are complementary to each other. But decentralized models, which constitute a fascinating and growing part of the literature of plan models, have been left out of this study because of the fact that there has not been much work on decentralized planning in India and that they have not yet reached the stage of computability. Hence, our main focus will be on multi-sector models which have reached the stage of being computationally workable and have been found useful in connection with actual plan preparation in India. These models may also be classified as *'Projection Models'* or *'Descriptive models'*[10] and *'Policy Models'* or *'Operational Models.*[11]

The literature on Indian Planning models has discussed the models covered under types (1) to (8) of the following schematic approach of this study. The present study extends the current state of Indian plan models into two directions: comparative dynamic optimising model and multi-sectoral multi-regional optimising model, i.e., types (9) and (10).

A Schematic approach of the present study

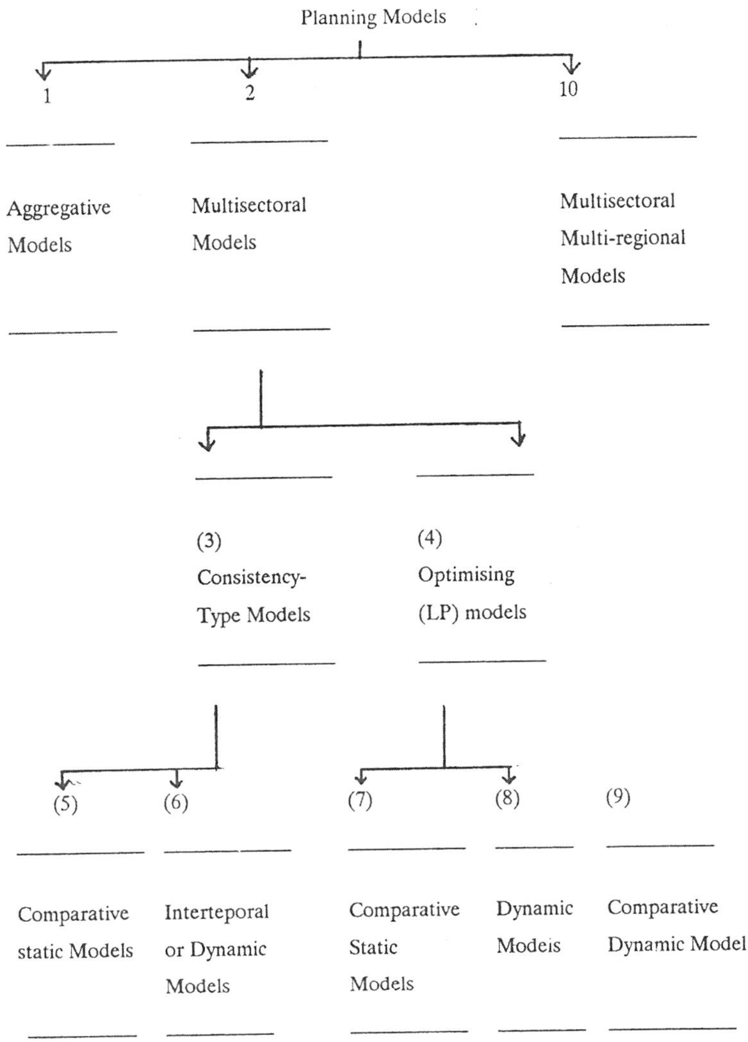

1.3 CHAPTER OUTLINE

We now briefly state the specific contents of our study:

In Chapter 2 through Chapter 6 we conduct a survey of the methodology of Indian planning models. In Chapter 2, we conduct a survey of those growth models which have some significance from the point of view of planning in India. In Chapter 3, we evaluate the comparative-static consistency-type planning models. In Chapter 4, we discuss the intertemporal consistency-type planning model. In Chapter 5, we make an appraisal of the comparative-static optimising planning models. In Chapter 6, we conduct a survey of the intertemporal optimising planning models.

In Chapter 7, we discuss the problem of the choice of planning techniques in the planning process, i.e., the permanent plan technique, the fixed plan technique, the sequential plan technique, the semi-rolling plan technique, the rolling plan technique, the technique of semi-continual planning revision, and the technique of continual planning revision with special reference to India. The justification of this chapter lies in the fact that all the Indian plan models surveyed in Chapter 2 through Chapter 6 have been formulated within the framework of the fixed plan technique. But the rolling plan technique is found to be more appropriate for Indian economy. And, thus, there arises a need to formulate planning models within the framework of the rolling plan technique. Such models are termed as 'comparative dynamic' models. These models incorporate the changes in initial conditions; and/or changes in exogenous forces; and/or changes in internal parameters.

In Chapter 8, we develop a comparative dynamic optimising planning model, i.e. the mathematical structure such a model can have; and also develop a method to compare the relative efficiency of the fixed plan technique and the rolling plan technique, and, then we point out the policy implications of these techniques.

In Chapter 9, we formulate a multi-regional multi-sectoral optimising planning model which can be operated within the framework of the fixed plan technique, the semi-rolling plan technique, and the rolling plan technique. A special feature of this model is the integration of human resource planning with economic planning through a general equilibrium approach.

In Chapter 10, we summarise the main points of this study and suggest certain elements of reality in the context of Indian economy which must be introduced in the formulation of planning models in future so that the gap between the theoretical and practical approaches to development problems can be narrowed down. Thus, we indicate certain promising directions for future research in the field of planning theories and techniques in India.

NOTES

1. A 'Sector' may be defined in a variety of ways, and *'multisector'* may refer to as few as two, but the underlying theory is essentially microeconomic in spirit. Walras, rather than Keynes, is the patron saint of multisector analysis. In this study we define 'multisector' in the sense of more than four sectors. We define a model having one to four sectors as 'aggregative model'.
2. The semi-input-output method has also been described and presented in ten Kate (1972), Cornelisse and Versluis (1969), Mennes, Tinbergen and Waardenburg (1969) and Hansen (1967a; 1967b). For the empirical applications of this method, see, Cornelisse and Tilanus (1965), Pronk and Schreuel (1969), Carillo-Arronte (1968), Netherlands' Economic Institute (1970) and Kuyvenhoven (1978).
3. This distinction is based on the tradeability of the commodities produced, and is similar to Little and Mirrlees' (1974) distinction between tradeable and non-tradeable goods. For discussion on tradeable and non-tradeable goods, see Hinshaw (1975) and Oppenheimer (1974, 1975).
4. For an excellent introductory and detailed discussion on SAM, see Pyatt and Thorbecke (1976) and King (1981).
5. See Lewis (1966).
6. In fact there were no conceptually satisfactory techniques of planning or more generally of making economic policy for development readily at hand when the Indian Plans were first being made.
7. For example, see Planning Commission (1973, 1981, 1986).
8. See Taylor (1975) for an excellent general study on theoretical foundations and technical implications of economy-wide planning models. He provides the potential model-builders with a fairly complete summary of the best practical and applicable planning techniques in general.
9. An interesting study can be conducted on the comparison of planning models used by centrally planned economies with those used by mixed economies. The main difference between these models would appear in the behavioural equations and in the constraints. The parameters of the centrally planned economy's model are likely to be influenced by the directives and the direct controls imposed by the 'central planning agency' and the constraints are also likely to be more rigid (than in a mixed economy model) in reflecting direct controls. In a sense, a planning model in a mixed economy can be said to be more open ended, since besides fixed values of instrument variables to attain policy goals it relies, in addition, on the equi-

librium forces of the market mechanism.

10. For example, Manne and Rudra (1965), Srinivasan et al. (1965), Bergsman and Manne (1966), Chakravarty and Lefeber (1965), Eckaus and Parikh (1968), Gupta (1973), and Planning Commission (1973, 1981, 1986).
11. For example, Weisskopf (1967, 1971), Manne and Weisskopf (1970), and Tendulkar (1971).

TWO

Growth Models in Relation to Development Planning

2.1 INTRODUCTION

Growth models can be viewed in three distinct ways as "analytical filling" devices, as "causal schemes of explanation" and as an example of "instrumental inference". From the point of view of development planning, the first and the third uses are very important.[1] From these points of view they do serve useful purposes. This is true despite the existence of numerous deficiencies from which existing models suffer. The main weaknesses of these models are that they (a) assume closed economy, (b) focus mainly on the allocation of resources between investment-goods and consumer-goods production, (c) ignore some of the central constraints on policy, and (d) study long-run equilibrium conditions rather than developments over a relevant planning period.[2] Furthermore, growth models cannot help us in determining many profound and complex problems, involving adaptations of institutional structure of a developing society, which deserve very careful attention.

However, these models have important implications for development planning. In so far as rapid capital accumulation can be shown to be a desideratum of economic policy, they can provide us some significant criterion for evaluating recommendations for such changes. In matters relating to the determination of volume and composition of capital stock alongwith the choice of technique of production we do get certain insights into the nature of optimal trajectories under certain well-specified restrictions on technology and preference. Even the concept of "steady growth", which is descriptively unrealistic, can provide us significant normative propositions.[3] After all, a capital using economy, no matter who manages it, will need to observe certain directional changes with regard to the composition of capital stocks, provided it has certain long-run interests in view. Thus, properly interpreted, growth models have important lessons for us which no capital using form of society, which is also a growing one, can afford to ignore.

The purpose of the present chapter is to conduct a survey of those growth models which have been already used or which have been designed to be used for planning purposes in India. These aggregative models trace consistent, and perhaps also optimal, paths of growth over time of such macro-economic variables as income, saving, investment, employment, etc. We begin with the First Five-Year Plan Model developed by the Planning Commission team. From this, we pass on to the models developed by Mahalanobis. So far as the degree of aggregation is concerned, Professor Mahalanobis has three models: a one-sector model; a two-sector model which resembles the Marxian scheme of expanded reproduction;[4] and a more generalized four-sector model with two factors of production, labour and capital. It is the four-sector model which has been used as the theoretical under-pinning of India's Second Five Year Plan. Finally, we discuss the wage-goods model of Vakil and Brahmananda.

2.2 THE FIRST FIVE-YEAR PLAN MODEL

The first identifiable planning model used in India was formulated by the authors of the First Five-Year Plan. This model is apparent in an implicit form in the numerical figures of the 'perspective plan' which embodies a projection of an aggregate growth path to be generated by capital accumulation financed largely by domestic savings. This model is a simple variant of the Harrod-Domar Model[5], with a sole modification of the distinction between the average and the marginal propensities to save. The savings function is assumed to be linear. A decreasing reliance on foreign aid is also assumed in spite of growing rates of interest. Capital-output ratio is assumed to be the same on the margin as on the average. Of course, this assumption is not realistic.[6] The model has no gestation period. And models without a realistic structure of gestation lags can not provide details about growth prospects when they are limited by stocks of goods-in-process. Such limitations are practically important, since planners usually are more interested in prospects over the near future. Even if the initial conditions of capital-goods formation in the process of gestation can be realistically specified, the adjustment to a set of balanced sectoral growth paths may dominate the economy for some years, depending on the investment lags assumed in the model.[7] It is also unrealistic to assume the Indian economy as a closed economy for which the model is essentially formulated. Moreover, the assumption of a constant marginal propensity to save for the economy allows this model to ignore the choice problem of planning over time which requires a weighing of present versus future gains. As pointed out by Bhagwati and Chakravarty (1969), the basic equations underlying the growth process in this model are the following:

$$(1)\quad I_t = S_t\ ;$$

$$(2)\quad S_t = aY_t - b\ ;$$

$$(3)\quad Y_t = \alpha K_t\ ;\text{and}$$

$$(4)\quad I_t = \dot{K}_t$$

Here I_t stands for investment at 't'; S_t for the corresponding amount of savings; and Y_t stands for income. All the equations except (2) are the same as in the Harrod-Domar model. Equation (2) introduces the distinction between marginal and average propensities to save. The model leads to the basic differential equation $\dot{K}_t = a\alpha K_t - b$ which can be easily solved to give us the time profile of capital stock and output. We get:

$$(5)\quad K_t = \left(K_o - \frac{b}{a\alpha}\right)e^{a\alpha t} + \frac{b}{a\alpha}$$

Here, we may notice that unlike the usual Harrod-Domar model, the rate of growth here rises from period to period provided, of course, $a > \frac{S_t}{Y_t}$. Thus an economy which decides to save more on the margin than on the average can hope to do better and better overtime in terms of its rate of growth. The asymptotic relative rate of growth of the system is given by the expression a α (for any specific t, $r_t < a\alpha$ where r_t is the relative rate of growth of income at time t).[8]

It may also be pointed out that the highly aggregative nature of the present model prevents it from being used as a tool in detailed quantitative policy making and conceals many structural aspects of the problem of a steady rate of growth.

2.3 MAHALANOBIS' ONE-SECTOR MODEL

In the course of a lecture delivered at the National Institute of Sciences of India, at New Delhi, on 4th of October 1952, Mahalanobis (1961) made out the following three propositions by using an operational model which provides three computational formulae for working out the consequences of varying the rate of investment in terms of varying long-term growth paths.

The first proposition is that the rate of growth of the economy(r) is determined by the rate of investment (α) and the national income coefficient of investment (β)[9], that is,

$$r = \alpha\beta$$

The second proposition is that the rate of growth of per capita net national income (η) is determined by the rate of investment, the national income coefficient of investment, and the rate of increase of population (ρ), that is,

$$\eta = \alpha\beta - \rho$$

And the third proposition is that if all the three coefficients α, β and ρ remain reasonably constant, then the per capita net national income would increase in accordance with the rule of compound interest, that is,

$$\eta_t = \eta_o (1 + \alpha\beta - \rho)^t$$

2.4 MAHALANOBIS' TWO-SECTOR MODEL

Mahalanobis (1955) then elaborated his one-sector model by dividing the economy into two different sectors, the investment-goods sector and the consumer-goods sector.[10] These sectors are assumed to be vertically integrated within themselves, i.e., sectors producing raw materials for consumer-goods are aggregated with the sector producing consumer-goods, and sectors producing raw materials for investment-goods are aggregated with the sector producing investment-goods. Now the question is whether aggregation into two sectors is possible? It is extremely difficult to isolate capital and consumption goods sectors in the industrial statistics at any reasonable level of disaggregation. There are two reasons for this. First, the capital-consumption dichotomy completely ignores intermediate goods, yet these make up the bulk of manufacturing output even in semi-industrialized economies. Second, at the common two digit classifications, most sectors produce at least two types of goods. For example, the motor-vehicle industry produces replacement parts (intermediate-goods), trucks (capital-goods), and cars (consumer-goods). Trying to force this diversity into two little boxes called capital and consumption is unrewarding.

Mahalanobis then assumed a closed economy. In this way he may be regarded as modern counterpart of mercantilists who could not grasp that balanced trade contributes to the welfare of the trading partners. One knows that the importance of foreign trade for development is a continuing theme in the economic literature. Both the classical 'trade as an engine of growth' doctrine and the modern 'two-gap' planning models reflect this importance.[11] Opening an economy to external trade has two important implications:

i. Given trade, domestic production and use of each commodity can differ, with production exceeding (falling short of) use in the case of exported (imported) commodities. Thus, even if there are no production commodity changes, with the introduction of trade welfare could be improved as long as there are substitution possibilities in consumption or use.

ii. In so far as technology permits substitution in production, introduction of trade makes it possible to reallocate resources in production along the lines of comparative advantage, thereby making an additional contribution to gross national product (GNP). Thus, trade contributes to welfare by efficiently reallocating resources between consumption and production.[12]

Similarly, external resource inflow into a country has important implications for two reasons. First, such an inflow augments the country's capacity to import.[13] Second, it enables the country's domestic expenditure to exceed its income or, to put it in familiar terms, it makes it possible for the country to invest more than it saves. Indeed, these two aspects of foreign resource inflow are at the very heart of the two-gap models of development.

The other assumptions of the Mahalanobis' present model are:

i. There is total non-shiftability of the capital stock from the consumption-goods to the investment goods sector.[14]

ii. The increase of consumption is a constant proportion β_c of the investment in consumer-goods industries.

iii. The increment in investment is a constant proportion β_k of the investment in investment-goods industries.

iv. A constant percentage λ_c of investment goes to consumer-goods industries, and the complementary percentage λ_k going to the investment-goods industries.[15]

v. Current production of investment-goods, which is a function of capacity in capital-goods sector, can be allocated freely (or subject to any exogenous constraint) between the two sectors.

vi. The production of consumer-goods equals consumption.

Then, Mahalanobis described the growth path of the economy in terms of the following curve:

$$Y_t = Y_o \left[1 + \alpha_o \left(\frac{\lambda_k \beta_k + \lambda_c \beta_c}{\lambda_k \beta_k} \right) \left\{ \left(1 + \lambda_k \beta_k \right)^t - 1 \right\} \right]$$

Where

Y_t = National income in year t;
α_o = the initial investment rate;[16] and
Y_o = the initial national income.

Thus, the growth pattern of the economy depends on α_o (which is given); the values of β_k and β_c which are determined by technological factors and conditions of productions and are not at the choice of the planner; and on λ_k which is the only policy instrument that the planner has. This implies that if a high value of λ_k is chosen, then, upto a critical period, the economy would grow at a slower rate but once the critical period is passed the higher the value of λ_k the quicker is the growth of the economy over a long period. This is because of the fact that a higher value of λ_k increases the magnitude $(1 + \lambda_k \beta_k)^t$ and lowers the value of the ratio

$$\left(\frac{\lambda_k \beta_k + \lambda_c \beta_c}{\lambda_k \beta_k} \right)$$

Of course, in the initial stage of development, the reductions in the

$\left(\frac{\lambda_k \beta_k + \lambda_c \beta_c}{\lambda_k \beta_k} \right)$ ratio brought by

a rise in λ_c may be larger than the increases in the expression $(1 + \lambda_k \beta_k)^t$ for small values of t; but with the passage of time $(1+\lambda_k \beta_k)^t$ would mean a higher rate of growth in the future.

The development philosophy embodied in this model is that when β_c is greater than β_k, in the initial stage of development the larger the investment in consumer-goods industries the larger will be the income generated. But there is a critical range of time and as soon as this is passed, the larger the investment in investment-goods industries, the larger will be the income generated. Hence, if we are interested in the immediate future we should invest relatively more in the consumer-goods industries. And if we are interested in the more distant future, we should invest relatively larger investment on investment-goods industries.

Moreover, pointing out that the rate of investment depends on how the capital stock was originally distributed between the two sectors, Mahalanobis made out the following three propositions:

1. If the ratio of investment in the investment-goods industries (λ_k) is larger than the corresponding ratio of the original capital stock (λ_o) then the rate of investment will gradually rise until it reaches a limiting value given by $\lambda_k \beta_k/\beta_k$.

2. If $\lambda_k < \lambda_o$, then the ratio will gradually fall until it reaches the same limiting value.

3. If $\lambda_k \equiv \lambda_o$ then the rate of investment is a constant and the rate of growth of national income is also a constant.

In this way, Mahalanobis demonstrated that a higher allocation of investment today to the capital-goods sector will entail a relatively favourable consumption level in the future. While he determined the allocation ratio exogenously, he clearly suggested that the capital-goods sector deserved higher priority in the initial stages of planning. Chakravarty (1969) and Das (1974) have also supported Mahalanobis' this result. They have shown that investment specialization appeared to be more relevant in an Indian type economy. In fact, as Chakravarty (1980) points out, in the 1960s a number of economists demonstrated that if the utility function was additively separable overtime, the optimal solution justified even a much stronger result than Mahalanobis' conclusion. They also pointed out that the optimal solution in this model would show either investment specialization or consumer specialization in the initial phases except for a razor's edge case which could in practice be ignored. This result was partly tested by Weitzman (1971) who relaxed the assumption of vertically integrated sectors and concluded that if there were no initial excess capacity in the system, then the three-sector model which allows for the existence of a pure intermediate sector need not differ in any essential way from the two sector model. The result would obviously extend if more than one pure intermediate sector was assumed.

As pointed out by Fox et al. (1966) the present model can be applied to a fixed or flexible target policy problem. For example, in the case of fixed target policy problem, it would be solved in terms of the λs which are the instrument variables, given a fixed pre-determined level of income at period t. In this sense the problem becomes a simple one-instrument one-fixed-target problem.[17] Alternatively, if national income is a flexible target, the policy problem consists of maximizing it, given a time horizon t. Thus, the programming formulation of the Mahalanobis's model becomes the following:[18]

$$\text{Maximize } Y_t = C_t + I_t \tag{1}$$

Subject to

$$I_t \leq I_{t-1} + \lambda_k \beta_k I_{t-1} \tag{2}$$

$$C_t \leq C_{t-1} + \lambda_c \beta_c I_{t-1} \tag{3}$$

$$Y_t = I_t + C_t, \qquad \lambda_k + \lambda_c = 1 \tag{4}$$

$$I_t \geq o, C_t \geq 0, \quad 0 \leq \lambda_k \leq 1 \tag{5}$$

$$\sum_{t=0}^{T} I_t \leq I_s \quad \text{for all } t = 1, \ldots, T$$

Where I_t = Investment in year t;

I_s = The total investment available over the whole period 1,2,...,T; and

C_t = Consumption in year t.

Chakravarty (1980) points out that the main limitation of the Mahalanobis model with regard to India is in its treatment of 'real wage' implicit in the model. Another unduly optimistic assumption of this model is a fixed capital-output ratio based on ignoring diminishing returns forever in Indian economy where food constitutes a primary constituent of the real wage basket and agriculture depends largely on land.

2.5 MAHALANOBIS' FOUR-SECTOR MODEL

Mahalanobis' (1955) four-sector model is an elaboration of his two-sector model. He divides the economy into four sectors, viz, (1) basic investment goods(k); (2) factory consumer goods (C.1); (3) household industries, including agriculture (C.2); and (4) services (C.3). For simplicity, let us term these sectors as sectors K, 1,2, and 3. The C.2-sector is further splitted up into two sub-sectors; (i) agriculture; and (ii) small and household enterprises.

The increase in national income (E), the investment (A), and the employment (N) are treated as variables. But the ratio of net income generated to capital investment β_k, β_1, β_2 and β_3; and the net investment required per engaged person θ_k, θ_1, θ_2 and θ_3, respectively, for each of the four sectors behave as parameters. The respective values of β's and θ's are assumed to remain more or less constant and, thus, are not sought to be influenced by planning during the period under consideration. The allocation ratios λ_k, λ_1, λ_2 and λ_3 also behave as parameters in the sense that they do not change during the planning period. The β's are assumed to be determined by the production conditions and the sectoral pattern of investments and, thus, are not influenced directly or explicitly by planning during the planning period. But the λ's are directly influenced by the planning and are assumed to be at the choice of the planner, of course, within certain limits. The value of $\lambda_k = 0.22$ is decided from considerations of long period changes; and the values of λ_1 λ_2, and λ_3 are obtained by solving the given set of simultaneous equations.

A target of total asset formation during the plan-period of five years is taken to be equal to Rs. 5600 crores on the basis of an average rate of investment of 9 per cent and from other considerations of financial resources. The rate of increase of national income (η) is assumed to be 5 per cent per year; and the number of total new employment to be generated during the planning period is taken to be equal to eleven millions. With these targets, the model is solved with the help of simultaneous equations; and, thus, by assuming the values of θ's and, β's the sectoral results with respect to A, E and N are obtained for the plan period. Further, by splitting up the C.2-Sector into two sub-sectors, i.e., (i) agriculture and (ii) small and household enterprises; and by assuming the values of β_h, θ_a and θ_h (where the subscripts a and h are used for the sector of agriculture and for the sector of household enterprises, respectively) the values of β_a, A_a, A_h, E_a, E_h, N_a and N_h are obtained.

Thus, corresponding to the four sectors, there were four output/capital ratios, β's, four capital/labour ratios, θ's; and four allocation parameters, λ's, showing the ratio of investment of each sector to the total investment. The allocation problem was presented by the following system of equations:

$$E_k + E_1 + E_2 + E_3 = E$$

$$N_k + N_1 + N_2 + N_3 = N$$

$$A_K + A_1 + A_2 + A_3 = A$$

in which E, N, A, were assumed as arbitrary exogenous variables.

"E_j's" represented sectoral increases in income;

"N_j's" represented sectoral increases in employment;

"A_j's" represented sectoral increases in investment; and

$$\sum_j E_j = E, \sum_j N_j = N \text{ and } \sum_j A_j = A$$

when j = sectors 1,2,3,K.

Hence the above system of equations could be rewritten as:

$$\lambda_k B_k A + \lambda_1 \beta_1 A + \lambda_2 \beta_2 A + \lambda_3 \beta_3 A = E$$

$$\lambda_k A/\theta_k + \lambda_1 A/\theta_1 + \lambda_2 A/\theta_2 + \lambda_3 A/\theta_3 = N$$

$$\lambda_k A + \lambda_1 A + \lambda_2 A + \lambda_3 A = A$$

The above system had three equations and four unknowns, λ's, of which λ_k was determined by the two-sector model. Thus the remaining three unknowns, λ_1, λ_2 and λ_3, could uniquely be solved from the above system of equations.

The Mahalanobis model has been evaluated analytically by several economists such as Bhagwati and Chakravarty (1969), Chakravarty (1968), Ghosh (1959), Fox et al. (1966)[19], Komiya (1959), Leela and Somasekhara (1972)[20], Little (1961), Mitra (1957), Prasad (1966), Raj (1961), Raj and Sen (1961)[21], Rudra (1975), Sengupta and Tintner (1963), Sengupta and Rao (1963), Streeton (1972), Taylor (1979), Tsuru (1957), Weitzman (1971), etc. This model engendered the following major criticisms:

1. The values placed on a number of coefficients have been shown to be quite questionable if not downright invalid. This criticism is particularly serious in view of the high degree of sensitivity of the solution set to small changes in these coefficients. There is no justification why λ_k, instead of other allocation ratios, should be taken as given exogenously.

2. The assumption of θ's being independent of β's is unrealistic. λ's are used in such a way as to suggest investment to be a single homogenous fund. Moreover, Mahalanobis also ignored the problem of timing of income increases and the gestation periods of investments.

3. Komiya shows that a simple linear programming exercise can show the inefficiency of the Mahalanobis' allocations as his solution is situated in the interior of the feasibility locus between incremental output and incremental employment.

4. Tsuru also finds himself unreconciled to the following statement of Mahalanobis:

"With an amount of total asset formation and with any given set of values of the β coefficient there would be, in principle, an optimum allocation of resources in relation to the basic objectives".

Rather, Tsuru's claim is that "the solving as such of a system of simultaneous equations of the kind set up by Mahalanobis is no guarantee that an 'optimum' will be struck". Moreover, he points out Mahalanobis' mistake of identifying investment with the output of sector-K. Similarly, Mitra explores some of Tsuru's comments in a little more detail and points out that Tsuru's rebuttal of the Mahalanobis' claim of optimum solution is indeed valid.

5. Although theoretically relevant and meaningful, it is practically impossible to implement the division of investment along Keynesian lines.

6. The Mahalanobis model is completely supply-oriented and does not make any allowance for demand considerations.

7. Mahalanobis' model, like Fel'dman and Domar models, in its concentration on technical rigidities in production plays down the importance of savings limitations on growth.[22]

8. As Rudra notes, Mahalanobis talked in a deliberately vague fashion about using data from different sources. He ignored totally the averaging technique and the way the coefficients for the intermediate goods industries are combined with those of the final goods industries. He never spelled out the statistical source of the parameters relating to labour-output and capital-output ratios. He also made no attempt to reconcile the model with the real situation, especially the presence of an open economy.

2.6 THE WAGE-GOODS MODEL OF BRAHMANANDA AND VAKIL

Brahmananda and Vakil (1956) put forward an excellent alternative approach to Indian planning at the time of the Second Five-Year

Plan formulation.[23] They neither imitated the growth models of developed countries nor followed the development strategy of the U.S.S.R. Their approach is fundamentally different from that of Mahalanobis. While the latter's whole emphasis is on the role of fixed capital, Vakil and Brahmananda's entire emphasis is on the role of wage-goods as capital.[24] As against the Mahalanobis' approach of unbalanced expansion of certain types of industries, their method of attack comprises an unbalanced expansion in regard to output of commodities. The social welfare function implicit in their approach is to minimize the time needed to reach full employment at reasonable levels of real wages.

They made the following assumptions to formalize their model:

1. There exists a large mass of disguised unemployment.

2. The wages are paid as advances in the beginning of the production period.[25]

3. The disguised unemployed must possess considerable savings potential since labour could be transferred from agriculture without lowering payment of wages consisting exclusively of food.[26]

4. The wage-good was assumed to be exclusively food.[27]

5. Labour could produce capital-goods without the assistance of other factors of production.

6. A mechanism existed by which average consumption on the farm could be kept constant subsequent to the transfer of labour, and the transferred labour's consumption on the farm be siphoned off to feed it while it was engaged in producing capital-goods. To be sure, the possibility of leakage in this connection is also recognised.

7. The whole of the hypothetical surplus might not be procurable and there might be a need to provide for slightly higher consumption levels than in agriculture to workers engaged in construction.

8. Investment and consumption are complementary and not competitive.

9. It is investment which is a variable and total investment is a multiple of the initial increase in investment financed by a given increase in the supply of wage-goods.

10. The investment potential concealed in relatively uneconomic techniques of production is different from that which is concealed in mass disguised unemployment.

11. The 'consumption multiplier', like Keynes multiplier, is to be understood in terms of equilibrium analysis.

The main propositions of Brahmananda-Vakil model can be summarized in the following terms:

1. The transformation of disguised unemployed into productive workers is prevented by the inelasticity in the supply of wage-goods. Thus, unemployment is only due to the prevalence of the wage-goods gap.[28] It is the inability of the economy to provide in the short-run the required surplus of wage-goods which is necessary to employ the disguised unemployed in investment, and that inhibits expansion in employment and in investment. Through a quick expansion of the output of wage-goods, a substantial proportion of disguised unemployed are transformed into productive workers. A major portion of this work-force will become available for employment in investment activities other than those connected with the wage-goods production.

2. The problem of unemployment and its consequent effects upon the standards of living can be overcome by supplementing domestic production through imports of wage-goods and/or by increasing the marketable surplus at home through export of population.[29] To the extent that the wage-goods gap is made good through domestic resources, mere importation of equipments cannot step up the volume of employment potential and hence of employment. The inflow of large quantities of equipments cannot reverse the trend towards retrogression.

3. The most important item in the wage-goods category is food. Land is the basic factor of production whose availability sets a limit to the expansion of food output. An increase in the productivity of land, other conditions being given, increases the net marketable surplus. It enables an increase to a multiplied extent of employment in investment. Therefore, the general emphasis upon new technological change should be on the discovery and invention of ways and means by which productivity of land can be increased. In this way, rapid technological progress does not lead to unemployment. The main emphasis in the wage-goods model is upon unemployment and capital accumulation, and the present approach seeks to harness the potentialities contained in technological progress and organisational changes.

4. In developing economies there is also an existence of mass employment in relatively inefficient methods of production.[30] The money value of the wage-goods consumed by a unit of labour in the inefficient methods of production is higher than the money value of the wage-goods consumed by the disguised unemployed. As the former, to a large extent, would have obtained wage-paid employment in the economy, their deployment in investment activities would not create any additional heavy pressures on the supplies of wage-goods. The money value of the wage-goods of almost all the labour force at present eking out its livelihood in investment in uneconomic methods of production, if released for investment purposes, would tend to bring about a substantial increase in the ratio of investment to employment.[31]

5. Through an adequate measure of forced savings, it should be possible to reduce the population pressure on land and to employ the labour force thus released in projects concerning the expansion of wage-goods and capital-goods industries. This in turn would enable the economy to reduce the proportion of the disguised unemployed to nil and thus to obtain a state of full employment.

6. A consumption multiplier formula is derived in which the multiplicant is an autonomous increase in the stock of wage-goods

in the hands of the planning agency. It will tell us how much investment will go up as a result of a given increase in the supply of wage-goods.[32] In it the relationship is between an increase in the supply of consumer-goods and increase in investment made possible thereby. It will also tell us by how much the consumption of wage-goods in the economy will have to go down, if a given increase in investment has to be self-financing.[33]

Brahmananda and Vakil suggest the following three stages of economic planning for implementation of their wage-goods strategy:

1. In the first stage of planning we should raise the rate of investment through forced and voluntary savings as the increase in employment in investment would be a multiple of the extent of resources thus obtained. Simultaneously, we should also introduce adequate organisational changes in the agricultural sector to bring about that rate of reduction in the proportion of disguised unemployment which is necessary in view of the planned expansion in investment. A major proportion of the new investments should go to the wage-goods sector so that the rate of growth of output of wage-goods is raised substantially above the rate of growth of population. Thus, the ratio of net revenue to capital stock would keep on rising and the rate of new employment in investment would always tend to be multiple of the extent of this rise determined by the value of the accumulation coefficient.[34]

2. In the second stage of planning we should concentrate our emphasis upon the development of capital-goods sector catering to the requirements of the consumer-goods sector.

3. In the third stage of planning we should initiate a quick rate of expansion in the standard of living of the labour-force in the economy. In this stage, it should be possible to develop various luxury industries and to provide for a substantial extent of outlay in regard to social amenities and other welfare services.

In this way the entire planning process becomes employment and accumulation oriented from the very beginning. All the improvements in technical progress would be absorbed in the economy. This process would result in a rise in the rate of accumulation in the initial stages and a rise in the standard of living later on.

Of course, the wage-goods approach to development is based upon the actual working of the Indian economy. But its main limitation, as pointed out by Bhagwati and Chakravarty (1969), is the assumption of a simple Austrian type economy: Labour → Capital-goods → Consumer-goods. The circular model of Marx and Leontief clearly points out that labour alone cannot solve the problem of greater capital formation.

Mainland China is the only country which has followed the wage-goods strategy. This approach requires a certain level of political will and the institutional mechanism to mobilise the limited domestic food surpluses for consumption of wage earners without causing the prices of food to rise in relation to those in the non-agricultural sector. These price increases have discouraged policy makers from following this strategy.[35]

The production increase necessary to release the wage-goods constraint depends upon the functioning of agricultural sector which operates under the diminishing returns. It can be achieved largely through technological change. But these technologies vary substantially in their distributive bias.[36] Therefore, they have important implications for the generation of employment directly in the agricultural sector. Moreover, the different demand elasticities among various income classes of wage-goods producers also affect the size of the marketable surplus of the wage-goods that is generated by the agricultural sector. The initial employment effect, and the consequent size of the marketable surplus, thus, in turn, affect the prices of wage-goods relative to non-wage-goods output as well as the level of real wages in the non-wage-goods sector. In this way, these factors are crucial in determining the rate at which the wage-goods constraint is released and off-farm employment is generated.[37]

NOTES

1. See Chakravarty (1980) for an excellent study on the relevance of growth models to development planning. Mathur (1979) outlines the logical difficulties of an economic nature encountered in the application of growth models to planned development. He discusses the applicability of the essen-

tial aspects of Keynesian and Robinsonian analyses to development planning. In an excellent study Koopman (1967) surveys the results of optimal aggregate economic growth models; and comments on the difficulties encountered and the desirable directions of further research.

2. The problem of optimal growth paths over time has been studied only under assumptions that are rather far from those which describe the policy choices faced by a developing economy. See, for example, Goodwin (1961), Stoleru (1965) and Uzawa (1964).
3. See Mathur (1965).
4. The Marxian two-sector growth model has been transformed independently into rigorous mathematical models of economic growth by Feldman in the Soviet Union of Russia and by Mahalanobis in India. Using the basic Marxian assumptions, but in a more formal framework, they have demonstrated that the rate of growth of the production of consumer-goods is a function of the share of investment in the producer-goods sector and its productivity there. Unlike the Marxian model of expanded reproduction, however, these two models could provide the planners with alternative plan variants showing what sectoral investment rates would be required to achieve various growth rates in income and consumption. It would, however, be clear that these models are valid under certain possibly untenable assumptions and are certainly non-optimizing. But the Harrod-Domar model relies largely on a capital theory of value in contrast to the Ricardo-Marx labour theory of value. While labour can be introduced into the system, it must be at a constant ratio of capital to labour. Just as Ricardo and Malthus made no provision for the effects of technological change, so did the Harrod-Domar model. The weaknesses of the Harrod-Domar model of growth led economists to explore more complex theories which allowed for changes in wage rates, as well as in interest rates, and substitutions of labour and capital for each other. For example, see the neo-classical models of growth, particularly Solow (1956, 1970) and Meade (1961).
5. Although Harrod (1939) is primarily concerned with the cyclical aspects of differences between the limits of growth set by the supply of capital and the supply of labour, his relations can be interpreted as a simple policy model of development alternatives. His model thus interpreted contains two equations corresponding to the supply-demand balances for capital and labour. If all the parameters are fixed, the maximum rate of growth will be determined by one of the two equations, and either capital or labour will be in excess supply. In his terminology the labour determined solution gives the 'natural' rate of growth and the capital-determined solution the 'warranted' rate of growth. In a policy model, however, some of the parameters become variables as, for example, the savings rate and growth rate at full employment. An increase in the rate of growth often requires a change in the structure of production in order to reduce the ratio of imports to total output. But Harrod ignores the balance of payments limitation to growth.
6. See Kuznets (1971) for a thoughtful review of the evidence regarding levels and stability of aggregate capital-output ratios.
7. This is the reason why authors such as Eckaus and Parikh (1968) and Chakravarty and Lefeber (1965) go to great lengths to include gestation lags in their models.
8. The technical note on the Sixth Plan of India (Planning Commission, 1981) presents the Harrod-Domar equation of the First Five Year Plan in the following simplified form:

$$V_t = V_o + \sum_{t=o}^{4} I_t^* ICOR^{-1} \text{ ; and}$$

$$I_t = V_t(1 - B)$$

Where

T = 5th Year (Terminal Period);
V = Value added, base year;
I^o = New investment;
ICOR = Incremental Capital-Value added ratio; and
B = Average propensity to consume.

9. β is the inverse of the marginal capital coefficient.
10. The present model is similar to the one developed by Fel'dman in the Soviet Union in the 1920s and later reviewed by Domar (1957) in an appropriate form. King (1989) makes an excellent comparison of the Mahalanobis and Feldman-Domar Models and concludes that they are strikingly similar and have very few differences of substance. Both lead to virtually identical policy prescriptions. Thus, these models should be considered as one model, i.e., the Feldman-Domar-Mahalanobis model.
11. One way to view the two-gap approach is as an extension of Harrod-Domar planning to economies with foreign trade, and it was so popularised by Chenery and Bruno (1962) and Chenery and Mac Ewan (1966). But more profoundly, two-gap models trace back to ideas about 'external stagulation' of under-developed countries proposed by Latin American structuralist economists Hirschman (1958) and Furtado (1964).
12. The extent of improvement in efficiency brought out by trade depends on the extent to which a country relies on trade.
13. This is always true in the short-run whether the capital inflow is in the form of grants, 'hard' loans, or direct private investment. However, loans and private investment naturally involve obligations in the future to amortize capital, pay interests, or repatriate profit.
14. The assumption of complete non-shiftability, though exaggerated, is not unrealistic in the absence of foreign trade.
15. $\lambda_c + \lambda_k = 1$.
16. It may also be termed as the initial investment-income ratio, i.e., $\alpha_o = I_o/Y_o$ where I_0 is the initial investment.
17. Even though there are two allocation ratios, there is only one effective instrument, since $\lambda_c + \lambda_k = 1$.
18. Weitzman (1971) extends the Mahalanobis model in optimal control terms.
19. Fox et al. (1966) have shown that the coefficient matrix in the four-sector Mahalanobis model is triangular. This implies the unilateral dependence of the consumption-goods sector on the investment-goods sector. This eliminates the possibility of affecting via external trade an increase in supply of investment-goods by a prior increase in consumption-goods.
20. Leela and Somasekhara (1972) examine the empirical validity of Mahalanobis' model.
21. An interesting extension of Mahalanobis' model is made by Raj and Sen (1961) to derive a number of alternative strategies of development.
22. See Taylor (1979).
23. An excellent and detailed critique of India's Second Five-Year Plan is given in Part I of Brahmananda and Vakil (1956). In Part II they develop the wage-

broad pattern of thought in the systems associated with Ricardo, Marx, Marshall, Keynes and Mrs Robinson; and compare their relevance to the developing countries.

24. The concept of wage-goods was brought into economic analysis by Ricardo. Then A.C. Pigou made a heavy use of this concept. Vakil and Brahmananda (1956) introduced this notion under conditions of development. In Sraffa (1960) the term 'consumption necessities' is substituted for wage-goods.
25. This assumption is in common with Marx and hence the wage-goods approach to development is related to the Marxian concept of variable capital.
26. In this way, Vakil and Brahmananda were following the tradition set by R. Nurkse and P.N. Rosenstein-Rodan.
27. A list of the wage-goods under Indian conditions is contained in Brahmananda (1978).
28. The size of the wage-goods gap depends upon the difference between the money value of the real wage consumed by an unemployed and the money value of the goods consumed by disguised unemployed multiplied by the number of disguised unemployed.
29. In this way, the present approach can be used to provide a rationale for the policy of importing food as a means to step up capital formation and generate extra employment. But, interestingly, no effort is made to link up this approach directly with the question of food aid. It is also possible to extend this approach to cases in which an increase in wage-goods supply is brought about as a result of various types of measures such as increase in output, reduction in the consumption standards, forced savings by procuring wage-goods from the producers, reduction in the value of disguised unemployed and reduction in the population pressure, and imports of food and other wage-goods in a closed economy.
30. Vakil and Brahmananda point out that from the analytical point of view, the investment potential concealed in relatively uneconomic techniques of production is different from that which is concealed in mass disguised unemployment.
31. It may be interesting to calculate the extent of additional increase in savings and investment thus possible as a result of the implementation of this approach. But no such attempt is made by Vakil and Brahmananda.
32. Keynesian multiplier indicates by how much the total income would go up as a result of an initial increase in investment.
33. Keynesian multiplier tells us by how much savings will have to go up, if a given increase in investment has to be self-financing.
34. Vakil and Brahmananda claimed that with appropriate coordinated measures a state of full employment can be achieved in Indian-type economy, within a period of about 10 to 12 years. The term 'full employment' meaning a complete eradication of disguised unemployment.
35. For a critical analysis of such policies in India, see Lele (1971).
36. The variations in the distributive bias of the different types of new technologies in agricultural production have been extensively discussed in the empirical literature. In the case of Indian agriculture, see Rao (1975).
37. Lele and Mellor (1981) highlight the importance of the wage-goods constraint to growth of non-agricultural employment in a traditional economy. See Mellor (1974) also for a detailed review of two-sector models in which the question of labour transfers has been treated in the context of development.

THREE

Comparative Static Consistency-Type Planning Models

3.1 INTRODUCTION

The results of numerical applications which are carried out on the basis of a relatively aggregate inter-industry description of the economy would emerge in terms of broad sectoral aggregates and macro-economic magnitudes. Of course, such studies and their results are of significant interest, but the degree of aggregation can be bothersome in practical planning. This is because of the fact that highly aggregate sectoral forecasts do not provide a good basis for communication between macro-planners and industrial specialists. In fact, there are a number of respects in which a more detailed quantitative analysis would yield more meaningful and significant dividends:

i. It is useful to set up inter-industry planning models on the basis of sectors or industries in terms of which the actual plans are formulated. Models which prescribe targets for the engineering sector as a whole are of little use to a planner who is interested in the future demand for railway wagons or diesel engines.

ii. A detailed empirical study can adjust to the differing quality of statistical information available for different sectors of the economy. Depending on the availability and/or suitability of the data, some sectors can usefully be treated in great empirical detail within the inter-industry framework of a model, while others are best aggregated or made explicitly subject to exogenous assumptions.

iii. One of the crucial problems in the strategy of economic growth concerns the pattern of industrialisation and foreign trade. Many models involve a degree of sectoral choice between domestic production, imports and/or exports. If such elements are to be meaningfully approached, it is essential that the relevant sectors be defined in fairly precise terms rather than as broad aggregates.

iv. A high degree of disaggregation permits one to unearth specific commodity shortages or bottlenecks that would be disguised at a higher level of aggregation.

v. For many planning purposes -- particularly as a basis for discussion between sector specialists and those concerned with macro analysis -- more disaggregated growth forecasts are desirable. These are almost always built around an essentially macro-economic construct, since the most detailed input-output tables rarely reach down to the plant (let alone the farm) in their classification. However, the tables do provide a half-way house between macro and micro; and are useful for precisely this reason.

vi. The degree of aggregation can be bothersome in practical planning as highly aggregated sectoral forecasts do not provide a good basis for communication between macro-planners and industrial specialists.[1]

vii. Most sectors include a great variety of products differing radically both in their input structure and in their sources of demand. This point assumes particular importance in the context of choice among alternative production, importing and exporting activities. If such choice elements are to be fruitfully approached, it is essential that the relevant sectors be defined in fairly precise terms rather than as broad aggregates.

Hence, multisectoral planning models, irrespective of their consistency or optimising variety, are decidedly superior to the aggregative models, discussed in Chapter 2. The subject matter of the present chapter is to conduct a survey of the comparative-static models of Manne and Rudra (1965), Srinivasan et al. (1965) and Planning Commission (1973, 1981 and 1986).

3.2 MANNE AND RUDRA MODEL

Manne and Rudra (1965) summarize some projections based upon a 30-sector inter-industry model for the target year 1970-71 over the base year 1960-61. They examine the effect on output levels and on imports of alternative assumptions regarding the growth of aggregate consumption and of investment. The effects of alternatives with respect to capital-output ratios assumed for agriculture and the degree of import substitution within the machine building industries are also examined. This is a conventional static Leontief inter-industry model with a few embellishments for the endogenous treatment of capital formation. Because of computer limitations and because most inter-sectoral choices were already obvious to policy makers, Manne and Rudra chose to model 'consistency requirements' in the static Leontief tradition rather than attempt an optimising study. Each choice between alternative activities is removed in the model either by specifying the proportionate mix or else the absolute level of all but one alternative. The model reports two alternative treatments of capital formation during the target year; one in which the entire item is determined exogenously and one in which the bulk of capital formation is calculated endogenously through multiplying each sector's output increase over the decade by its own capital-output ratio and stock-flow conversion factor of 17 per cent (that is, totally exogenous and partially endogenous).[2] The stock-flow conversion factor is worked out on the assumptions that the flow of investment rises smoothly from the base to the target year, a two year gestation lag, and the investment growth rate in the neighbourhood of 8.7 per cent per year. Through this stock-flow conversion factor, the model avoids 'edge-effects' and contains a built-in rationale for investment activity during the target year. But in either case, inventory investment is determined endogenously through the relations induced inventory investment in item i = $0.4\,(x_i - x_i^o)$.

The 30-sectors are divided into the following three independent groups of industries of which neither the first nor the second has significant inter-industry sales outside itself:

i. Agriculture based production and processing for final consumption, i.e., sector FF;

ii. The mining, metals, machinery and wood products industries, which comprise the investment goods producing sectors at the focus of the Indian import substitution strategy, i.e., sector MM; and

iii. Intermediate product industries, including fuel, power, transport, and chemicals, i.e., sector UI.

Table 1. A (3 x 3) Input-output Table for India

(1959-60 Producer's Prices: value in Rs. Crore)

Producing Sectors	Absorbing Sectors MM	FF	UI	Final demand	Gross Output
MM	1063.3	26.7	44.1	2138.2	3272.3
FF	10.5	2057.3	38.5	7753.4	9859.7
UI	136.6	171.3	335.9	496.0	1582.8
Value added	2061.9	7604.4	1164.3	-10830.6	0
Gross Output	3272.3	9859.7	1582.8	0	14714.8
Percentage	22.23815	67.00533	10.75652		

Table 1 suggests that a shortfall in organising FF output will have a first order impact upon household consumption, and a shortfall in MM will have a first order impact upon the investment widely throughout the entire economy. Thus, it implies that at all stages of economic development, the MM sector is the principal source of fixed capital formation and import substitution. This implies that the domestic production will have to be expanded more rapidly than the aggregate volume of investment if the foreign exchange bottleneck is to be broken.

To derive the matrix of coefficients A from Table 1 we divide the items in every column in the indented matrix by the gross output level of the corresponding sector. Thus,

$$A = \begin{bmatrix} 0.32494 & 0.00271 & 0.02786 \\ 0.00321 & 0.20866 & 0.02432 \\ 0.04174 & 0.01737 & 0.21222 \end{bmatrix}$$

The inverse of (I-A) correct to five decimal places is the following:

$$(I-A)^{-1} = \begin{bmatrix} 1.48464 & 0.00624 & 0.05269 \\ 0.00845 & 1.26457 & 0.03934 \\ 0.07885 & 0.02821 & 1.27305 \end{bmatrix}$$

Thus, the gross output levels, X's, may be written as

$$\begin{aligned} X_1 &= 1.484\,Y_1 + 0.007\,Y_2 + 0.053\,Y_3 \\ X_2 &= 0.009\,Y_1 + 1.350\,Y_2 + 0.041\,Y_3 \\ X_3 &= 0.079\,Y_1 + 0.032\,Y_2 + 1.273\,Y_3 \end{aligned}$$

Where Y's denote levels of final demand.

It can be noticed that for the Indian economy, the pattern of interconnectedness in 1960-61 was such that a one per cent increase in final demand for MM sector would imply an increase in gross output level for the same sector of 1.48 per cent, a negligible increase of 0.009 per cent in the demand for output of FF sector, and a slightly higher increase of 0.079 per cent in the output level of the UI sector. Since investment is largely equivalent to final demand for the MM sector, it may be argued that for the Indian economy investment is largely autonomous in character. The same applies to FF sector. Thus, it may be concluded that raising investment or consumption demand are largely independent questions.

Table 2 shows that an overwhelming fraction of India's household consumption is provided by the FF sector which is also a principal earner of foreign exchange through exports.

Table 2. Sectoral Distribution of Final Demand: 1960-61

(1959-60 Producers' Prices: value in Rs. Crores)

Producing Sectors	House-hold consump-tion	Govt.con-sumption	Gross fixed capital	Additions to stocks	Exports	Imports	Others	Total final demand
MM	248.6	197.8	2002.2	26.1	56.3	-550.9	153.3	2138.2
FF	7189.8	104.9	0	197.9	388.1	-322.0	194.7	7753.4
UI	503.7	32.0	0	7.1	16.4	-240.1	176.0	496.0
Value added	4662.0	1054.3	276.0	·	172.1	-11.1	0	6145.1
GNP	2604.0	1380.0	2278.0	231.1	632.9	-1090.5	529.9	16566.3

"One of the most significant insights obtained from the numerical exercise is this: everything does not depend upon everything else. At least within the Indian economy it appears that there is an almost block-angular structure of current account transactions. The bulk of such transactions takes place within two virtually independent complexes: one based upon agriculture and the other upon mining, metals, machinery, and forestry products. The first of these sectors is the predominant source of consumption goods. The second is the source of investment goods, and appears to be the strategic point for import substitution. A third and smaller complex produces items that may be described as 'universal intermediates'".

"The block-angular structure[3] of current transactions implies short-run (but not long-run) independence between agriculture and the investment-goods sector. Block-angularity suggests that success or failure in raising agricultural output will have an immediate impact upon the supply of consumption goods, but only second-order effects via the income generation process upon the agriculturists' demand for industrial products. That is, the output targets for the key industrial sectors depend primarily upon whether the government is sufficiently bold to maintain a high rate of aggregate investment... . This course of action entails a distinct risk of inflation, but might nonetheless be worthwhile from the long-term view point of growth in productive capacity both outside and inside agriculture".[4]

This economic structure implies that successful implementation of agricultural plans would be essential in order to achieve proposed household consumption targets but would have only second-order importance (via farmers' income changes) on the demand for industrial production. On the other hand, output targets for key industrial sectors would depend upon Government's willingness to maintain high aggregate investment rates regardless of the behaviour of agriculture (which depends upon good monsoons and other stochastic phenomena). A shortfall among industrial production targets would directly affect the domestic investment programme and the import substitution strategy India had planned for conservation of foreign exchange. Moreover, under-achievement of output targets among intermediate product would have diffused impact throughout the economy. Thus, the present model attempted to derive investment patterns which were consistent with future production targets rather than to focus directly on consumption planning.

In this model exports are determined exogenously and are assumed to grow at a rate of 5.5 per cent per year. A minor volume of imports is tied to specific commodities as a result of bilateral clearing agreements. No formal constraint upon the deficit on merchandise account is placed. The current account balance of payments is not a fixed resource constraint, as it would be in a linear programming model. Competitive imports and other parameters are adjusted during the course of numerical experimentation so that the trade gap would be in a feasible range of what India might expect to secure from foreign loans and grants. Since these are not policy but target variables, these adjustments imply confidence that import licensing or an active import substitution policy were economically, politically, and institutionally feasible and would induce the desired results.

Since sectoral levels of production and competitive imports do not substitute for each other as functions of the relative scarcity of domestic factors of production as compared to the exogenous supply of foreign exchange (exports and the foreign trade gap), the model is insensitive to relative costs and cannot be used directly to explore India's international comparative advantage.

If more foreign aid were available to India than was predicted by the authors' adjustment of it, it would not be absorbed in the terminal year resource allocations implied by the model's solution.

Therefore, the planner must use the estimate of foreign aid judiciously. There is nothing implied by the solution about feasible or efficient levels of foreign capital inflow. The judgements of feasibility come from outside the model. Import licensing arrangements might be set up to attempt to induce the import pattern projected by the model, but even doing this probably would not lead to the sectoral output targets calculated by the model. Thus, the consistency model is designed to explore the implications of structural change at the normative rather than operational policy level.

The present model is of an open-loop type which assumes in effect that the government has sufficient fiscal power so that it is unconstrained by the feedback link that operates in a market economy from the production process back to the distribution of incomes, savings and the generation of domestic expenditures. Unlike a closed-loop model, no explicit feedback link is provided here from the process of production back to the generation of income and in turn back to the principal components of gross domestic expenditure.

In this way, the present exercise explores the implications of two alternative views of aggregate development: (a) an ambitious development programme that is premised upon vigorous government action; and (b) a more pessimistic view of what would be feasible. These implied different ten years average growth rates for the aggregates of gross capital formation, government consumption, household consumption, and gross domestic expenditure. Beyond this, variations in the values of other critical parameters permitted the authors to generate a much wider range of solutions for the interpretation and discussion with policy makers. Runs differed from one another by (i) the degree of endogenous investment left to the model; (ii) changes in the agricultural sector's capital-output ratio; (iii) altering the degree of block-triangularity found in the technological matrix; and (iv) evaluating the effects of the machinery import substitution programme. The two alternatives represent altogether different evaluations of India's rural development prospects -- hence differ strikingly with respect to the assumed rates of growth of aggregate household consumption: 5.4 per cent versus 3.6 per cent per annum (with 2.4 per cent compound rate of growth of population). But these two projections are found to be identical in terms of government consumption.

The model considers three alternatives for totally exogenous investment. The first two cases are based directly upon the final demand projections A and B, and the third is a hybrid. It provides for gross fixed capital formation at the high rate of programme A, but for the household consumption at the low level of programme B.

The static Leontief system in the model is closed by making endogenous the capital capacity expansion, inventory investment, and some imports, but set household consumption as a terminal target.

3.3 SRINIVASAN ET AL. MODEL

Srinivasan et al. (1965) use the Manne-Rudra model with the only significant difference of shifting the terminal year of the plan from 1970-71 to 1975-76. The theoretical framework, the sectoral identification, and the data base is also the same. This model makes some 16 variants by assuming two alternative target year aggregate consumption levels; two time horizons, 1960-61 to 1975-76 and 1970-71 to 1975-76; two sets of import coefficients corresponding to optimistic and pessimistic anticipation about import substitution; and two alternative concentration ratios, corresponding to two degrees of inequality reductions. This model also makes some changes in the technical coefficients, import coefficients and inventory coefficients.

3 4 THE FIFTH PLAN MODEL

The heart of the framework of the Fifth Five-Year Plan Model's (Planning Commission, 1973) reasoning consists in applying an open static Leontief model for ensuring terminal year consistency amongst the output levels of different sectors. This model consists of three parts: macro-economic model; input-output model; and consumption model.

The Macro Model

The macro-model gives information on the macro-economic projections based on a gradualistic time path for gross domestic product (GDP) at factor cost which is consistent with a desired average compound growth rate over the plan period as a whole. Total gross investment levels for the planning period have been estimated by applying a global incremental capital-output ratio to alternative growth rates, on the basis of a postulated value for GDP in 1973-74. Since the incremental-capital-output-ratio for a particular sector is liable to fluctuate with the degree of excess capacity prevailing in that sector as well as vary in the light of time structure of investment envisaged for the sector, therefore independent checks have been carried out on the overall marginal capital-output ratio. Aggregate public consumption as well as exports are exogenously estimated and the aggregate private consumption is obtained as residual after allowing for public consumption.

The Input-Output Model

The input-output model considered is a static Leontief inter-industry model with provisions made for endogenous estimates of import requirements and for redistribution of private consumption from the richer to the poorer sections of the population. Deliveries of different sectors to public consumption, to exports and to gross fixed investments are estimated exogenously in this model, while those relating to private consumption are estimated through a separate consumption model. Sectoral changes in stocks are obtained as fixed proportions of the increase in output levels of the different sectors. Control is exercised with the aggregate change in the stock level of the different sectors. The aggregate terminal year net imports of all types of goods and services are obtained with the help of this model and is used to derive domestic savings necessary for achieving the desired level of investment. Thus, sectoral imports are estimated endogenously through constructing suitable import coefficient matrices but without distinguishing between competitive and non-competitive imports. Conceptually, non-competing imports do not appear in the model at all.

The year 1973-74 is adopted as the base year for the purpose of projection. The basis of the projection of output levels is the inter-industry current flow matrix for the year 1965-66. The input-output table considered is for 66 sectors, representing current flows in value terms of producers' prices. The coefficient matrix based upon producers' prices is more stable than one based on market prices as the latter distorts the true production coefficients due to imposition of non-uniform taxes.

Consumption Model

The approach of this model is designed to test the feasibility of bringing the lowest 30 per cent of the income recipients upto a specified minimum consumption standard by 1978.[5] This would involve a 60 per cent rise in the average per capita consumption of this group over the five year period. It is further assumed that income redistribution would not effect the overall rate of growth of GDP, and that a reduction in the average per capita consumption of the top 30 per cent of income recipients of 3 per cent (instead of an increase of 16 per cent with no distribution) would therefore be required.[6]

Sectoral private consumption sector used in the input-output model is estimated separately for rural and for urban areas through a separate consumption model, after taking into consideration the desired levels of monthly aggregate per capita consumption for the lowest 30 per cent of the population.

Sectoral private consumption has been estimated by projecting the consumer demand for a sector by different expenditure classes with the help of the consumption model, where the total private consumption, as endogenously estimated in the macro-model, has been used. The following assumptions are also made for this purpose:

1. The sectoral consumption pattern by persons in different classes would remain practically same throughout the plan period.

2. In order to fulfill the objective of narrowing down the gap between urban and rural areas in terms of per capita consumption, the per capita consumption is assumed to increase at a faster rate in rural India than in urban India.

3. The distribution of monthly per capita aggregate expenditure amongst population in urban and rural areas is assumed to be log-normal for each.

The aggregate public consumption has been estimated for terminal year of the plan period at an overall growth rate of about 7 per cent over the base year.

Several alternative exercises with the model are carried out with different assumptions on the growth of GDP and exports, in some cases considering import substitution and the reduction in the expenditure distribution. The extent of import substitution is judged partly by the capacity constraint on the domestic production levels and partly by the objective of self-reliance with regard to the balance of payments. The stock coefficients for different sectors are derived partly by considering the stock-flow conversion factors and partly by means of observed inventory to output relationships. Then, the models are solved by Gauss-Siedel method of iteration using electronic computer.

One of the most interesting result of this exercise is the effect that redistribution of consumption would have on the production levels of most industrial sectors. In 22 of the 66 sectors consumption redistribution causes a change in the annual growth rate by more than one per cent. Requirements for foodgrains and textiles are appreciably increased, while consumer durables are significantly lower. But the feasibility of this type of redistribution policy depends in the first instance on the possibilities for limiting upper income consumption through taxation, which in the Indian context would have to be mainly in the form of indirect taxes on luxury consumer goods.[7] In principle, it should be possible to compute the level of excise taxes needed on the basis of the price elasticities for each commodity. If this income transfer is found to be possible, feasibility will then depend on the supply elasticities of food production and the ability of Indian policy-makers to change the supply structure of the economy. And both these conditions require judgement which falls beyond the scope of the consistency model.

The present model does not analyse the process of income generation of the instruments for intervening in it. But it does represent one of the most significant attempts to explore the implications of distributional policies for planning. Similarly, static tests of consistency ignore the dynamics of the redistribution problem. They fail to study the short-term supply imbalance caused when half-completed investment projects or new investments with gestation lags would impede the restructuring of the economy to meet a target of redistribution consumption. But unless policy instruments are found to maintain the new purchasing power within the working group for a time period sufficient for the pattern of domestic supply to permanently adjust to the newly imposed pattern of demand, the goal of consumption redistribution cannot be permanently maintained.[8]

Thus, from the methodological point of view the present model does not contain any novel feature that has not been used before in other similar planning models. The macro-model is a variant of the Harrod-Domar model; the input-output model is a variation of the static-open-Leontief model; and the consumption model is identical in assumptions to the exercises made by Manne and Rudra (1965) and Srinivasan et al.(1965). It may also be pointed out that though this model has the weaknesses of not being able to analyse the process of income generation or the instruments for interfering in it yet it does represent one of the most significant attempts by a government body to explore the implications of distributional policies for planning.[9]

3.5 THE SIXTH PLAN MODEL

The Technical Note of the Sixth Plan of India by the Planning Commission (1981) provides a detailed structure of the model system. But it omits the macro-model which is explained by Alagh and Majumdar (1982) and Majumdar and Panda (1982). This model covers a fifteen year period from 1980-81 to 1994-95, divided into the following two sub-periods:

i. The Sixth Plan period of five years from 1980-81 to 1984-85; and
ii. The perspective plan period of ten years from 1985-86 to 1994-95. The model is comprised of a core model, a macro model and five major sub-models.

In the core model, the year 1979-80 has been taken as the base year. In developing the projections of output levels, the base year table has been constructed in the following two stages:

i. The 225 sectors input-output table for the year 1968-69 has been aggregated to 89 sectors; and

ii. the 89 sectors table has been updated to 1979-80 at 1979-80 prices.

The agriculture sector is split into ten different sectors. A distinction is made between 'commodity by commodity' and 'industry by industry' input-output tables. The model uses the former approach under industry technology assumption.[10] Sectoral final demands are estimated at the market prices and then converted to factor costs using indirect tax (less subsidy) rates. Tax rates are adjusted to arrive at given total indirect tax less subsidy. This core model is composed of the following seven blocks: (i) Input-output; (ii) Investment; (iii) Private consumption; (iv) Financial resources (domestic savings, both private and public); (v) Imports; (vi) Employment; and (vii) Perspective Planning.

The agricultural sub-model provides estimates of capacity outputs in agriculture which are fed into the core model as exogenous variables. In this model alternative estimates are made for alternative weather scenarios.

The export sub-model estimates export values, sector-wise and time-wise, by econometric, technical and other normative assumptions which again enter as exogenous values in the core model.

By using relevant demographic relations, the demographic sub-model works out population, its rural and urban break up and the labour force, feeding these as inputs into the core model.

The last two sub-models (on autonomous investment and public consumption and on long term objectives, with both cardinal and ordinal values) try to quantify the social and economic goals of the plan as the planners perceive them. They appear as targets in the plan and enter as exogenous variables into the core model.

The private consumption vector for 1979-80 at purchasers' price has been generated by consumption sub-model using aggregate private consumption 1979-80 at 1979-80 prices. The private consumption vectors, separately for people below and above the poverty line in rural and urban population, have been derived on the basis of a LES for 13 groups of commodities and services and relevant demand functions for commodities within each LES group.[11]

Within each LES group there is a set of Engel Curves/demand functions covering all the 89 sectors of the input-output model. The LES and Engel Curve/demand functions have been developed separately for people below and above the poverty line in rural and urban areas.[12]

In this model imports have been estimated separately for the intermediate uses, consumption and investment. But there is no distinction between competitive and non-competitive imports.

In this model investment outlays by fourteen sectors are estimated endogenously through the use of investment functions. Parameter estimation of these functions constitutes the most noteable achievement of the Sixth Plan modelling exercise. Incremental capital-output ratios (ICORs) have been estimated, initially, for fourteen sectors and then utilised to estimate ICORs for the 89 sectors of the input-output model. Investments are classified into three categories; (i) replacement; (ii) induced fixed investment including inventories; and (iii) autonomous investment. The terminal year gross investment is estimated through investment functions in three components: (i) construction; (ii) machinery and other fixed inputs; and (iii) change in stock.

The basic structure of the macro-model is similar to the Fifth Five-Year Plan model with only one difference that this model estimates terminal year investment endogenously while the fifth plan model estimates private consumption. The macro-model provides insights into the estimation of aggregate private consumption and savings. The aggregate private consumption is obtained as a residual in this model.

The model tries to capture the constraints dealing with demand, financial resources, supply/capacity for activity sectors, demand-supply balance, foreign exchange, land and natural resources, manpower, welfare programme, public sector financing, tax/fiscal private sector investment financing and welfare goal. A large number of endogenous variables are taken as exogenous in working out the resource allocation process, both intertemporal and intersectoral.

There is also an induction of the matrix of labour coefficients in different sectors of the input-output commodity matrix.

In this model, the gross output has been made dependent on: (i) the production technology; (ii) the exogenous element of the final demand; (iii) the consumption propensity of the community; and (iv) the rate of growth of the economy stipulated for the future. The model also demonstrates that once an economy reaches its limit to total saving, the post-terminal growth rates and the plan growth rates pose a problem of trade-off which means that the post-terminal growth rate can increase relative to the plan growth rate only by increasing the community's propensity to save.

The capital to output relations in the model are based on the hypothesis that investment in a period with gestation lag of L years would be spread by equal amounts over L years.

The demand equations of perspective plan period are almost the same as those of the Sixth Five-Year Plan period. But the supply equations of the perspective plan are different in the sense that they are much less restrictive. In the long range perspective, supplies are less constrained in most sectors where their necessary capacity would be developed and, therefore, demand is taken as the guiding indicator for resource allocation;[13] whereas in the short range perspective it is the capacity that sets the upper limit of growth and it is demand management which acts as the adjusting factor.

Then the present open-loop type model is solved uniquely by giving alternative values to the remaining key policy variables until the system is reduced to a state with only one degree of freedom. In this way, a maximum growth path is chosen which fulfils all the constraints.

In this model there is separate sub-system on material balances, which is used to disaggregate the macro and sectoral dimensions into their detailed physical units and to check overall consistency.[14]

The present model determines endogenously the growth rate in gross domestic product during the perspective period subject to the total investment during the Sixth Plan period, making it possible to examine the trade-off between the social objectives during the medium and long-term plan periods.

The model runs at constant prices in the accounting sense and incorporates the effects of price changes in the foreign sector by calculating the impact of terms-of-trade changes on foreign savings. It adjusts domestic resources on the basis of actual (ex-post) price changes. It is capable of accommodating (ex-ante) price changes arising out of projected inflation based on cost considerations. It is also capable of taking into account relative price changes in the domestic sector.

The Technical Note of the Sixth Plan points out the following three salient features of this model:

i. The system of supply equations is an extended and modified version of the Harrod-Domar equation. It is primarily meant to accommodate sectoral disaggregations, investment lags, and the existence of a foreign trade sector.

ii. The system of demand equations is also an extended version of Leontief's input-output system. It endogenises consumption imports and investment.[15]

iii. The set of inequality relations with given upper bounds ensures that the demand should not exceed the supply in any of the markets dealing with commodities, services, capital, labour, foreign exchange and non-renewable resources. Similarly, the set of inequality relations with lower bounds ensures the attainment of minimum welfare targets of the community.

This 'Technical Note' of the Planning Commission points out the following analytical gaps in this model:

i. The treatment of private consumption is not strictly on a 'closed-loop' basis.[16]

ii. The income distribution and the production structure of the economy are not explicitly functionally related.

iii. The model is run only for terminal years although it is well known that the feasibility of a production target and that of a demand supply balance in the market can be tested only when examined as a flow overtime.

iv. In order to ensure a technical feasibility examined from capacity considerations at the terminal year of the plan, a simplifying assumption of exponential spread of investment between the base and the terminal year of the plan has been assumed. This might create problems of input-output imbalances, when checked on an annual basis.

v. A rough check is done by assuming some selected sectors of the final demand as the balancing "item". This aspect needs more articulation.

vi. The role of the private sector, the impact from the changes in relative prices and problems of spatial allocation of resources should be paid more attention.

In an excellent comparative study of the Fifth Five-Year Plan model and the Sixth Five-Year Plan model, Majumdar and Panda (1982) also point out the following deficiencies in these models:

i. Redistribution of income is the most effective instrument in achieving the primary objective of basic needs. But as admitted in the Technical Note of the Planning Commission (1981, p. 17) "the income distribution and the production structure of the economy are not yet explicitly functionally related." The work of Sinha et al. (1978) has made some preliminary attempts to construct a matrix showing distribution of sectoral value-added by six different income classes. In this regard it is high time that the Planning Commission should go in for developing a 'closed-loop' formation on a firm basis.

ii. An expanded capital flow matrix to estimate the requirement of different capital goods should be built up and used to ensure consistency amongst the sectoral growth from consideration of both current inputs and capital inputs.

iii. This model assumes constant prices, whereas higher tax rates, increased money supply and other internal and external factors bring in inflationary pressure causing erosion of real content of the plan resources and deceleration of growth. This vital aspect of Indian planning process needs immediate attention.

In addition to the above mentioned deficiencies, the following questionable points of doubt also remain to be discussed:

i. Now what is questionable is that the planners have adopted the input-output tables of 1968-69 with some modifications for the base period. But at a theoretical level, there are serious assumptions involved in taking over of the input-output table of one particular year as the basis for a plan for ten years later. The input-output coefficients would have undergone a change because of the very fact of rising capital-output ratio. Similarly, the structure of prices also keeps on undergoing a change. A change in one price in Leontief type input-output table involves a change in all prices.

ii. Another point of doubt arises over the present model on its incorporating several different theoretical systems. Naturally, there are bound to be problems of reconciliation among them since any theoretical system is based on certain assumptions and technical procedures which may not be the same for each, and when taken together, may tend to be contradictory.

iii. Similarly, the present model specifically mentions that investment has been endogenously chosen. But it does not make clear as to how the consumption growth rate is chosen.

3.6 THE SEVENTH PLAN MODEL

The basic structure of the Seventh Plan Model and its working are the same as in the Sixth Plan Model. The model comprises of a 'core' and seven major 'sub-models'. The core model consists of (i) a macro-economic model; (ii) an input-output model; and (iii) investment model.

The *macro-economic model* consists of a number of national income and expenditure identities and this in combination with input-output model determines investment in the terminal year endogenously. It also determines resources available for investment.

In *the input-output model,* vectors are developed which correspond to scalars in macro-model for government consumption, gross fixed investment and changes in stock. The value of total imports provides the crucial link between macro-economic model and input-output model. Coefficient matrices for the technological thrusts of Seventh Plan are based on 115 sector input-output table for 1973-74 of CSO duly updated by RAS method and revised. The input-output model uses 50 sectors corresponding to 115 sectors of the CSO table.

Investment model derives investment requirements at broad aggregate sector levels and converts investment by destination into that by origin.

The Seventh Plan Model has the following seven major 'submodels':

Agricultural Sub-Model

This model goes into the allocation of land area among different uses and also distribution of irrigated area among different crops. It incorporates separate dimensions for the eastern region. This is a new feature in the Seventh Plan.

Poverty Sub-Model

This model captures the income distribution process underlying the Seventh Plan and estimates the number of people crossing the poverty line through the combined effects of general economic development and anti-poverty programmes articulated in the plan strategies.

The Industry Sub-Model

The structure of this sub-model is the same as has been used in the Sixth Plan.

Consumption Sub-Model

This model attempts to forecast the demand for different goods and services for private consumption, given a certain growth pattern of the economy, a projected growth in population, its rural-urban composition and a base period consumption distribution. Subsequently, the consumption patterns are adjusted in the light of likely changes in income distribution resulting from specified redistributive policy measures proposed by the Government for the future. For estimating the consumption demand for different goods and services, econometric estimations of expenditure elasticity of demand are derived from the past data. For this purpose, LES consumption functions are used. In the model, the private consumers have been divided into four groups -- rural, urban, separately for below and above the poverty line.

Investment Planning Sub-Model

For projecting investment by destination, econometric simulation model is used. The estimated investments by destination are then converted into sources by the use of a capital flow matrix. Finally, they are dovetailed with the main input-output model to check their consistencies. For the purpose of the plan exercises investment has been separated into eleven national income sub-groups. Besides, they have been also separated between public and private sectors. (Investments by destination in the Sixth Plan were not separated between public and private.) The investment planning sub-model of the Seventh Plan is further modified in order to take care of replacement, modernisation, productivity improvements and new capacity generation.

Export-Import Sub-Model

The plan projections for exports are done in this sub-model. It is a simulation model and parameters are basically estimated by econometric estimation procedures. It has three specifications in estimating the future export projections:

1. Exports which are dependent on domestic production capability;

2. Exports which are dependent on world demand, their relative prices and degree of India's penetration into the international market; and

3. Exports of new commodities.

Giving the exogenous policy packages, their impacts on exports are assessed and built into these projections.

Imports have been separated into two groups: bulk imports and non-bulk imports. (A third group, foodgrains, figures only in the import mix in the base year 1984-85.) In this model a provision for contingency imports has also been built into. This is done to meet any uncertainty, specially due to weather and changes in terms of trade which have been experienced often in all other earlier plans. This level of contingency is conditioned by foreign exchange availability. The extent of import substitution is determined, among other things, by restraining domestic demand or by adopting a policy mix resulting in increased output.

Financial Resources Sub-Model

In this model attempts are made to estimate the financial resources available to support the necessary investment requirements of different sectors. This model can be broadly divided into three groups:

a. for the public sector,

b. for the private sector separated between corporate and non-corporate, and

c. for the rest of the economy.

As pointed out by Gupta (1986), in this model a device has been evolved whereby the resources calculation in real terms, i.e., at constant accounting price, would take account of any automatic adjustment needed for the likely increase in inflation in future over the plan period.

In this way as pointed out by Gupta (1986) and the Planning Commission (1986), the following notable changes have been incorporated in the Sixth Plan Model to formulate the Seventh Plan Model:

1. a public sector investment planning;

2. inflation and the changes in the relative prices in the domestic sector between consumption and capital goods as an explicit factor in public sector plan resources assessment;

3. the quantification of major basic needs by developing a separate additional sub-model to supplement the Sixth Plan Model-frame;

4. a more disaggregated poverty sub-model;

5. for the first time, in the Seventh Plan Model an attempt has also been made to relate, on the one hand, the physical increase in the availability of basic needs and the financial allocation on these heads and, on the other hand, the real (physical) supply of basic needs and their impacts on development in future;

6. another new feature of the Seventh Plan Model is that, in its agricultural sub-model, it incorporates separate dimensions for the eastern region of India comprising of States of Bihar, West Bengal, Orissa and East U.P.; and

7. investments by destinations have been separated between public and private sectors. Besides, the investment planning sub-model is further modified in order to take care of replacement, modernisation, productivity improvements and new capacity generation.

NOTES

1. Only if the input coefficients of a group of industries are identical, or if the demand for the output of those industries remains always in fixed proportions, then no information will be lost by aggregating all of them into a single sector. See Chenery and Clark (1959).
2. The stock-flow conversion factor is a device for tying capital stock variables, which outline the planning horizons, to current investment, which by itself

would give no intra-horizon capacity benefits, given long gestation periods.

3. If the block-angular structure is characteristic of other economies then this would provide a short-cut description of production which would prove equally useful to the policy-maker and the theorist. A two-sector or a three-sector model (with only limited shiftability of capital from one to another sector) is a fruitful way to theorize about the process of economic growth.
4. Rudra (1964) makes an attempt to quantify the magnitude of the second order inflationary effects from different alternative assumptions for the rates of growth of agriculture and industry.
5. The same target is earlier tested by Manne and Rudra (1965).
6. A similar exploration of the implications of alternative income distribution has been earlier made by Srinivasan et al.(1965).
7. Bardhan (1973) explores the use of indirect taxes as the principal instrument for redistribution.
8. For a provocative examination of some of the theoretical reasons for the unequalizing spiral of income concentration see Bacha and Taylor (1971).
9. See Krishanan (1973), Tendulkar (1974a, 1974b) and Nanjandayya and Majumdar (1974) for an excellent and detailed evaluation of the Fifth Five-Year Plan Model.
10. See, United Nations (1968) for details regarding the distinction between 'commodity by commodity' and 'industry by industry' tables and the different assumptions under which they may be used.
11. Following Ashok Rudra's earlier work, the present model adopted LES approach as in the well known writings of Richard Stone for the U.K.
12. See, Planning Commission (1978) for certain salient features of the results of the present model.
13. These would exclude very long gestation sectors like coal, power, railway, steel, irrigation, etc.
14. The material balance technique has been extensively used in the official plan models in India since the Third Five-Year Plan.
15. In the Fourth Five-Year Plan model only imports were endogenised in the input-output system. In the Fifth-Five-Year Plan model consumption and imports were endogenised in the input-output system.
16. This has been the case in earlier plan models also.

FOUR

Inter-Temporal Consistency-Type Planning Model

4.1 INTRODUCTION

The purpose of this chapter is to examine the inter-temporal consistency-type planning model of Bergsman and Manne (1965, 1966).[1] This model may be regarded as another step forward in the field of methodological innovations ushering in a more realistic planning procedure in Indian planning literature. A comparative-static model omits all inter-temporal problems, for example, lag structures of capital gestation and learning functions required to reach full capacity, which characterize dynamic or inter-temporal models. Besides, static input-output models have no explicit theory of investment so that the vector of final demands for capital goods is on the same footing as all other final demand components. But this situation is radically altered in a dynamic input-output model incorporating an accelerator-type investment theory in which current demands for investment goods are made to depend on future expected rate of growth of output. Thus, through the use of a dynamic Leontief model, we can formally take into account the accumulation of sectoral investment into capital stocks and the capacity limits the latter place on production.

The explicit recognition of both inter-temporal and inter-sectoral relationships in a planning model has a number of advantages. It, first of all, offers a better approximation to the real context in which policy is made than do the static and aggregate models. The model solutions include period-by-period calculations of the uses of capital and of requirements of other inputs in each sector, the level of investment in each sector, the deliveries by each sector of goods for consumption and investment, and other final demand. These results make possible a more effective analysis of many important issues of development policy, such as the savings and investment implications of particular goals, the effectiveness of foreign aid, and the content of balanced growth.

4.2 BERGSMAN AND MANNE MODEL

Bergsman and Manne extend the comparative static models of Manne-Rudra (1965) and Srinivasan et al. (1965) into an inter-temporal framework by tracing out alternative time paths for each of the thirty sectors through the Fourth and Fifth Five-Year-Plans, making 1965-66 as the reference period. By postulating aggregate growth and import substitution targets and then deriving the implications for production, investment, and the balance of trade, this model intends to quantify some implications of alternative paths of economic growth for India. But the particular mix of policy instruments--physical, fiscal and monetary--that would be best suited to achieve the postulated targets is not specified by the model. The model imposes no constraints on the magnitude of the balance-of-trade deficit in any year as its main purpose is to compare the balance-of-trade time paths under alternative strategies for the Fourth and the Fifth Five-Year Plans. It also intends to be of some use in estimating the absolute levels of foreign exchange needs as implied by a specified set of assumptions relating to growth and performance of the economy. Thus, the primary aim of the present exercise is to explore balance-of-trade time paths under alternative growth and import substitution strategies and to explore some specific effects of time-lags between investment and output.

The model assumes the availability of certain 'shock absorbers' -- i.e., demand-supply gap for each commodity is assumed to be filled by imports of producers' goods or by consumption shortfalls of food and fibres, or by increases in domestic output of services -- for bridging the gap between domestic supplies and total demand. Each sector's output is assumed to grow at a constant rate during the Fourth Five-Year Plan and at another rate during the Fifth Five-

Year Plan. The model is 'almost consistent' because of the domestic service sectors where domestic production could create bottleneck during years too close to the base year for output to be expanded. The model considers two alternative time paths of aggregate domestic expenditure, and for each time path three alternative assumptions concerning import-substitution targets (differing in the assumed ratios of imports to domestic production for each sector) are considered. Thus, each of the six possible combinations of aggregate growth and import substitution are explored. In both alternative growth paths the model determines induced investment endogenously. But exogenous investment, government consumption and household consumption are determined exogenously. The model also investigates an export promotion variant.

Imports are divided into two parts: competitive imports and non-competitive imports. Non-competitive imports are specified as endogenous variables related to output levels. Competitive imports are a residual supply category defined as the difference between excess demand and production, and are called 'equilibrating' since they represent changes in planned import-substitution.

Some parts of the terminal year investment demand are given exogenously by the static consistency model used to set the plan targets; other parts are estimated endogenously as adjustment factors. The endogenous investment specification is derived from the accelerator relationship.[2] The terminal year accelerator incorporates exogenous post-terminal growth rates set as target rates of sectoral capacity expansion. Thus, this exercise derives a consistent set of output levels and induced investment for each of the two target years. Then, the output levels, the input-output coefficients, and the exogenous final demands for the intermediate years are interpolated log-linearly. Inter-industry demands are calculated by input-output method. The induced investment demands for each year are generated through multiplying capital coefficients by future output increases--i.e., through an acceleration relationship. Dynamically consistent sectoral supply (output and import) patterns are tested with a simulation technique.

The computing procedure of the present exercise has the following notable characteristics:

i. By postulating shock-absorbers the model resembles an open-loop simulator rather than a fully consistent model.[3]

ii. Unlike a recursive dynamic input-output model, the interpolation procedure of the present exercise ensures a virtual match of all domestic output levels, excluding the service sectors, for the initial year with the estimates of initial conditions.

iii. Output is assumed to grow along a log-linear trend line during the Fourth Five-Year Plan implying a sufficient flexibility of the short-run accelerator so that the output increases in the first years of the plan remain unconstrained of the project starts that were under way during the final years of the earlier plan.

Export evaluations of the balance of payments gap and of savings need vary considerably among different solutions of the model, depending upon the import requirements of alternative dynamic investment programmes computed by the model. The dynamic input-output model alone gives inadequate tests of economic feasibility of both exogenous targets and endogenous variables.

The solution strategy in the present model involves backward recursion from the consistent terminal year targets to the known initial conditions. The model generates consistent demand and supply patterns for three points in time, between which the authors interpolate to obtain estimates of sectoral values of output, input-output coefficients and all exogenous final demands in the interplan years. Sectoral investment is made consistent by using the accelerator specifications. An unusual feature of this model as compared to other models is its use of interpolation technique to approximate time paths of crucial variables.

The most striking result of the model is that even though faster import substitution in the capital-goods sectors requires higher imports to be used in building up domestic capacity and, therefore, larger trade deficits in the early years, these are more than off set by the imports saved in later years. Thus the sum of trade deficits during the ten years (whether discounted at zero per cent per annum) is less in the case of faster import substitution strategy. This implies that a larger external resource flow in the early years (to build up capacity in import substituting industries) decreases the total aid (over the ten years) needed to sustain the growth targets.[4] The authors also feel that there is an immediate additional cost (which can be measured both in additional import requirements and in additional investment requirements) attached to import substitution or export promotion in the capital goods industries because it takes machines to make machines. They point out that the additional foreign exchange costs are more than recovered over the present planning period of ten years.

To evaluate the present model justifiably, it may also be pointed out that the Bergsman-Manne log-linear trajectories are arbitrarily determined and do not represent optimal paths with respect to any objective. The necessary implication is that the efficiency of the trajectories may be improved by injecting some optimizing principle. Since in the model the rate of growth of private and public consumption is given and the focus is on the foreign exchange requirements of alternative import substitution policies, the minimization of foreign exchange costs of production and investment may provide such a principle. Similarly, the extreme rigidity of fixed import-output ratios does not permit allocation according to real cost advantage. If some endogenous choice were permitted to in the framework of an optimizing mechanism, decreases in the implied foreign exchange requirements might be experienced.

We know from the experience of developed economies that in addition to investment, technological change has a fundamentally important role in bringing about economic growth. There is a reason to believe that the same must be true, possibly with even greater force, in the case of developing economies. We might expect this change to manifest itself both in the structure of the input-output tables and in the magnitudes of the capital-output ratios. The Bergsman-Manne computations are based on input-output tables which show no further change during the period 1970-71 to 1975-76. In addition, the capital coefficients remain constant over the entire ten year period. Similar observations could be made about the demand coefficients. These may be correct assumptions, but if they happen not to be, they will have strong implications for the computed savings and foreign exchange requirements.

It may also be pointed out that there are many ways to bring about consistency in a dynamic model. Some model builders relax the rigid requirement for a balanced transition from 'known' initial conditions. This is especially true when they use a lagged accelerator because it is difficult to estimate the sectoral capital formation-in-process at the initial year.[6] Bergsman and Manne judged that it was most realistic to ignore the model's prediction that the urban construction industry might not expand sufficiently in the short-run. Others might have taken this as a binding constraint and shifted investment around throughout the intra-plan period in order to compensate for the deficient capacity as quickly as possible.[7] In the mean time, output levels could be held below their interpolated values. Similarly, when possible, other elements of demand such as consumption and inventory accumulation might be varied during early years of a plan.[8] A final 'shock absorber' in the real world is excess capacity, which permits supply to vary at a rate different from changes in demand. This seems to be important in solutions to dynamic optimizing models.

NOTES

1. Several studies on 'dynamic consistency input-output' models have been conducted outside India. See, for example, Adelman et al. (1965) for South Korea; Clark and Taylor (1971) for Chile; Hawaylyshyn et al. (1976) for Tunisia; and Johansen et al. (1968) for Norway.
2. Bergsman and Manne replace the Manne-Rudra stock-flow conversion factor by an accelerator.
3. In a closed-loop model, i.e., negative feedback simulator, demand-supply gaps trigger policies designed to reduce their magnitude.
4. The pattern of aid utilization in the dynamic optimizing model of Chenery and Mac Ewan (1966) is very similar to that reported by Bergsman and Manne, and is typical of planning models in which capital inflows early in the planning period can be used without rapidly increasing costs to build up capacity with a long-lasting pay off, as in Bruno (1974).
5. See Lefeber (1966) who evaluates the Bergsman-Manne exercise and raises certain doubts about the underlying assumptions and their implications. He also attacks the title of the present paper and points out that the term 'almost feasible' would have been more accurate than 'almost consistent'.
6. A criticism frequently levelled at input-output models is that they have no past. Unlike econometric models, their behaviour is seldom verified over an historical period. Hence, initial conditions for dynamic models which incorporate multiple year investment lags are usually simplified in one of two ways: (i) point estimates are made from actual observed figures, and (ii) the gestation lag is reduced to one period by aggregating time. Celasum (1972) introduces non-uniform gestation lags into a Bergsman-Manne type multi-sectoral simulation model for Turkey. Bergendorff and Clark (1973) use a

three-year lagged accelerator to estimate initial year capital utilisation and partially finished investments by forcing the endogenous variables of the model to track the actual path of all sectoral and aggregate values given for each year of a five-year pre-plan period.

7. Taylor, Ide and Sheshinski (1971) have developed a simulation programme which incorporates an incremental investment-shift function to minimize sectoral supply shortfalls while maintaining full intersectoral consistency.
8. Two schools of thought prevail among development planners concerning the realism of and likely speed of adjustment to an optimal growth path. For example, Manne (1970) describes the computational advantages of a 'gradualist path', of consumption, while Eckaus and Parikh (1968) consider it an unrealistic requirement to expect consumption to grow smoothly during a period of transition from unbalanced to balanced growth.

FIVE

Comparative-Static Optimising Planning Models

5.1 INTRODUCTION

A consistency model does not seek to maximize any explicit welfare function. Given an exogenous policy decision, such as the growth rate of consumption, we work out a consistent and interrelated set of figures pertaining to variables such as consumption and capital stock. Now the question is whether an explicit welfare or utility-maximization approach has any conceptual or practical advantages over the consistency approach.[1] It may be apparently said that the utility-maximization approach is the more appropriate one, since whatever can be done with the help of consistency approach, can also be done by the utility-maximization approach. An optimal path must necessarily be consistent, but the consistent path need not necessarily be optimal. In addition, the utility-maximization procedure, which is based upon explicit functional relationships by nature, may help us in generating a set of alternative optimal courses of action through a uniform parametric procedure. Secondly, in most problems of development overtime, there are inescapable elements of choice, especially where durable capital equipments are employed. Thus, one necessarily has to fill in the choice elements to get a causally determinate path for policy purposes.[2] In a mere consistency approach there may be a danger of the choice elements to be filled in a very casual manner, or in a manner in which their rationality is not quite evident. By its very nature, the utility-maximization approach would necessarily be systematic and would be based on considerations of economic efficiency. Finally, the utility-maximization approach based on constraints gives us an idea of shadow prices of various scarce resources in the light of the objective function that we maximize.[3] In an optimization problem, each constraint has a value corresponding to the lagrange-multiplier that shows how the maximum or the minimum value of the objective function would be altered consequent to a slight shift in the constraint set caused by a parametric shift.[4] Furthermore, if, in practice, there are several constraints other than those implied by technology and/or balance of payments conditions under which an actual planner would have to operate, the maximization of utility function subject to these additional constraints would yield additional shadow prices for these constraints. These additional shadow prices would serve as a very useful, though negative, purpose for showing a welfare loss to the society as a whole as caused by these constraints. Thus, the optimizing of utility maximization approach possesses some additional advantages over the mere consistency approach.[5]

In this chapter we examine the comparative-static optimizing models of Frisch (1960), Sandee (1960), Weisskopf (1967, 1971) and Tendulkar (1971). The technique of analysis which has been used in these models is that of linear programming (LP). The great advantage of this technique is that it provides a means for efficient and systematic exploration of the economy's choice set, as delimited by input-output and other constraints.[6]

5.2 FRISCH'S MODEL

In the present model Frisch (1960) considers the 'coming year' planning problem and the problem of the asymptotic pattern of the economy and gives the theoretical set up and the basis numerical tables for formulating an asymptotic problem and the corresponding coming year problem. By 'coming year' he means a period "so short that the targets contained in the plan for this period can be considered as something definite on which action is to be taken more or less immediately after the beginning of the period, without awaiting new information or analysis."

Frisch's set up is based on a 26 x 26 interflow matrix. The first 22 sectors, which are divided into four major categories, of the matrix represent the productive enterprise. The interflow coefficients are determined from the matrix of Rupee values by dividing each element by the corresponding column sum. A fairly larger part of the system is assumed to be constant. All the interflow coefficients except those in the investment column are assumed to be constant. The export surplus is one of the free variables that is to be disposed of with a view to achieving whatever goals we may want to formulate. The other variables to be used for this purpose are the investment parts of the output of all the production sectors as well as the primary factor's inputs to be used directly for investment purposes and the taxes on investment. To indicate the expected change in the total levels of activity in various sectors as a consequence of given investment into any individual investment-receiving sector or as a consequence of any given total pattern of investment defined by the way in which the investments are distributed over the investment-receiving sector, Frisch introduces multiplier coefficients.

Frisch, then, introduces upper and lower bounds to his analysis. He conditions that the current planning year consumption should not fall below the total initial level of consumption. Similar conditions are incorporated for each of the three consumption groups: (1) agriculture plus animal husbandry; (2) textile consumption; and (3) services of house property. Government consumption on current account is not explicitly related to the productive activity, as are that of other sectors (through the introduction of input coefficients). Total government outlay or intake is assumed to be fixed at the initial level. Current consumption coefficients are assumed to be non-negative constants.

In the current year linear programming problem, the upper bounds are introduced by taking account of the existing capital capacities in various sectors, and by taking account of the immobility of labour. Frisch only considers the capital capacities, K_k, only for the 22 production sectors and does not consider any such capacity for the rest. The capital capacity that will actually exist in sector K at the end of the coming year is defined as follows:

$$K_k = K^o_k + J_k - D_k \quad (K = 1,2,3,...,22)$$

Where, K^o_k, J_k and D_k are the initial existing capital capacity, the gross investment, and the depreciation in sector K in the coming year, respectively.

Frisch argues that "in general K_k will be different from the asymptotic value $\bar{K}_k$ because it will be impossible in the course of one single year to pass from the actual situation to one that is compatible with the asymptotic pattern". Thus, he is interested in minimizing the difference between the two patterns K_1, K_2,...,K_{22} and $\bar{K}_1$, $\bar{K}_2$,...$\bar{K}_{22}$ when $\bar{K}_k$ and K^o_k are given and J_k and D_k are variables. This is the same as to maximize:

$$\sum_{k=1}^{22} \left(\bar{K}_k - K_k^o\right) \quad \left(J_k - D_k\right)$$

Frisch defines the preference function as follows:

F = 16 U + 4V + W

Where U = millions of new jobs created annually;

V = annual rate of investment; and

W = net annual increase in India's net foreign assets.

All these three variables, U, V and W, are expressed linearly in terms of the 24 basis variables.

Thereafter, Frisch considers "the way in which the population and the economy may develop in the course of time partly under the impact of objective natural forces and partly as the result of a planned activity". He defines the asymptotic state as a 'balanced state', characterized by absence of under-employment and over-employment; and deficient capacity and excess capacity in each sector of the population is assumed to grow, given the 'technical' and 'behaviouristic' coefficients; technical coefficients that characterize production, and behaviouristic coefficients that explain consumers' and producers' reactions.

In case of balanced development the model has

$$K^t_k = K^{e\,ct}_k \quad (K = 1,2,...,22,24,25,26)$$

Where K_k is a constant that expresses the Rupee value of the total production in sector K in the year t=0; and e^Ct is the factor by which the total population is multiplied each year.

Similarly, we have for all the other time functions

$$C^t_k = C^{e\,ct}_k \quad (K = 1,2,...,22,24,25,26)$$

$$J^t_h = J_h^{e\,ct}, \text{ etc. } (h=1,2,...,24)$$

Where C_k is the rupee value of the consumption of goods in sector K in the base year, t=0; and J_h is the rupee value of the total investment in sector h in the base year t=0; etc.

Frisch considers an asymptotic problem characterized by the following assumptions:

$$K^t_h = b_h x^t_h \quad (h = 1,2,....,22 \text{ but not } 23,...,26)$$

$$D^t_h = d_h x^t_h \quad (h = 1,2,...,22 \text{ but not } 23,...,26)$$

$$N^t_h = n_h x^t_h \quad (h = 1,2,...,22,24,25,26 \text{ but not } 23)$$

Where K^t_h is the size of the capital that is present at the point of time t;

D^t_h is the total depreciation that takes place between t and t+1;

N^t_h is the employment in sector h in period t;

X^t_h is the flow in the period extending from t to t+1; and b_h, d_h, n_h are the given constants independent of time.

The investment lags are assumed to be given constants. In terms of investment lags the time relation between capital capacity, gross investment and depreciation is given as:

$$K^t_h = K^{t-1}_h + J^{t-Sh-1}_h - D^t_h \ (h = 1,2,...,22)$$

Where J^t_h is the gross investment in sector h during the intermittent period between t and t+1; and S_h is the investment lag in sector h.

The levels of activity x^t_h (h = 1,2,..., 22) are taken among the basis variables in the asymptotic problem and, therefore, no matrix is inverted as was done in the coming year problem. The assumption of constant consumption is also dropped in the asymptotic problem. It is assumed that the Government administration per head of population does not increase.

Finally, as a preference function Frisch introduces

$$f = C_1 + C_2 +,...,+ C_{22}$$

Which means that he simply wants to maximize total consumption of home produced consumer goods.

5.3 SANDEE'S MODEL

Sandee's (1960) model is based on an assumed economic situation in 1960, and analyses the Indian economy in 1970. The economy is divided into 13 sectors. An assumption is made that investment over the 10 year time-span, treated as one time period, increases in a monotonic linear fashion. In order to make the model as compact as possible, the investment and inventory matrices are converted into the corresponding flows and added to the technology matrix. The model has no explicit problem of the post-terminal period.[7] Labour is assumed to be free. Foreign trade is specified to be in balance; however, the structure of the model is such that a unit of export costs less than the imports required to produce it. Thus, exports have to be supplied with specific maximum and minimum (import) levels. These levels serve to bind the model. Investment is restricted to less than a certain fraction of consumption, a constraint that is always active. There is, however, no upper-level constraint on investment except in agriculture.

Capacity is not distinguished from production; and non-competitive imports are not recognised. The model involves only two macro-variables: aggregate consumption and gross investment. They are connected together by an inequality which implies a marginal propensity to invest 24.9 per cent. The investment relations in the model ignore wear-and-tear and investment-output lags. Many input-output coefficients are employed in the same way as Leontief used them originally.

In the initial period of the model, it is assumed that all productive capacity is fully used so that all growth of output will have to come from new capacity. Capital-output ratios relate the new capacity required to the increment in gross output. The required fixed capital is then divided into three categories: heavy equipment, other equipment and construction. Attention is also paid to inventories in the model. To maintain constant stock-output ratio, it is assumed that the normal levels of inventories held are proportional to the output-levels.

There are sixteen linear equations that relate to 30 variables occurring in the model. This leaves 14 degrees of freedom. Thirty five defined constraints, expressed in terms of 30 variables, are introduced in the model so that the occurrence of unrealistic values can be prevented. The constraints are divided into four groups: (1) constraints relating to foreign trade; (2) constraints on investment comprising an upper-limit and lower-limit to investment in each of the sectors; (3) constraints on consumption; and (4) constraints concerning the agricultural stimulants - fertiliser, irrigation and agricultural extension. To simplify computations, the 30 variables are left aside, and the algorithm uses only 21 slack variables and the target function, which is expressed in terms of 14 slack variables. The objective function relates to the maximization of the sum of sectoral consumption levels in the target year over the base year subject to constraints.

Since in the present model the balance of payments in the terminal year is assumed to be such as to require no import surplus, Sandee pays no attention to any parametric variation in foreign aid availability. This question has been reportedly posed by many model builders in India since then.

Carter (1967) extends Sandee's model into a non-linear function of the simple log-type which is shown to be relatively easy to handle.

He demonstrates the usefulness of the cardinal utility approach by reformulating the Sandee model to remove the upper and lower bounds on each consumption good. He incorporates a log-linear objective function of the Stone-Geary form:

$$U(t) = \sum_i \alpha_i \log\left[C_i(t) - C_i(O)\right],$$

Where the coefficients are marginal expenditure shares.[8] He also includes substitution effects in consumption demand.

Bruno (1966, 1967) has also extended the Sandee-type of programming model in a number of interesting ways. First of all, he considers non-linearities in export demand functions by introducing piece-wise linear functions. But a much more important feature has been the introduction of a constraint on the size of skilled labour. Not only does he operate with a general labour constraint, but more specifically, he assumes that skilled labour may turn out to be a bottleneck in a growth process. Even if the assumption of a labour surplus economy holds in a general way, skill limitations may prove real, and then, the pattern of optimal production and trade may become very sensitive to the assumption of a constraint on skill. This is shown by different rankings of trade activities, depending on whether or not the assumption of a skill shortage operates.

5.4 WEISSKOPF'S MODEL

The purpose of Weisskopf's (1967, 1971) exercise is to generate alternative patterns of domestic production and imports subject to a set of predetermined goals of final demand in the terminal year.[9] The choice between production and importing activities, recognised explicitly in the model, makes it differ from a straightforward consistent-requirements planning model. The economy is divided into two parts: the industrial part[10] and the rest of the economy. The industrial part is disaggregated into 147 sectors which are classified into 9 groups, and whose levels of output, imports and so on, are determined endogeniously through the operation of the choice mechanism of the model. A distribution equation balancing supply with demand corresponds to each of 147 endogenous sectors. To almost each of these endogenous sectors there corresponds a distinct domestic productive activity with which is associated a single sectoral output, a production function in the form of a vector in a current flow matrix, and an incremental fixed capital structure in the form of vector in a capital matrix. But there are exceptions in this context in case of joint production, alternative techniques of production, and non-competitive imports. Another notable aspect of Weisskopf's model is that it pays great attention to the dual formulation of the model.

The non-industrial part of the economy is exogenous of the model and affects it only as a source of demand for the products of industrial sector and makes an impact on the balance of trade. Thus, there are no overall distribution equations for these exogenous production activities of the economy.

Five distinct sources of demand for imports are identified within the model:

1. demand for competitive imports;

2. demand for non-competitive imports for those few sectors whose products are relatively heterogenous and a fraction of the total demand or in few sectors the entire demand is to be satisfied only by non-competitive imports;

3. demand for non-competitive imports of agricultural raw material which are related via fixed coefficients to the endogenous production activities which use them as inputs;

4. demand for imports for the exogenous part of the economy excluding agricultural raw materials; and

5. demand for non-competitive imports of the parts of the engineering sectors.

Two stock-flow conversion factors, η^F and η^W, are introduced in the model; η^F approximates, for the endogenous activity as a whole, the ratio of target year fixed capital investment demand to the addition to fixed capital stock between the base and target years; and η^W, a working capital stock-flow conversion factor, approximates the ratio of target year inventory investment demand to the addition to inventory stock between the base and target years. Each of the stock-flow conversion factors is applied uniformly to investment demand from all of the endogenous activities of the model.[11]

Labour resources, measured in terms of their total wage cost, are required by each of the domestic production activities of the model. Estimates of exports are specified exogenously on the basis of independent projections for the target year. Thus, there is no explicit balance of payments constraint in the model as, given the exogenous exports, the cost of foreign capital flow is included in the objective function through foreign exchange costs. Other constraints in the model include the usual commodity balances, constraints on capacity, and lower bounds on competitive imports as a proportion of domestic availability. The model assumes a two-year average investment-output lag.

The objective function relates to the minimization of weighted sum of the domestic and foreign primary resource costs.[12] The former are the labour costs (wage) associated with achieving terminal year targets. The latter are the foreign exchange costs of financing the competitive and non-competitive imports required to achieve the given targets. The element of choice in the model is brought into play by variation of the effective rate of exchange between the rupee and the dollar. The resulting re-allocation of domestic and foreign resources is reflected by changes in the values of the aggregate capital-output and import-output ratios. Values of the two ratios vary not only with the effective rate of exchange but also significantly with the targetted rate of growth of consumption, and in the case of import ratio with the alternative assumptions.

Given the final demand targets, a set of basic assumptions about export prospects and non-competitive import requirements, the basic structural coefficients, and the initial conditions of the economy, the model is solved under a variety of parametric assumptions about the future in order to provide alternative optimal solutions for the terminal year. Increasing import substitution is being induced in the model by increasing the relative weight of foreign resources in the objective function.

Then, Weisskopf compares the qualitative nature of the macro-economic results of his study with the results obtained from aggregative two-gap models of a similar kind.[13] The qualitative nature of the macro-economic results in the present study shows that potential domestic savings cannot be put to use beyond a point when exports are limited exogenously, and when non-competitive imports are required in fixed proportions for domestic production or investment or both. In this situation the growth of domestic output cannot be increased for lack of foreign exchange to purchase specific complementary imports. At this point, a higher growth rate can be attained only by working directly on the foreign exchange constraint by increasing exports, reducing non-competitive imports, or receiving additional foreign aid (net capital inflow). By contrast with the results of an aggregative model, the results of the present multisectoral model, which involves a wide range of substitution possibilities between domestic production and imports, show a relatively smooth approach of the foreign exchange bottleneck. But there does not arise possibilities for further substitution when all possibilities for import-substitution are exhausted. In the process, the overall import-output ratio in the economy gets depressed to a minimum level well below its base year value and the overall capital-output ratio rises above what it would have been with less import substitution. Thus, the rigid implications of the aggregative model are tempered by the introduction of choice among linear activities at the sectoral level.[14]

Thus, in the present model, the resource augmenting aspect of foreign capital inflow is depicted in two ways. If the growth targets with respect to consumption, exports, investment and so on are unchanged while the relative weight of the foreign resource cost in the objective function is varied, a trade-off between external capital inflow and domestic savings is derived. Obviously as the relative weight of external resource cost is increased, more domestic savings and less foreign capital are used to achieve the given targets, and the substitution of domestic savings for foreign resources becomes increasingly costly. Alternatively, one can view the economy-wide incremental capital-output ratio as a measure of efficiency of investment in the model. As the relative weight of foreign resource cost increases, the capital-output ratio rises, reflecting increasing cost of import substitution or, equivalently, the increasing productivity of foreign resource flow.[15] Interestingly, an important aspect of the optimizing solution noticed by Weisskopf is the almost complete insensitivity of the solution to changes in final demand.[16] The reason given for this phenomenon shows the importance of Samuelson's non-substitution theorem in comparing alternative optimal configurations.[17]

Weisskopf suggests the following three ways through which a greater degree of realism can be achieved by widening the area of choice: First, "export levels could be made a function of the effective rate of exchange in those sectors for which there is a significant price elasticity in the demand for or supply of exports.[18] Secondly, the sectoral composition of consumption -- which was fixed (at the margin) in the present form of the model -- could also be allowed to adjust to some extent of the relative scarcity of domestic and foreign resources. Finally, alternative techniques of production for domestically produced goods and services could be introduced -- where appropriate -- in the form of additional linear production activities".[19]

It should be emphasized that the present model does not trace out the time path of the economy from the base to the target year. To arrive at any judgement about the over all feasibility of the alternative strategies as described, it would be necessary to consider explicitly the dynamic implications of the static solutions.

5.5 TENDULKAR'S MODEL

Tendulkar's (1971) present study explicitly incorporates two primary bottleneck constraints on economic growth, namely, domestic savings and foreign exchange.[20] There are several multisectoral models which introduce only the trade constraints bringing out the import financing role of foreign capital inflow.[21] But Tendulkar introduces the savings constraint in order to focus also on the savings supplementing role of foreign assistance, in a multisectoral framework.[22] This formulation is contended to be better suited to highlight the interaction between domestic and foreign resources and its effects on economic growth. The model incorporates both the balance of trade and the savings as primary constraints. Two variants of the basic model have been developed and applied to Indian economy for empirical investigation:

i. *The open-loop variant:* It assumes that domestic savings can be raised to any extent required so that foreign exchange availability becomes the only binding constraint on investment, i.e., a purely-trade-limited (PTL) growth process.[23] The domestic financing of consumption and investment is regarded as exogenous to the system and the optimization process is carried out unconstrained by the availability of domestic resources and subject only to the availability of the primary resource of foreign exchange.[24] The policy implications of the PTL growth process is that the government has sufficient fiscal and monetary control over the economy so that the mobilization of domestic savings does not pose a binding constraint. In this growth process there is free scope for choice in the process of resource allocation between aggregate consumption and investment. However, when the PTL growth process involves raising the domestic savings well beyond the institutional and behavioural limits, the implied investment strategy is unlikely to be successful. It is in such situations that the second variant of a closed-loop variety becomes relevant.

ii. *The closed-loop variant:* It treats the problem of domestic financing as endogenous to the system through an explicit feedback from the process of production to the generation of incomes and, in turn, back to the principal components of gross domestic expenditure. The feedback is accomplished by the introduction of the domestic savings constraint through the specification of the marginal savings propensities for wage and non-wage income earners. The criterion function is optimized subject to the availability of the two primary resources of foreign exchange and domestic savings.[25] Consequently, we get a simultaneous trade-and-savings limited (TSL) growth process. In a closed-loop model, some or all wages are exogenously fixed, and there are fixed coefficients relating wage and profit income to gross output. The fixed propensities to save and to consume out of these forms of income restricts the scope for choice between consumption and investment. The closed-loop assumption is logically consistent with the existence of unemployment and yet a positive shadow price for labour. These features are difficult to introduce into open-loop models.[26]

By dividing the economy into 32 sectors, Tendulkar empirically investigates the two variants of the model over a planning horizon of 15 years. The open-loop variant follows Weisskopf in terms of the supply of foreign exchange as the factor limiting growth. The gross capital formation over the planning period is obtained by dividing the target year levels of gross induced fixed investment (assumed to have a gestation period of two years) and inventory plus exogenous investment (assumed to have no gestation period) by a stock-flow conversion factor and adding them together. To derive the stock-flow conversion factor, Tendulkar assumes: (a) a planning horizon of 15 years; (b) an average investment-output lag of two years; and (c) an exponential rate of growth of gross investment of 8.7 per cent throughout the plan.[27]

The two alternative systems considered by Tendulkar have been found to lead to two different sets of policy prescriptions in optimally adjusting to varying levels of foreign aid. The results of the present exercise can be summarized in the following way:

1. In a closed-loop framework, for the same level of foreign aid as in the open-loop, the average rate of growth of private consumption and that of gross national product (GNP) declines in comparison with the open-loop solution. In the open-loop variant foreign aid increases private consumption faster than the closed-loop variant. The open-loop system reacts to additional capital inflow by adding maximally to consumption more than to investment. The situation is reversed in the closed-loop system.

2. In a closed-loop system the sectoral output mix produces a somewhat higher aggregate gross incremental-capital-output-ratio (ICOR). But the ratio of aggregate gross investment to GNP in the target year is lower in this framework. It can be shown through the Harrod-Domar mechanism that this lower growth rate results from the reduction in the proportion of GNP diverted to gross investment and the rise in the aggregate ICOR.

3. A marginal dollar is found to release only the trade bottleneck in the open-loop variant, whereas it directly and simultaneously

breaks the savings and the trade bottlenecks in closed-loop system. This reveals a multiplier effect of foreign aid on gross investment in the closed-loop system and consequently results in higher marginal productivity of foreign aid than in the open-loop variant. The marginal productivity of a given level of foreign aid declines faster in the open-loop variant than in the closed-loop system.

4. In the closed-loop system foreign aid plays the savings supplementing role in all its aspects. The additional foreign aid with unchanged domestic savings specifications makes possible a higher growth rate, inter-alia; a higher level of aggregate personal savings; a declining marginal savings ratio; and a downward sloping savings ratio in the target year despite a rising target year ratio of gross investment to GNP.

5. The personal savings ratios in the open-loop system remains consistently higher and declines faster than the closed-loop system for expanding levels of foreign aid. This implies that the conflict between the social and individual preference goes on narrowing down with higher availabilities of foreign capital inflow.

6. The closed-loop variant is found to be of more relevance for economic planning in such an economy where the central government does not have full control over the rate of savings but is obliged to operate within the framework of institutionally given savings constraints.

Conceptually, the single-period comparative static framework adopted in this study is restrictive in investigating the consequences of a given assumption about savings which involves intertemporal decisions in giving up immediate consumption in favour of higher future increments in the same. From this point of view, an explicitly dynamic framework is preferable. In a general dynamic framework, the result concerning the greater effectiveness of foreign assistance in the presence of savings constraint does not hold time-point by time-point.[28] In a dynamic model, it is necessary to assess the effect of a given time-stream of foreign assistance as a whole. The relevant criterion would be the evaluation of alternative time-streams of foreign assistance in terms of changes in the corresponding discounted present values of consumption over a given horizon under closed and open-loop versions.[29] The result would hold under this criterion.

The present model may be improved in certain other ways also as suggested by the author himself. First, the treatment of the final consumption basket in a proportional form is an unrealistic assumption, especially when incomes are undergoing structural changes. The introduction of Engel elasticities and variations around them, along the lines of Bruno (1974), would provide a better alternative. Secondly, exporting sectors should be more disaggregated. Thirdly, the agriculture sector should be given more attention. The technological transformation of such decentralized sector may be handled with incremental production processes, along the lines of Sandee (1960), with appropriate bounds to incorporate the limitations imposed by institutional and time factors. Finally, the pricing procedures should have all the information uniformly in market prices.

NOTES

1. For a detailed discussion and rigorous exposition on the question of consistency models versus utility-maximization models, see Chakravarty and Eckaus (1964a) and Chakravarty (1969).
2. In the case of models involving heterogenous capital-goods these difficulties become especially acute. See, for example, Chakravarty (1969, Chapter 6), Hahn (1960) and Samuelson (1967).
3. For a critical review of planning model methodology in relation to the use of the 'dual' of an optimizing framework and the derivation of shadow prices for decentralized decision making and the evaluation of investment projects, see Bruno (1975).
4. See Samuelson (1947), Chapter IV.
5. Bergendorff, Clark and Taylor (1973) point out that an optimizing model provides a 2 or 3 per cent better forecast of the frontier of the choice set in terms of its own welfare function then that resulting from a consistency model. However, the efficiency gains by optimization over projection models have not been explored much in the literature.
6. Besides providing a useful computational means to consider trade-offs implicit in the input-output system, linear programming, in principle, may be used for decentralized planning since solution of the model provides a set of shadow prices with Walrasian interpretation.
7. Eckaus and Parikh (1968) discuss this problem extensively.
8. For a review of consumer demand theory, see Brown and Deaton (1972) who discuss complete systems of demand equations derived from maximization of specific utility indices.

9. Weisskopf's present study is an extension of the aggregative two-gap models of Chenery and Bruno (1962), Mc Kinnon (1964), and Chenery and Strout (1966), who have emphasised the two independent constraints on growth imposed by savings and by foreign exchange, in the direction of multi-sector model. Bruno (1967) provides some methodological guidance to Weisskopf.
10. At that time the endogenous industrial part of the economy accounted for about 25 per cent of India's net national product and 17 percent of the total labour force. However, the endogenous sectors account for about 80 per cent of current imports. And in terms of gross domestic expenditure 50 per cent of total investment and 33 per cent of total consumption is directed to the products of the endogenous sectors.
11. In principle, it would be more accurate to apply distinct stock-flow conversion factors to each of the domestic production activities, since the variables on which the values of η^F and η^W depend are likely to differ as between different activities.
12. It is theoretically possible for the model to prefer imports to domestic production in foreign exchange minimizing solutions if the minimal foreign exchange content of domestic production actually exceeds the corresponding import price. But this is not the case in the present study.
13. For example, Chenery and Bruno (1962), McKinnon (1964), and Chenery and Strout (1966).
14. By overcoming specialization problem, Ali (1979) makes the optimal volumes of both exports and imports endogenous in the free trade solution; and thus makes an improvement on Weisskopf's model.
15. Adelman and Chenery (1966) provide estimates of the actual effects of aid on the growth of the national product. In their pioneering study, they analyse both the past and the future effects of external resources on Greek development in order to determine the productivity of foreign aid.
16. Manne (1963, 1966) also noticed a similar phenomenon. Weisskopf's study is constructed on Manne's lines.
17. The non-substitution theorem asserts the invariance of techniques to a change in the final demand, provided that there is only one primary factor and no joint production and that technology shows constant returns to scale. For the initial, independent statements of the theorem, see Samuelson (1951) and Georgescu-Roegen (1951). For formal proof of the theorem, see also Koopmans (1951) and Arrow (1951).
18. Any such modification would involve the approximation of non-linear functions reflecting diminishing marginal net earnings from exporting activities.
19. See, Chenery and Raduchel (1971).
20. A pioneering study in this area is conducted by Chenery and Bruno (1962) who, in an aggregated one-sector framework, formulates a single-period model for Israel which incorporates both the constraints simultaneously. Tendulkar's present model may be regarded as a multi-sectoral generalization of their work. Like Tendulkar, Mac Ewan (1971) also incorporates both trade and savings constraints into a consumption-maximizing model. But Ewan's study is unique in its treatment of distributional problems in a developing economy made up of two distinct regions. Given different factor endowments, technologies, and demand structures in each region, he analyses the pattern of regional comparative advantage under alternative assumptions about the inflow of external resource and political preferences.
21. For example, Chenery and Kretschmer (1956), Chenery and Uzawa (1958), Bruno (1966) and Weisskopf (1971).

22. The exercises by Eckaus and Parikh (1968) and Bruno (1966) approach the savings constraint as a lower limit on incremental consumption whereas Tendulkar's model imposes savings as an upper limit on investment. Eckaus and Parikh include the savings constraint in the Guide-path II version. Bruno mentions the savings constraint in his theoretical framework of the model but fails to include it explicitly in the solutions. However, through varying capital-inflow, he works out the implicit savings rates in his solutions.
23. As an alternative possibility we may consider a purely-savings-limited growth process which may apply to oil-rich economies with non-scarce supplies of foreign exchange.
24. An 'Optimal growth' theorist would immediately detect that this is a comparative static analogue of the Ramsey-type optimal savings models which are based upon open-loop assumptions. In Tendulkar's model foreign exchange is the primary resource, whereas in the Ramsey problem labour is the autonomous factor limiting growth. For an excellent survey of optimal growth models, see Koopmans (1967).
25. Phelps and Pollak (1968) discuss a dynamic analogue of the closed-loop variant in the framework of the optimal growth theory.
26. The closed-loop assumption underlies the Sen-Marglin choice of techniques models. For a complete discussion of the differences between open-loop and closed-loop hypotheses, see Marglin (1967).
27. Assumptions (b) and (c) are numerically the same as those of Manne and Rudra (1965).
28. For details, see the result of Blitzer et al. (1969).
29. The two-gap approach is an extension of Harrod-Domar planning to economies with foreign trade, and it was popularized by Chenery and Bruno (1962), and Chenery and Mac Ewan (1966). But more profoundly, two-gap models trace back to ideas about 'external strangulation' of underdeveloped economies proposed by Latin American structuralist economists Hirschman (1958) and Furtado (1964). Mc Kinnon (1964) presents a two-gap model with imported investment goods underlying the trade constraint and derives the conclusion in the manner of Harrod-Domar. Marris (1970) presents a useful critique of two-gap calculations of 'aid requirements'. Taylor (1971) analyses phasing of investment in a two-gap model similar to that in the Chenery and Mac Ewan model using optimal control theory. One may utilise the neo-classical two-gap variant of Nelson (1972) to investigate the effects of tariff or exchange rate changes.

SIX

Inter-Temporal Optimising Planning Models

6.1 INTRODUCTION

As pointed out in earlier chapters the explicit recognition of both inter-temporal and inter-sectoral relationships in an optimising planning model decidedly makes it superior to aggregative and/or comparative static models on theoretical as well as empirical grounds and makes possible a more realistic analysis of many important issues of development policy. The inter-temporal, inter-sectoral optimising planning models of Chakravarty and Lefeber (1965), Eckaus and Parikh (1968), Manne and Weisskopf (1970) and Gupta (1973) may rightly be regarded as another step forward in the context of methodological innovations approaching a more realistic planning procedure in India. The purpose of this chapter is to conduct a survey of these linear programming (LP) models.

It may also be pointed out here that for obvious computational reasons, dynamic optimising models have finite horizons as well as all the adhoc characteristics of the static models. Dynamic models can be seen as static programming models which repeat themselves over time. Successive periods are linked together through capital accumulation equations. But in a dynamic optimising problem, strict limits are imposed on the number of sectors and periods to keep the problem manageable.[1] The degree of aggregation can be bothersome in practical planning as highly aggregated sectoral forecasts do not provide a good basis for communication between macro-planners and industrial specialists; and putting two or three years in one time period means that the model can say little about very short-term changes in the economy. These limitations of dynamic linear programming models limit their usefulness.

6.2 CHAKRAVARTY AND LEFEBER MODEL

Chakravarty and Lefeber (1965) formulate an eleven sector finite horizon discrete time period planning model for India.[2] Their objective function is to maximize the discounted sum of consumption over the planning period. The choice of terminal conditions in the form of equality relationships on the types and amounts of capital goods to be bequeathed to the future introduces the post-plan future of the economy. The discount rate is assumed to be arbitrary and remains constant over the plan horizon so that the Strotz (1956)-type 'regret' phenomenon can be avoided. Consumption is defined as a composite commodity, consisting of different commodities consumed in fixed proportions. This assumption of a fixed-consumption pattern implies that the model assumes identical constant returns to scale test for each individual, ruling out explicit consideration of the effects of changes in income distribution on consumption patterns. Similarly, composite goods consumption variable avoids the non-linearities which may be associated with explicit demand elasticities and also circumvents the problem of separately weighting each good that enters consumption. But it is undoubtedly a significant abstraction.

The model incorporates three types of constraints: technological, market-determined and political. The Leontief production coefficients give the technological constraints. The economy is assumed to operate below full capacity if it is optimal to do so. The gestation-lag is assumed to be three years but investment is not assumed to be distributed uniformly over the lag period. Ability to export only limited quantities of goods of different types refers to the set of market-determined constraints. Therefore, export levels are given exogenously. The assumption that the consumption level in a particular year cannot be less than the consumption level in the previous year augmented by a growth factor introduces the set of political constraints.

The model assumes that only a stipulated amount of foreign aid is available period by period which, with the given amount of exports, determines the total foreign exchange available. Foreign aid, government demand for goods and services, exports and the annual replacement requirements are stipulated exogenously. There are only two scarce resources in the system: the sectoral capacities and the supply of foreign exchange.

Imports are divided into two parts: non-competitive and competitive. The non-competitive imports are assumed to be in fixed proportion to sectoral domestic outputs. The ceilings placed on the sectoral allocation of the foreign exchange available after satisfying non-competitive import requirements are represented by the competitive import-coefficients. Import ceilings in all import sectors as well as import floors, where necessary, are imposed in the model.

The solution to the model generates a complete specification, period-by-period, of the resource uses for various types of production and the flows of goods to various uses. These are consistent with the constraints and optimize the maximand of the model.

The theoretical framework of the model is combined to the Indian data to perform certain computational experiments. One of the computations is designed to check the consistency of India's Third Five-Year Plan. The other computation is an independent solution which shows very explicitly the logical consequences and implications of an endogenous determination of terminal targets based upon an explicit post-terminal extrapolation of the rate of growth of consumption and other major demand components. The results of the two computations are compared to have an insight into the effects of alternative methods of target setting on the level of attainable consumption.

Since it brings out the logical implications of an endogenous selection of targets, the qualitative pattern of investment allocation indicated by the model is of much importance from the methodological point of view. The endogenously determined terminal target solutions have the merit of making completely explicit assumptions concerning present and future technology, demand, and other variables and parameters. This may lead to the clarification of some of the implicit assumptions underlying terminal conditions that are obtained by non-explicit method.

The rate of discount is arbitrarily assumed to be 10 per cent and the minimum required annual increase in aggregate consumption is set to be 2.5 per cent in one experiment and 5 per cent in another.

The results of one computation show that in a model where all the relevant relationships are linear, where consumption is taken to be of fixed composition, and where the time-lag is assumed uniformly to be three years, the initial year consumption is of strategic importance. Another experiment where the targets are determined according to the needs of exogenously specified post-plan growth rates of private and government consumption, imports and exports--arbitrarily fixed to be at 5 per cent, 2.5 per cent, 4 per cent and 3 per cent, respectively--is experimented to analyse the methodological implications of an endogenous selection of targets. In this experiment the major constraining sectors throughout the plan period are the consumer goods rather than the capital goods sectors.

The results of the model are sensitive with respect to the change in the capital coefficient for agriculture as in view of diminishing returns in agriculture, the agricultural output cannot be significantly increased without introducing new techniques which will require new industrial output. Other areas for sensitivity test concern the set of assumptions regarding the foreign trade sector, assumptions relating to the post-terminal rate of increase of government demand for goods and services and the length of the planning horizon.

The findings of the model about the shadow rate of foreign exchange provide important qualitative insights into policies concerning the allocation of resources. If, as is the case in the present model, infant industry arguments and employment considerations etc. are not at issue and existing capacity can be partially underutilized without constraints, then foreign exchange (over and above that is needed for non-competitive imports) is in no sense a strategic resource of growth. The manner in which the investment figures for the terminal year are derived in the present model is different from that employed by Sandee (1960) or Manne and Rudra (1965). This model brings the post-plan period into focus in terms of investment in the terminal year. This had certain conceptual advantages over the converse procedure used by the earlier model-builders. Srinivasan

(1965) raises a conceptual question relating to the way in which the terminal conditions are specified in the model. He suggests the method of setting terminal conditions in a way which would maximize indefinitely sustainable per capita consumption. This method has both conceptual and policy determination merits, especially in the context of an economy such as India with massive and rapidly growing population.

Similarly, Bhagwati and Chakravarty (1969) also point out two limitations of the procedure of envisaging terminal conditions: (i) in a model involving an infinity of time, no indefinitely sustainable growth rate can exceed the growth rate of the labour force; and (ii) the composition of consumption, which in this model is pagged till eternity, could be expected to change if, as planned, income levels are going up year by year.

6.3 ECKAUS AND PARIKH MODEL

Eckaus and Parikh (1968) present an excellent set of models for planning and analyzing the inter-sectoral and inter-temporal allocation of resources. These models are applied to development planning in India to illustrate their scope and utility. These models are addressed to the problems of determining the optimal levels of savings and investment overtime and the related problems of inter-sectoral and inter-temporal distribution of investment and output, and the use of foreign exchange resources.[3] There is a basic theoretical structure common to all of them which is much similar to that of Chakravarty and Lefeber (1965). Production processes are assumed to require fixed capital and intermediate inputs in fixed proportions and have constant returns to scale. Private consumption is taken to be a composite commodity and is assumed to be consumed in a fixed proportion in each period. Aggregate consumption is assumed to increase monotonically with time. The different gestation lags for each sector are specified externally to the model. Fixed capital and foreign exchange are the only scarce factors in the model. Labour supply is assumed to be unlimited. In some of the models a savings constraint is imposed to relate the maximum permissible level of net savings to the net national product. This is another way of introducing social goals and a behavioural constraint into the models as it describes indirectly the limits on willingness of the society to sacrifice present for future consumption. Exports and public consumption are exogenously determined. Imports are divided into two categories: non-competitive imports and competitive imports. The objective function of the model is to maximize the discounted sum of aggregate consumption in each of the plan periods. Eckaus and Parikh argue that "this particular objective is chosen because it reflects directly... improvement in the average standard of living... . In a programming model, goals of economic policy can be stipulated not only by what is chosen to be maximized, but also by the content of the constraints." But we feel that for other objectives built in as constraints the efficiency frontier that linear programming solutions draw represents merely minimal attainment of these other objectives and is in no sense optimal. A different objective function will yield quite different social optimal from the particular optimum explored here. It would be wrong to base the strategy for economic planning for a country like India with a massive and growing volume of unemployment and a difficult foreign exchange situation exclusively on an approach based purely on the maximisation of aggregate consumption. This basic structure is combined in various ways and over different planning periods to develop four different models illustrating different aspects of model building and analyzing different problems. The authors themselves make it clear that "since the theoretical structure of the model is an extension of existing economic theory rather than an innovation, surprises are not be expected in the qualitative results. The sectoral and temporal detail generated by the solutions does make those results quantitative and thus more useful in determining strategies for growth".

While in the '*Target Model*' the terminal conditions are stipulated in the form of required minimum terminal capital stocks in each sector, in the '*Transit Model*' the terminal conditions are set endogenously from a specification of required post-terminal growth rates of consumption, exports and imports. The '*Guidepath Models*' are formulated in order to investigate issues that require a long planning horizon taken to stretch to 10 and 30 years in alternative solutions; and each successive time period is aggregated to three years' duration.

The Guidepath Models embody techniques for endogenously changing consumption proportions and for shifting resources from traditional to modern methods in the agricultural sector. The terminal conditions in the Guidepath models are determined, as in the Transit Model, by specifying minimum post-terminal growth rates for various final demands. The Guidepath-I and Guidepath-II versions differ in that an explicit savings constraint is enforced in the latter model. Lastly, a '*Guide-post Model*' is used to obtain year-by-year details for the early years of a desired long-term path which is obtained as a solution of Guidepath Model.

Thus, for their initial work (the 'Target' and the 'Transit' Models) Eckaus and Parikh experiment with a fairly complex dynamic structure: three year gestation lags, with individual time periods each of one year in length. Subsequently (for the 'Guidepath' and the 'Guidepost' Models), they adopt the simplifying assumption that the individual time periods and gestation lags are of the identical length of three years. These simplifications are adopted partly for analytical convenience and partly because of the difficulties of gathering the data for more realistic lag structures.

There are no external economies or diseconomies introduced in the model as all production relationships are accounted for directly in inputs and outputs. Inventory accounting is made an explicit part of the model inspite of the fixed inventory coefficients. In this model, and in similar models, investment is related endogenously to increases in capacity and output. In effect, these models handle investment through a multi-sector version of the rigid acceleration principle.[4]

Each model is solved for a variety of alternative specifications of behavioural, technical, and policy parameters in order to determine the sensitivity of the results to changes in such parameters and to illustrate the range of issues that the models can analyze. Each solution of a model generates for each sector and each period all the uses of capacity, foreign exchange, and output that are consistent with the maximum value of the objective functions and the constraints.[5] To show the detailed overall working of the economy period-by period national income accounts are compiled.

In addition each solution provides a set of shadow prices, determined in terms of composite commodity, corresponding to various constraints which indicate the value, in terms of the maximand, of a marginal adjustment in a constraint with all other constraints remaining unchanged.

To control the 'flip-flop' tendencies,[6] Eckaus and Parikh impose a minimum growth requirements for consumption in one version of their model and maximum savings rates in other versions. The first type of constraint may be interpreted as an elaboration of the objective function in the form of a constraint. The second may also be interpreted in this way or as technical constraint because investment cannot, of course, exceed the available savings.[7]

Eckaus and Parikh's experience suggests that if reasonable results are to be obtained from open-loop linear models of a labour surplus economy, it is dangerous to reject the postulate of diminishing marginal utility. Alternatively, for such an economy, it may be preferable to adopt closed-loop distributional constraints of Sen-Marglin type. Diminishing marginal utility can be handled through the discrete-time maximum principle, or through non-linear programming, or through piece-wise approximations with linear programming.[8]

6.4 MANNE AND WEISSKOPF MODEL

Manne and Weisskopf (1970) intend to quantify the implications of alternative time patterns of the inflow of external assistance at a macro-economic and at a sectoral level.[9] The model's principal interest lies in quantifying the marginal productivity of foreign aid inflows, the implications of self-reliance by the mid-seventies, and the trade between the near-term and long-term growth of consumption. The model generates internally consistent sectoral paths for domestic production, imports, exports, consumption and investment over the planning period of eight years spanning over 1967-68 to 1975-76. The time-lag is assumed to be of two years. For each individual time period the sectoral investment allocations and the sectoral import substitution activities are among the choice elements. A 30-Sector input-output accounting framework for mining, manufacturing, power and transport organizes the domestic production activities. These sectors are divided into two groups: 17 labelled as 'production-oriented' and 13 as 'consumption-oriented.'[10] The focus of India's import substitution programme is on the production-oriented sectors. The consumption goods industries are in effect assumed to provide negligible inter-industry deliveries. All other, mining, manufacturing and power, together with rail and road transport, sectors are endogenous to the model. The exogenous sectors include agriculture and services.

From the methodological point of view, the authors rightly suggest that the model differs from its predecessors in three principal respects: First, the 30 sector inter-industry model is reduced to 17 aggregated sectors to reduce the number of activities and items that enter into the linear programming optimization. Secondly, the objective function of the model is to maximize consumption levels attained at various points of time. During subsequent time periods, consumption is constrained to branch from the given initial year's level, to fit at all periods within a two-parameter class of 'gradualist' paths: the near-term and the long-term growth rate of consumption. Finally to reduce the likely horizon effects, a certain condition is imposed on the sectoral allocations of investment during the terminal period using the long-term growth parameter of the gradualist consumption path to ensure that these allocations will be in 'turnpike' proportions. A limited amount of experimentation with this terminal condition suggests that the optimal near-term consumption path is not necessarily sensitive to the arbitrary choice of an eight years planning period.

By determining the aggregate consumption (C) via the objective function subject to the gradualist path constraint, calculating the aggregate net investment (I) as the sum of the endogenously determined investment requirements for capacity expansion of all sectors, the level of net foreign aid (F) in each period; the model gives a full set of macro-economic accounts. Given C, I and F, the corresponding values of net domestic savings and net national product follow from standard macro-economic accounting identities. Similarly, the foreign trade aggregates (total exports and imports) may be calculated directly from each solution. Exports are specified exogenously for each time period, and the corresponding sectoral export levels are determined as linear functions of the aggregate quantity of exports.

Aggregate imports are defined as the sum of four groups: imports of goods that are competitive with those of the production-oriented sectors, and whose individual values are determined by the model; imports of fertilizers and of principal imported raw materials for fertilizers which are fixed exogenously; imports of foodgrains which are also fixed exogenously; and imports of all other commodities--classified together as 'maintenance imports'--a total projected as a constant proportion of the value of net national product.

Thus, the model involves variables corresponding to each of the production-oriented sectors and also contains variables representing the principal macro-economic magnitudes. From any given solution, a complete set of macro-economic accounts may be estimated, together with implications for each of the endogenous sectors. The model operates under the assumption of complete flexibility of the initial year's sectoral investment allocations. Then the problem is stated as one of the assigning non-negative values to 236 variables so as to maximize the initial period's consumption increment, subject to 228 inequality constraints. In this way, Manne and Weisskopf show how the number of intermediate goods balances can be reduced when some of the sectors supplying them are modelled without resource substitution possibilities.

The model summarizes the macro-economic implications of two alternative choices for the asymptotic growth rate, g=8 per cent and 6 per cent, and the consequences of three alternative aid programmes. The higher the value of g, the higher becomes the rate of investment during the Fourth Five-Year Plan, and the greater becomes the base for future expansion of consumption. It is shown that with g=6 per cent rather than 8 per cent there is a higher initial increase, and the absolute level of consumption remains higher throughout the eight year planning period, irrespective of the aid inflows pattern. In 1977-78, the more austere programme (g=8 per cent) overtakes the less austere one (g=6 per cent). This trade off between near and distant future consumption is of the same order of magnitude as is predicted by the Fel'dman-Domar-Mahalanobis aggregative model of labour-surplus economy with a single capital good, a constant incremental output-capital ratio and a constant marginal propensity to save.

Other significant findings of the present exercise are that the aggregate incremental capital-output ratio, as well as the shadow price of foreign exchange, increases as the rate of decline in aid flow increases; and the more rapid the path of self-reliance, the greater the share of the investment budget that is allocated to the capital-intensive import substituting sector.

6.5 GUPTA'S MODEL

Gupta's (1973) model covers a time period of ten years and has three broad types of structural systems: a conventional open input-output type of transaction flows, with observations for only one, or at the most two years; a behavioural equation system purporting to approximate to the economic behaviour of consumption, inventory holdings, imports etc., based on time series or cross-section data; and a set of inequality restraints and boundary conditions, either on the target and the instrumental variables or on the individual coefficients and the relations between them.

Capital and skilled manpower are regarded as the major constraining factors. The capital constraint works in terms of the capacities of the initial period and the supply of savings. The objective function of the model is to maximize the discounted sum of aggregate consumption over the plan period. Other major alternative objectives, such as balance of payments considerations, guarantee of a minimum level of consumption, and reduction of idle capacity and wastage, are all accommodated by the content of the constraints. A constraint relating to the terminal capital stock is imposed to ensure a desired rate of growth of consumption in the post-terminal period. The discount rates are pagged at three alternative levels of 10 per cent, 20 per cent and 30 per cent per annum; and the ranges of their sensitivity are also explored.

The present model can be divided into two stages: the 22-sectors steady-state and the 6 sectors transient-state. Data from 7 separate submodels (export submodel; import submodel; consumption/income submodel; public expenditure and tax submodel; macro-economic model; skilled manpower model; and tax model) are fed into the steady-state model at different iterative stages of its solution, in order to arrive at the final results given in terms of gross output, fixed and working capital, replacement investment, imports, value added requirements for skilled manpower, intermediate demands, and saving investment gaps with their fiscal implications.

In the steady-state of the model, two broad alternatives (defined as pessimistic and optimistic) are attempted, based mainly on different export assumptions, owing to the uncertain effect of rupee devaluation in India at that time. The first alternative is defined as pessimistic and the second as optimistic. The basic assumptions of the first alternative are that exports are exogenous to the model and devaluation has no effect on the volume of exports and imports; current inputs and replacements investments are related to gross output in fixed proportions; marginal fixed capital and inventory holdings are related to marginal gross output and intermediate imports are proportional to sectoral outputs, while capital-goods imports are related to net fixed capital formation and time, no consumption goods are imported, and the whole of the import surplus is balanced by foreign aid (i.e., foreign aid is endogenous). In the second alternative, it is assumed that devaluation has its full effect in the reduction of prices of export goods and that net foreign aid will amount to zero in this period. All the other assumptions of the first alternative are retained.

The transient-state of the model comprises four submodels (export submodel, import submodel, the public expenditure submodel and the consumption-income submodel) and one principal model. Its main purpose is to lay out the inter-temporal movements of the relevant economic variables in the context of the objectives of the plan. The parameters of the principal models refer mainly to the coefficients of production functions in comparatively disaggregated form. They are confined to estimating the current flow coefficient matrix, the capital flow coefficient matrix, the inventory flow coefficient matrix, and the replacement flow coefficient matrix. Originally, they are all derived in a 22-sector classification; but subsequently, they are abridged into 4 sector classification before being fed into the transient-state model.

The model assumes a gestation lag of roughly one and a half year for the incremental capital/capacity ratios. Imports are divided into three categories; intermediate imports; non-competing imports contributing to the capital formation; and consumer-goods imports going to households, government and corporate sectors as direct consumption.

In this transient-state of the model, the choice between the alternative patterns of development of the economy is computed. There are three major types of constraints in this model: technological constraints; foreign aid constraints; and behavioural constraints. The first and third types of constraints are assumed to be given exogenously, and the second becomes the policy constraint. Hence, the alternative optimal development patterns are explored almost exclusively in the light of alternative aid assumptions.

Both the steady-state and transient-state models satisfy all the technical conditions by using the base-period current and capital flow matrices for developing their production relations and observing the capacity constraints that arise from the problems of resource availability. The constraining effect of land, however, is not explored. The constraining effect of labour is taken care of in the manpower submodel. The behavioural feasibility of this model is mainly tested in the savings/income submodel.

The savings constraint in the present model is policy-oriented and not behavioural, and being much-less stringent it only guarantees against a fall in per capita consumption over the plan period, compared to the base year. However, the model's solution permits an improvement in the per capita consumption, which suggests that the plan period as a whole has no effective savings constraints.

From the technical view point, the present linear programming models are said to contain two major limitations: high sensitivity of the plan outlays to the discount rates used; and 'flip-flop' behaviour in the movement of some of the major macro-variables like consumption and output. This means that consumption shows a tendency to concentrate at the tail-end of the plan period, and the rate of growth of output falls sharply near the end of the plan. But the first objection does not appear significant in this study and the second objection is removed by using time discount rates in the objective function and by introducing a monotonicity assumption in the movement of output.[11]

The results of the model can be summarized in the following way: firstly, the higher the level of foreign aid, the less the strain on the domestic economy in achieving certain goals, and the higher the value of its social maximand. Secondly, the larger and more favourable the supply of foreign resources, the quicker the growth of capital stock, and the greater the supply of consumption goods to the society over the plan period. Thirdly, the productivity of foreign aid is very high in plan formulation in developing economies. Evidently, therefore, any error in forecasting the aid supply is quite likely to disrupt the entire structure of the plan. The sensitivity of plan allocation to aid changes decreases as the economy moves to a higher income-and-growth path. Finally, the capital-output ratio increases mainly due to the faster growth of the capital-intensive sector relative to others.

NOTES

1. This is true even when all possible substitutions are made to introduce the number of constraints in the model. Bruno et al. (1970), Manne and Weisskopf (1970) and Bergendorff et al.(1973) describe such reduction procedures.
2. The logic of an inter-temporally consistent multi-sectoral planning model was first outlined by Chakravarty and Eckaus (1964) who pointed out the basic difficulties without computing numerical growth paths. The present model by Chakravarty and Lefeber is a generalisation of the models presented in Eckaus and Lefeber (1962) and Lefeber (1964): and has been further discussed and developed by Eckaus (1967), and Eckaus and Parikh (1968).
3. There have been several theoretical studies on the problem of determining the optimum level of savings, see, for example, Ramsey (1928), Sen (1961), Chakravarty (1962), Tinbergen (1960). But to my knowledge, no survey exists as yet on Ramsey-optimal savings models. Clear introductions of such models are given by Arrow and Kurz (1970) and Dorfman (1969).
4. The present model is extended by Eckaus (1973) to illustrate the maturation version of the absorptive hypothesis.
5. In contrast to Eckaus and Parikh (1968) and Chenery and Mac Ewan (1966), the model by Bruno et al. (1970) exhibit, on the whole, fairly smooth behaviour of consumption and other variables over time even without extra path constraints on consumption.
6. 'Flip-flop' (also called bang-bang) behaviour means that the solutions tend to extremes in time or in whatever dimension they can find which will permit the maximization of the objective function of the model. For example, the objective function of a planning model typically calls for the maximization of consumption over some plan period. If there is a choice between raising consumption in nearer or more distant time periods, the model solu-

tion will generally tend to delay any increase in consumption. It will plough back as many resources as possible until the latter part of the plan period. Then, near the end of the plan period as much of the available resources as are divertible will be put into the kinds of output and the uses of output which increase the objective function most rapidly, consistent with all the constraints on the problem.

This 'flip-flop' behaviour results because of the thorough-going linearity in the model. In effect, therefore, the simplex algorithm searching along the feasible set of solution points for an optimal position ends up at a vertex, that is, at an extreme position.

But this 'flip-lop' behaviour is not inevitable with dynamic input-output technologies. From the work of Tsukui (1968) it can be seen that this problem can be avoided through closed-loop model with savings constraints. Similarly, in Bruno et al. (1970) solutions are avoided through primary resource constraint by imposing an upper bound upon labour employment. By definition, this type of upper bound is a redundant in a labour surplus economy.

7. Still another method to control the 'flip-flop' tendencies of inter-temporal programming models is to introduce both upper and lower limits to the level of investment.
8. For more on these three alternative computational techniques, see Kendrick and Taylor (1971), Luenberger (1972) and Westphal (1971).
9. Manne and Weisskopf's study is closely related to the studies of Chakravarty and Lefeber (1965), Eckaus and Parikh (1968) and Chenery and Mac Ewan (1966).
10. The original 147 sectors of the Weisskopf's (1967, 1971) exercise are aggregated into 30 sectors and all of the physical and money values are converted into 1967 prices.
11. In formulations which do not contain these two assumptions, the 'flip-flop' behaviour becomes marked: consumption moves along the minimum level (constrained as lower bound in the model) and jumps to a very high figure in the terminal year of the plan.

SEVEN

The Choice of Planning Techniques in the Planning Process

7.1 INTRODUCTION

An underdeveloped economy attempting to have planned development has to face a number of problems, one of which is that of choosing between alternative planning techniques in the planning process -- that is, the *permanent plan* technique, the *fixed plan* technique, the *sequential plan* technique, the *semi-rolling plan* technique, the *rolling plan* technique, the *semi-continual revision plan* technique and the *continual revision plan* technique.[1] as regards the method of these techniques each has its strong points as well as problems, and each is considerably more complex than its predecessor.

The desirable mode of planning technique in the planning process should be determined on the basis of the availability of certain prerequisites to the respective techniques. In the absence of these prerequisites, the prospect of the more complex and apparently more suitable planning technique may lead to unintended results. Therefore, the purpose of this chapter is to discuss, within a theoretical framework, the problem of the choice of planning techniques in the planning process.

7.2 THE BASIC THEORETICAL POSSIBILITIES

The choice of an appropriate planning technique involves two fundamental decisions that must be made in advance of any specific plan and in any specific institutional setting. First is the choice of a *horizon* (H), that is, the time interval covered by the plan. Second is the choice of a *period* (P), that is, the time interval during which the plan remains in effect before it is revised.[2] The combinations of these decisions would determine the nature of planning techniques, the theoretical possibilities of which are shown in the following table:

Basic Theoretical Possibilities of Planning Techniques in the Planning Process

Type of Technique / Characteristics	Permanent Plan Technique (PPT)	Fixed Plan Technique (FPT)	Sequential Plan Technique (SPT)	Semi-Rolling Plan Technique (SRPT)	Rolling Plan Technique (RPT)	Technique of Semi-continual Planning Revision (TSCPR)	Technique of Continual Planning Revision (TCPR)
Period (P)	α	Finite	Finite	Finite	Finite	Zero	Zero
Horizon (H)	α	Finite	α	Finite	Finite	Finite	α
Relationship between P&H	P = H	P = H	P < H P rolling	P < H P rolling H fixed	P < H P rolling H rolling	P < H	P < H
Possibility of implementation	No	Yes	No	Yes	Yes	No	No

The techniques of the rolling plan and the semi-rolling plan can be further classified into time planning, event planning and hybrid planning. In the *time planning* technique, the plan is revised after a fixed time interval has elapsed. In the *event planning* technique, the plan is revised after a certain event or set of events occurs. The event that triggers the drawing up of a new plan is usually closely related to the goals of the decision maker (e.g., a new fiscal plan is drawn up in the event of war or inflation). *Hybrid planning* technique represents a combination of time planning and event planning. In this case either time or some event(s) can trigger the formulation of a new plan (e.g., an Indian type of Parliamentary system in which a new Government is elected if there is a vote of no confidence or five years have elapsed since the last election).

In any system involving uncertainty, revising plans on the basis of events is preferable to revising plans on the basis of time alone. A major problem of event (or hybrid) planning, however, is simply that of identifying the event(s) which would trigger the new plan. The event(s) should summarize relevant information available concerning the state of the system, involving certain significant changes in some fundamental variables of the system. Given a relevant index or set of indices, the particular level(s) which would trigger the formulation of a new plan would generally depend on the cost of planning and the opportunity cost of not revising the plan.

The choice of a particular horizon and period depends upon certain factors, e.g., the degree of uncertainty concerning the decisions to be made, the cost of planning, the cost of processing new information, and political, social, legal and other constraints. Keeping in view these determinants of a horizon and a period, we can discuss the plausibility and practical possibilities of adopting these techniques in a real world situation.

As regards the *permanent plan*, the gross uncertainty of the future period beyond a certain future point makes this technique of no relevance and inapplicable or impracticable to real world situation. Similarly, in the case of semi-continual plan revision technique and the continual plan revision technique, a zero period would also be highly undesirable and impracticable because there is usually some information about the near future and decisions as to this near future are closely inter-linked to those pertaining to the present; there is no time available to revise the plan; and the computational facilities and resources to revise the plan are hardly available in any developing economy.

7.3 THE FIXED PLAN TECHNIQUE

In the fixed plan technique the plan period is equal to the plan horizon over some finite interval. This technique implies the ability of the Planning Agency to determine the course of the economy over the entire planning period/horizon, and under these circumstances a new plan can be instituted only at the expiry of the old one. This type of plan formulation is so simple that there remains no possibility of major political hagglings. At the initial period, optimum targets upto the terminal period are set. The government and the people are motivated to move along this optimum path by resisting the temptation of backslide.

But against this, the rigid nature of the fixed plan technique has grave disadvantages. *Administratively*, it implies that an additional rigidity is superimposed on a system already teeming with rigidities. Necessary and desirable adjustment to unforeseen changes or correction of errors may not be made even in the light of the latest available informational basis, and the adaptations that are made will tend to occur abruptly between plan periods. *Psychologically*, too, the temptation to revise the plan downward when no formal provision for this is made can have demoralizing effects.[3] Similarly, the inhibitions against stepping up efforts when things turn out better than anticipated is strengthened.

Another disadvantage of this technique is that of the lack of *flexibility*. This technique is without the provision for possibilities for change as the period unfolds and new developments impinge on the economy. Too many things are so neatly tied in that a basic change can only be made when a new plan is formulated, and even then, there is every possibility of the past commitments to limit the area of manoeuverability. What a dangerously naive procedure it is to work out a plan for certain uncertain long years to come at a given date and then to petrify and to stick to it, regardless of what is going to happen in the course of this period. To be bound by the figures in this system may lead to misallocations of resources. It may also destroy the authority of the Planning Agency because decision-makers, private and public, may find the planners' documents increasingly irrelevant to immediate needs. Consequently, they may either ignore them to lobby against the Agency as a plan without relevance soon ceases to carry authority. Poor performance of national economic projections, if repeated for a considerable period, would eventually destroy the credibility of a plan. Moreover, towards the latter part of the plan, which started with a process of capital formation in projects with long-gestation periods, the time period remains too short for investment decisions in many sectors and giving them up half-way through is often less economic than either not having them at all or completing them. Similarly, in this technique the choice of terminal investment conditions are necessarily arbitrary.

Needless to say, in this dynamic and living world of imperfect knowledge and uncertainty, the planning technique must be flexible enough to absorb and utilize all the new information that are available at any time. Plan implementation is much more difficult than plan formulation since formulating a plan is an exercise of imagination, while implementation is a struggle with reality.[4] One should not stick to plans to an undue degree because they are 'plans' but treat them more like working hypotheses which are revised when new information indicates a change in the premises or conditions. Thus, when reality is found to differ from expectations, the plan must be revised accordingly to cope with the changing facts. Furthermore, a plan needs to be modified periodically as new data becomes available and new ideas arise. New projects might become known that are better than those that were known previously. With the passage of time new data and the results of recent research are bound to become available and to enrich our knowledge. Moreover, from time to time, a new programme of action is needed in which all the new information can be used. It implies that the results of the development strategy during a period in the past can be taken into account and an attempt can be made to profit from the results obtained--both the positive and the negative results.[5] Similarly, the changing political electorate may also retard the implementation of the plan. The current population may be concerned with those events in the near future in a much different manner than those with more distant, and the passage of time necessitates an extension of this period of original plan in the form of a re-evaluation and a modification of the original programme in accordance with the changing tastes. We should note here that whatever else democratic theory may or may not imply, we must consider it axiomatic that a democratic government reflects only the preferences of the individuals who are presently members of the body politics.

It is well known that the process of economic development implies more output; and also changes in the technical and institutional arrangements under which production and distribution take place. Development also implies greater efficiency; changes in the composition of output and in the allocation of inputs by sectors; and change in the economic activities that occupy the labour force and foreign trade. Similarly, inventions and innovations take place. Productivity increases and costs lower through a 'learning-by-doing effect'.[6] All these developments make it necessary to revise the plan periodically in the light of new informational basis because of the fact that an appropriate data system for economy-wide planning would have to contain a mechanism for updating or revising existing data.

The *development planning models* in the context of the fixed plan technique would either be of a 'static' or of a 'comparative static' or of a 'dynamic' nature. The model's parameters which may be imprecise or random are usually estimated from observed statistical data which may contain measurement errors. The model itself may be incorrect as the underlying economic theory could be erroneous. Therefore, it should be recognised that the uncertainties which circumvent policy are not simply those derived from the need to forecast the values of exogenous variables; they also arise from the imperfections and limitations of economic theory and econometrics. In general, we do not know for certain the future values of exogenous variables. It may be due to imperfect information or due to the general unpredictability of the phenomenon. Under uncertainty possible investment levels as well as their probabilities are unknown; they are subjectively estimated by the policy makers. As time passes, the government will obtain new information which may suggest a revision in its earlier estimations of investment levels and probabilities of their occurrence. Thus, the existence of uncertainty may cause us to change policies as we get new information.

Similarly, in most economies, information is available in a highly dispersed form. Even the most disaggregated development planning models used by the Planning Agency take into account only a limited account of information, and that too in a form that may not necessarily be accurate on account of the almost inevitable aggregate bases.[7] Additionally, in a country like India there is the problem of concentration of income and wealth in private hands which may not necessarily be adaptable to the planners' need of an 'optimum plan'. Further, even if the central planners owned all the non-human property, there would remain important problems pertaining to people's preferences for jobs and commodities.[8] Hence, the need to revise plans.[9]

In this way, the theoretical and practical planning work under the fixed plan technique does not deal with planning under uncertainty. As pointed out by Sarris and Adelman (1981) in their excellent work, projections of likely paths of exogenous variables are made and then the plan is formulated to fulfil some objectives given the assumed structure of the economy and the projected path of the exogenous variables. The plan is then based on the "medium" variant, and the information on how the investment strategy differs under the alternative variants helps the Planning Agency to cope with different policy regimes. Surprisingly, it is known *a priori* that the exogenous variables and the behavioural representation of the economy will deviate from their assumed values by some random magnitudes; but this information is not taken into account systematically in the initial preparation of the plan. Therefore, when during plan implementation unforeseen contingencies arise, the original plan is usually hastily adjusted to the contingency or even completely scrapped. By this time, the original planning furor has usually dispersed: the plan has served its political function; hence, the attention of the chief policy makers has shifted from it; and short-term stabilization considerations, arising at least partly out of the unforeseen contingencies, take over the centre of the stage in economic policy analysis. Instead of reformulating the plan, it is hastily patched up. If the disturbance imparted by the unforeseen event(s) is large, the plan is abandoned entirely. Thus, the absence of good contingency planning, namely planning that allows for subsequent adaptation to random events, is a major reason why formal planning is perceived by most policy makers and heads of planning offices to be an essentially irrelevant exercise, useful mostly for window dressing and political mobilization.[10]

7.4 THE SEMI-ROLLING PLAN TECHNIQUE

In the semi-rolling plan technique the plan period is rolling within a fixed planning horizon. The overall planner breaks the planning horizon into a sequence of plan periods due to the complexity of formulating a trajectory over the entire interval (t_o, t_n). In this technique we formulate a plan for a horizon of 'n' time periods and after each period, in the light of the latest available information, we keep on re-formulating new plans for rest of the planning horizon, i.e., n-1,..., {(n-(n-1)} periods, respectively. This may be done by either sticking to the initially projected terminal level of the economy or by changing it. In this way, the plan period remains constant at each stage of the planning process. The planning horizon keeps on decreasing by the size of a plan period at each stage. In the final stage, the plan period and the planning horizon remain identical to each other.

In general, the semi-rolling plan technique implies that there is a long-term plan (covering the entire plan horizon) which specifies selected states of the economy for various time periods t^{*}_{1}, t^{**}_{2}, ...,T^{***}. For the first period a short-term plan is worked out which borrows targets from t^{*}_{1}. However, in view of more recent information and facts, and limitations brought to light by the analysis of implementation possibilities, the Planning Agency may end up with targets for the first period T^{**}_{1}, which may not necessarily be identical with those contained in t^{*}_{1}. Furthermore, t^{**}_{1} may be more disaggregated as compared with t^{*}_{1}. This plan then also specifies the intended use of the instruments. Next for the second period a target t^{*}_{2} which is specified partly on the basis of the long-term plan t^{**}_{2} and partly influenced by experiences from the first period and dynamic conditions relating the possibilities in the second period to the achievement in the first period. This plan specifies the intended use of instruments t^{**}_{2} which is deemed necessary for achieving t^{**}_{2}. In the same way one proceeds from period to period.

The semi-rolling plan technique is in between the fixed plan technique and the rolling plan technique. It shares the characteristics of these techniques in parts. In the initial period, it embodies the characteristic of flexibility which is a feature of the rolling plan technique. Towards the final periods, it embodies the characteristic of rigidity which is a feature of the fixed plan technique. In this way, the related advantages and disadvantages of these techniques are also associated with this technique in an essential way.

7.5 THE ROLLING PLAN TECHNIQUE

In this technique both the period and the horizon keeps on rolling, i.e., the plan is revised at the end of each period and an additional period is appended to the original horizon so that a future planning horizon of constant length is maintained. Thus, in this system of planning we formulate a plan for a horizon of 'n' periods in which initially we project an optimum path for the development of the economy to achieve a certain level of development on the completion of the 'n-th' period; and after each period we keep on formulating another optimum plan for a horizon of another 'n' periods, irrespective of the targets achieved or not-achieved, making use of the projected path only for one period. Thus, in this form of planning, old programmes may be scrapped and new ones can be instituted at points in time before the expiration of the original plan.

The rolling plan technique is more suitable in those situations where the economy is faced with large *uncertainties* with reference to certain natural and/or economic factors which make it irrelevant to take a long or medium term prospective regarding the future course of events in the economy. Under these circumstances, the rolling plan technique offers the flexibility of adjusting to the changing exogenous factors from period to period. Even in the normal course of planning, the ex-ante coordination involved in the planning process has to be based on the incomplete and uncertain informational basis available at the time of plan formulation. As a result, there is a certain amount of inevitability about some discrepancies between forecasts and actualities, and hence, the need for a built-in capacity to correct mistakes. This is expected to be provided by the rolling plan technique. The dichotomy of short and long-term planning is largely in conflict with reality because in real life information flows of relevance for both the present and the future are inextricably interwoven. This technique would integrate them and take care of the dynamic equilibrium in the continuous process of structural change in the economy.[11]

Under uncertainty the rolling plan technique allows the planner to adapt to the economic state as well as to exogenous shocks. In addition, structural changes may be *imbedded* in the planner's state space to allow adaptation to technological change and changes affecting the dynamics of the economic system. Uncertainty imposes upon the planner the task of deciding what to do in future periods while at the same time not making a commitment to a particular action. One can point out *two different classes of uncertainty* which an economy faces. One class consists of stochastic fluctuations of a recurring nature such as yearly swings in international process of raw materials or domestic agricultural yields.[12] The second class consists of very unlikely events of potentially catastrophic consequences, such as an embargo on exports or imports or an earthquake. The distinction between these two classes of uncertainties is important because they require different conceptual treatments. A recurring event can be dealt with by means of a feedback type of adjustment rule, while a highly unlikely but major event usually gives no prior signals which one can use as an early warning system for changing immediate plan prior to the realization of the catastrophe.[13]

The stationarity property of the rolling plans clearly has computational advantages over decision-making procedures which follow finite horizon plans to completion and then recalculate the next plan. From the practical viewpoint, there are two additional advantages also. First, the initial period decision rules of a medium or long-term plan will be more reliable and relevant, while the decision rules of latter periods become increasingly inaccurate as the effects of uncertainty accumulate. Secondly, the division of time into horizons or periods of five to seven years may tend to generate cycles in investment starting and completion which are not efficient from an overall point of view.[14] It may be shown that the stationary rolling plan comes closer to the optimal solution of the infinite horizon plans, while incorporating much of the realism and tractability of finite plans. Moreover, the rolling plan method is more realistic since it does not require infinite foresight.

The necessity to revise a plan may also result from some political process wherein only those currently alive may vote directly or indirectly on the length of the planning period and horizon; and where their consideration of future generation is different from their own. Moreover, since the current population constitutes the only group of the society capable of expressing explicitly its preferences, and since the composition of this group is continually changing, plans once formulated may become obsolete. The constantly changing composition of the population then necessitates planning revision.[15] The logic of this planning system is that the society (i.e., all individuals in the society, regardless of when they will live) might have been unable to determine the course of the economy for the entire planning horizon and the current population may find the plan unacceptable or undesirable, then they will wish to revise the plan. Today, it will be rational for a man to jettison his optimal plan of yesterday, not because his knowledge of the future is different, but because today he is a different person with a new discount function--the old one shifted forward in time.[16] As we all know, if an individual is free to reconsider his plan at later dates (even though his original expectations of future desires and means are verified) he will not generally obey the optimal plan of the present month, i.e., his future behaviour will be inconsistent with his optimal plan. This potential inconsistency may be resolved through planning revision. Therefore, at each moment in time the current population should be free to formulate and to begin implementation of its own T-year plan. Thus, in this technique of rolling plan, planning ceases to be a one time exercise and becomes a process of improvisation, refinement and continuity with a very high degree of sensitivity imparted to the entire idea of development. In this way, the rolling plan technique permits an extended vision on society's goal at the same time that changed circumstances renew the planning process rather than making its work obsolete.[17]

The development planning models in the context of the rolling plan technique shall be methodologically of '*comparative dynamic*' nature which can deal with the changes in the initial conditions, and/or changes in the exogenous forces and/or changes in the internal parameters.

The *rationale of the rolling plan* technique is that the more upto date the statistical base period, the more reliable are likely to be near term policy recommendations generated by the comparative dynamic models formulated under this technique. This is because of the fact that effective planning, to a great extent, involves developing an efficient flow of information which is not generally one way, but is multi-lateral involving important feedback at all levels between decision makers, planners, researchers and statisticians. Since this technique ensures flexibility of adjusting to the changing exogenous factors from period to period, it has both the advantages of administrative and psychological nature which are lacking in the fixed plan technique. Moreover, the rolling plan technique has the advantages of a clearer perspective, a better view of the priorities and a constant time horizon for investment decisions. It fulfills the purpose of planning by making a rational adjustment of means to ends in the light of changing circumstances, including new experiences and new ideas generated in the process of plan formulation and plan implementation. It increases flexibility in the process of planning development of the economy and thus liberates efforts for progress so that favourable opportunities can be seized and pitfalls avoided.

However, there are also *dangers involved* in the use of rolling plans. One may object to this system of planning on two counts: First, there may be the absence of sufficient discipline in ensuring that serious and sincere efforts are made to achieve the targets once they are initially set. Second, with rolling plans there might be no day of reckoning when targets are compared with performance. But we do not see any reason why, with rolling plans, targets cannot be compared with performance. Of course, frequent comparisons of targets and performance may, in practice, be less likely to occur when plans are revised from time to time than would be the case with conventional fixed terminal date planning. The objection concerning the possible absence of sufficient discipline in ensuring that serious effort is made to achieve the targets once they are initially set is important, and underlines the need for periodic comparisons of past targets and performance and assessment of that performance.

But under the rolling plan technique of the planning process there remains always a possibility for the politicians in power to pressurize the Planning Agency to roll over the planning objectives not in response to non-political exogenous factors as implied by the technique but because of political compulsions and inabilities to opt for hard policy options as this provides them to evade their commitments by lowering the commitments from time to time and not by raising the levels of achievements. In this way, this technique becomes a device for covering up slippages in the practice of planning and achievement of goals. Similarly, projects and policies which for one reason or another are not interesting to the government but have to be included any way can be conveniently stashed away in the last years of the plan and then ignored.

The foregoing considerations suggest the following essential *prerequisites* for the successful and efficient working of the rolling plan technique:

1. It is very important for the planning process to have a good *monitoring mechanism* to provide regular and intensive assessment of how plans are being carried out. Important questions include why planned aggregate or sectoral production targets have not been achieved, or why unexpected price increases have occurred, or trade balance estimates have deviated from ex-ante projections. Although some of this performance monitoring will have to be done qualitatively, quantitative monitoring is also desirable. Quantitative checks prove more useful in the planning office's attempts to persuade other agents to adhere more closely to the plan. In addition, such monitoring is important in learning about how to improve the planning process itself. There are a number of requirements which have to be met by the planning office in the development of an effective mechanism for these purposes, for example:

i. Continuous efforts must be made in correcting and updating economic data. Changes in the most strategically significant input-output coefficients have to be made consistently.

ii. The new updated data should be used to test, at regular intervals, the structural specification of the various planning models which are being used. If an input-output model is being used, the components of the final demand vector, especially consumption and capital-formation, should be checked annually.

iii. The models themselves may have to be returned with revised estimates of certain exogenous variables, such as the level of net foreign aid, the exchange rate, or the marginal savings propensity.

These steps should provide considerable help in reducing the gap between the planned and the actual situation.[19]

Thus, there must be a very efficient monitoring system regarding the progress of various projects, the diagnosis of plan targets and the suggestion for possible corrective actions. This has to be organised in a decentralized fashion with two-way information flows going to and from a centralized agency overviewing this work at the Planning Agency. This monitoring mechanism will have to be supplemented by an equally efficient short-term forecasting system which is expected to indicate the course of various key variables in response to the latest informations regarding uncertain factors and controllable policy-variables.

2. The monitoring system and the short-term forecasts would make an assessment of the planning objectives in the light of evolving circumstances. This would be related to *dynamic long-term perspective* which would make it necessary to initiate certain corrective steps of the discrepancies, if any, between the plan targets and achievements. These corrective steps would require certain decision-making power and technical expertise involving certain decision taking capabilities with the Planning Agency. An efficient administrative apparatus will have to back these capabilities so that the corrective decisions may be transmitted for implementation and the political sanction may be ensured for their effectiveness. It would also require basic moral character and discipline to ensure that the socially accepted objectives remain fixed. This would be particularly more important when redistributive social objectives requiring political will are in the forefront. In an operational sense, this would require a close and continuous rapport between the Planning Agency and the Government with the required discipline on the part of the government to keep their commitment to the objectives fixed and on the part of the Planning Agency to make them realise this in case short-term political compulsions come to dominate.

3. Then, there must be a centralized agency for ensuring *coordination* and giving appropriate signals for action. These signals would have to take effect through an administrative apparatus. This would require the capacity to discriminate on the basis of incomplete and uncertain informations, the consequences of emerging non-political circumstances. These circumstances may be either of temporary nature requiring no action or may be having significant effects on medium and long-term perspective requiring changes in strategies.

In this way, these basic pre-requisites of the rolling plan would lead to the strengthening of the implementation process which is perhaps the most important part of any planning system. The smooth operation of this technique would depend on the availability of the above mentioned essential prerequisites and an adequately prepared institutional framework. The flexibility under the more sophisticated rolling plan technique would succeed provided the pre-requisites for its effective use exist whereas if they do not, less sophisticated fixed plan or semi-rolling plan techniques may prove more effective.

Therefore, we may make out the following observations on the assumption that a certain level of these essential pre-requisites is given:

Proposition

The rolling plan technique is essential in any economy where (i) nature's unforeseen changes affect the whole economy; (ii) foreign economic relations are crucial; and (iii) domestic activities are not fully controlled by the State. Hence, the need to reallocate resources in the light of fundamental revisions relating t critical assumptions is certainly obvious.

Corollary-I

In a closed economy which is free from nature's unforeseen changes and where domestic activities are fully controlled by the State, the fixed plan technique is certainly better than the rolling plan technique if we take into account the simplicity and the cost of formulating a plan. In such an economy critical assumptions remain the same and their is obviously no need to reallocate resources.

Corollary-II

In an open economy which is free from nature's unforeseen changes, where domestic activities are fully controlled by the State, and where foreign economic relations are regulated by the State monopoly and are not at all crucial, the fixed plan technique is certainly better than the rolling plan technique if we take into account the simplicity and the cost of formulating a plan. Obviously, in such economies the critical assumptions remain unchanged. Therefore, there arises no need to reallocate resources.

7.6 PLANNING TECHNIQUES IN THE INDIAN PLAN LITERATURE

Since the inception of planning in India, we have a three-tier system of the planning process. In this system there is an 'annual plan' which is formulated within the framework of a 'Five-Year Plan'. The five-year plan is formulated within the framework of a 'perspective plan' of fifteen years or so. The formulation of an annual plan implies the adoption of the '*fixed plan*' technique. The relationship between the annual plan, where the period is one year, and the five-year plan, where the horizon is five years, is that of a '*semi-rolling plan*' technique as the period keeps on rolling and the horizon remains fixed. On the other hand, the relationship between the five-year plan, where the period is five years, and the perspective plan, where the horizon is fifteen years or so, is that of the '*rolling plan*' technique as both the period and the horizon keeps on rolling, i.e., after every five years we have a new five year plan and a new perspective plan of fifteen years' or so. But surprisingly, all the Indian plan models have been formulated within the framework of the fixed plan technique representing either the static or the comparative static or the dynamic versions of this technique. So far no attempt has been made to formulate a 'comparative-dynamic' type of planning model within the framework of the rolling plan technique.

If we survey the Indian planning literature, we find that the basic logic of the rolling plan technique has always been recognised but, of course, without giving it any explicit recognition in the formulation of plan models. For example, during his stay at the Indian Statistical Institute from the end of 1954 to the spring of 1955, Frisch wrote a number of memoranda on various technical aspects of national planning. And in one of these memoranda he writes:

> "In principle the coming period may be something different from a year... . The period... should be so short that the target contained in the plan for this period can be considered as something definite on which action is to be taken more or less immediately after the beginning of the period, without awaiting new information or analysis. This means that the 'coming period' cannot be something as long as, say, five years.

"Realistic planning in the changing world of today must be a continuous process. It must be influenced by the newest and best information that is available at any time. A plan cannot be petrified for, say, five years in advance. The future possibilities are taken account of in the asymptotic pattern, while the immediate action is decided by means of the 'coming year' plan".[20]

One can easily make it out that Frisch has talked about the logic of the rolling plan technique in a clear manner.

Almost in the same tune, Mahalanobis spoke on 11th of September 1955 in his radio lecture on 'Approach to Planning in India':[21]

"Planning must be flexible and continuous. There should be general framework for five years; and detailed annual plans should be prepared every year. Targets, projects and policies must be continually re-assessed and formulated in the light of new experience. Also we must always keep in view the growth of the economy over a long period of 10 or 15 or 20 years, so that a balance can be secured between short-term and long-term objectives."[22]

Mahalanobis again explained the logic of the rolling plan technique in one of his papers' concluding remarks:

"The type of planning visualized above would be necessarily a continuing process and would have two broad aspects. One would be the current planning directed to projects included in the annual plans within a framework of a five-year plan. The successive five-year plans themselves would have to be fitted into a larger framework of perspective planning with a wide horizon of 10 or 20 or 30 years or even more."[23]

Similarly, the Indian Planning Commission (1978) has explicitly recognised the need of adopting the rolling plan technique in the Indian planning process:

"It has, therefore, been proposed to adopt the Rolling Plan system which will have the following features:

(i) Year to year targets will be set for sectoral outlays and output for major sectors within the Five-Year Plans.

(ii) The horizon of the Five-Year Plan will be extended by working out these selected sectoral targets for one additional year at the end of each year.

"As far as major investment decisions are concerned, the Rolling Plan system will have the clear technical advantages of projections from a base level which is adjusted annually, continuous correction of errors and a constant time horizon for investment decisions. This will introduce a significant degree of realism and flexibility in the process and reduce the chronic and increasing shortfalls in targets and achievements observed in the past. The system will also be better adopted for coping with fluctuations and uncertainties."[24]

From the above analysis we can very rightly conclude that since the inception of planning in India, Indian planning literature has been involving all the three types of planning techniques in the Indian planning process, i.e., the fixed plan technique, the semi-rolling plan technique and the rolling plan technique. Thus it can be said that the rolling plan technique is not a new methodological innovation to our existing planning literature. But, of course, this technique has neither been explored theoretically nor has it found any application in the formulation of plan models. It should now attract the attention of the researchers to work out its operational implications so that we may enrich our planning literature in the coming years.

7.7 CHOICE OF AN APPROPRIATE TECHNIQUE FOR THE INDIAN PLANNING PROCESS

The Planning Commission (1978) of India has itself accepted the shortcomings of the Indian planning process in the following words:

"Some of the specific major shortcomings of the planning process, which a close examination of the past planning process has revealed, are listed below:

i. The successive Five-Year Plans tended to assume higher levels of savings and investment in real terms, and consequently, a much higher rate of growth than was warranted by objective consideration. As a result, there has been growing gap between plan projections and actual achievements in all sectors of the economy.

ii. The plans could not make any allowance for fluctuations in agricultural output within the plan, nor was there a machinery for adjustment of the plans to unforeseen external events. The consequence of both (i) and (ii) was that the Third, Fourth and Fifth Five Year Plans were disrupted by inflationary crises and the unplanned dusts in developmental outlay unnecessitated thereby resulted in disruption of plan priorities.

iii. The planning process provided for one mid-term appraisal only and the corrections made in the course of such a review proved to be inadequate. Thus, if demand or supply in one sector did not develop according to anticipation, the necessary changes in other related sectors were not made adequately in time.

iv. Towards the later part of the plan period in a fixed Five-Year Plan the time horizon was too short for investment decisions in many sectors.

v. The plans were based on models which provided for theoretical inter-sectoral consistency for the terminal year of the five-year period, and the likely imbalances that might arise from year to year were not provided for.

vi. Given the character of the mixed economy, planning of the large self-employed sector in agriculture, household and services was minimal. The private corporate sector could be given incentives or regulated, but targets were only indicative since firm production and investment plans were initiated by the sector itself. Some correction of targets is, therefore, inherent in the system. In addition, in the past there were major slippages even in the public sector plans where targets were set."[25]

Now, let us take the example of the performance of the Sixth Five Year Plan which envisaged an annual growth rate of 5.2 per cent. But during this plan period the real growth rate varied widely from year to year. It was as high as 7.8 per cent in the first year but slided down to 4.5 per cent in 1981-82 and 1.6 per cent in 1982-83 and, after recovering sharply to 7.8 per cent in 1983-84, slipped again to 3.5 per cent in the terminal year. Thus, the annual growth rate was around 5.0 per cent, lower than the targeted growth rate of 5.2 per cent.

In an excellent and detailed study on the growth cycles in the Indian economy since the beginning of planning, Chitre (1982) shows that the Indian economy has not been free from substantial short-term fluctuations in economic activity.[26] He identifies five growth cycles for the period 1951-1975. The causes of these have been the fluctuations in agricultural production; the fluctuations in the private business investment in fixed capital and inventories; the fluctuations in money and credit; the fluctuations in the world economic activity; and the fluctuations in the public sector investment in fixed capital and stock. Chitre further points out that the fluctuations in the public sector investment in fixed capital and stocks have been quite sharp in India over the twenty-five years of planning, and they seem to have accentuated rather than mitigated the fluctuations arising out of the other causes. The causes of this may be exogenous factors like wars; or changes in the ideology of the plan strategy; delays in plan formulation and implementation; lack of flexibility to quickly adjust to unforeseen opportunities or difficulties; or alternative spells of overstraining the economy followed by a reaction to it; or fluctuations in agricultural production; or changing conditions of the world economy. Alternations of a high and low public investment with consequent alternations of phases of high and low growth may be desired by the 'industrial leaders' in the planned developing economies, for the same reasons for which Kalecki (1971, Chapter 12) argued that alternations of high and low public spending with consequent alternations of periods of high and low employment is desired by them in advanced capitalist economies. The country's foreign exchange situation also has an important bearing on investment in fixed capital by the public sector and the private sector, and therefore, for the growth cycles in the economy.[27]

As regards the nature of Indian economy, one may point out its following main characteristics:

i. Agriculture, depending on the nature's unforeseen changes, is the dominant sector of the economy in almost every aspect (national income, foreign trade, industrial production, etc.).

ii. Foreign economic relations are crucial, for example, foreign aid is crucial in project investments and utilization of industrial capacity. And, also expectations of peace and tranquillity would lead to higher domestic savings and less capital flight.

iii. Domestic activities are not fully controlled by the State, since India has a democratic set up of government within the framework of a mixed economy not only in terms of ownership of the means of production but also in terms of inter-dependence of decision making. The government influences private sector decision-making only indirectly through its manipulation as prices, taxes or tarriffs; and sometimes directly through licensing schemes and credit rationing. On the other hand, the private sector usually wields considerable influence with the government which values the private sector's entrepreneurial role. The private sector includes industrialists (both foreign and domestic), small businessmen, farmers, landlords, artisans and important labour unions. There is rarely, if ever, complete mutuality of interests among them. Most of the productive resources are privately owned and the choice of occupations and commodities is entirely left to private individuals.

iv. In Indian economy information is available in a highly dispersed form. Even the most disaggregated models used by the planners take into account only a limited amount of information, and that too in a form that may not necessarily be accurate on account of the almost inevitable aggregative basis.

v. Finally, but most significantly, we must pay our attention towards our experience over the past decades which shows that it has become a general practice of the government to accept the advice of the Planning Commission whenever politically convenient and ignore it whenever politically unpalatable. Part of the blame for this sorry state of affairs also lies with the Planning Commission, which, in the past, concentrated more on the quantification of the political slogans than on concrete programmes and consequences of the policy-frame associated with the alternative levels and combinations of social objectives. It has also been guided not much by realism but by considerations of aiming high under the naive and untested premise advocated by the politicians that somehow aspirations would bring forth the required efforts for their achievements. (Of course, planning by its very nature is bound to be completely sterile in the absence of a policy-frame provided by the political leadership. But the Planning Commission must not become a cog in the machine of control and coordination under central political authority and must remain an independent advisory body for central and state governments on the tasks of development planning. It should not be a planning department of the government rather than an independent body. As laid down in the original 1950 Resolution of the Government of India constituting the Planning Commission, it must constitute an independent expert advisory body. It should not be bound by any responsibility as an executive branch of the Central Government and should be free to propose alternative policies and plan programmes, leaving it to the government to make its own choice.)

From the above analysis, we may conclude that there is always a very high possibility of unexpected changes in strategic areas such as agriculture, foreign trade, domestic activities etc. which shall call for adjustments and reallocation of resources. Therefore, comparative dynamic planning models formulated within the framework of rolling plan technique shall be more appropriate to the nature of Indian economy than any other type of planning models formulated within the framework of fixed plan technique; if we concentrate on a realistic planning system and assume a certain given level of essential pre-requisites for the successful working of the rolling plan technique.

NOTES

1. Habr (1966) and Goldman (1968, 1969) make an early contribution to the theory of planning techniques.
2. Intriligator and Sheshinski (1981) make an excellent formal analysis of these aspects of planning in a dynamic stochastic maximization problem.

3. See Myrdal (1968).
4. See Lewis (1966).
5. See Tinbergen (1967, pp. 162-163).
6. See Arrow (1962).
7. See, for example, Kornai (1969) who has developed the most disaggregated planning model for Hungary by dividing the economy into 491 sectors.
8. This would be evident to any reader of the socialist economies.
9. Using a numerical linear-quadratic formulation which allows for both the cost of uncertainty and progressively acquired information on uncontrolled factors, Deleau and Malgrange (1974) find that for a five year horizon, revision near the end of the period (year 3,4,5) is favoured. Their numerical results suggest that a four-year period is optimal, with the plan being revised in the fourth year.
10. Sarris and Adelman (1981) propose a methodology, based on the ideas of stochastic control theory, that can be applied in an operational manner for devising a set of adjustment rules for coping with actual departures from the forecast conditions under which the plan is formulated.
11. In his classic work, Goldman (1968) investigates the dynamic properties of a rolling plan within the framework of a one-sector neo-classical optimal growth model. Dasgupta (1978) compares the results of Cass (1965) and Samuelson (1965) concerning the catenary turnpike theorem with Goldman's results on rolling plans and shows that the former set of results implies the latter and vice versa. Easly and Spulber (1981) examine the steady state properties of rolling plans in a stochastic discrete time framework. Day and Kennedy (1970) have examined 'recursive decision systems' of which rolling plans are a special case. Recently Spulber (1986) has defined the principal economic issues involved in economic planning with rolling horizons.
12. Sarris and Adelman (1981) discuss this class of uncertainties.
13. See Blitzer et al. (1975) for a thorough survey of planning models in which uncertainty is neglected. Johansen (1977) reviews the short-run macro-economic stabilization issues under uncertainty. Cheng (1980), Helpman and Razin (1978) and Pomery (1979) review the literature on trade under uncertainty. One of the first empirical treatments of sectoral investment planning under uncertainty was by Manne (1961). Jabara and Thompson (1980) incorporate uncertainty into a static linear programming model. Kornai (1975) also makes a partial-equilibrium attempt to incorporate uncertainty into planning by using an objective function that depended on the expected value and variance of profits of the investment in one industry. Roumasset (1976) gives a useful overview of the rules that are usually used in risk programming which can be adopted by national planners. Some other studies incorporating uncertainties are by Weitzman (1971), Brada (1971, 1973), Brainard and Cooper (1968), Ruffin (1974), Adelman and Robinson (1978), Dervis et al. (1982), Batra (1974, 1975), Bardhan (1971, 1973), Das (1977), Mayer (1976), Kemp (1976), Ruffin (1974) and Turnvosky (1974).
14. See Johansen (1977, p. 209). One may also see Radner (1975), Arrow and Kurz (1970), and Mirrlees and Stern (1972) and Day (1975).
15. See Yaari (1964) who argues for the bequest motive on the part of individuals.
16. See Strotz (1956) and Koopmans (1950) for a detailed discussion on this point.
17. Tinbergen (1967), Lewis (1966) and Myrdal (1968) have also emphasized the need of plan revision. For a discussion of the value of being able to

postpone decisions until more information is available, see Marschak et al. (1967). Deleau and Malgrange (1974) discuss the problem of information about uncertain factors on which policy must be based. See Inagaki (1970) for a discussion on a shifting finite time horizon.

18. See Tendulkar (1977) for an excellent and detailed discussion on this point.
19. See Tinbergen (1956, 1964) for an excellent discussion on this point.
20. Frisch (1960, p. 57).
21. This speech explains in a general way the approach to planning as recommended in the Draft Plan Frame of March 17, 1955.
22. Mahalanobis (1961, p. 54).
23. Mahalanobis (1955).
24. Planning Commission (1978, p. 119).
25. Planning Commission (1978, p. 119).
26. For a work which examines fluctuations in comparatively long period trends in India's economic activity over about a century period to independence in a broad sweep of analysis, see Ghosh (1979).
27. An excellent study can be conducted by investigating the mechanisms operating during growth-cycles and the effects of the growth cyclical fluctuations on the economy for developing an appropriate policy stance towards these short-term fluctuations in economic activity. Similarly, one can also analyse the nature and causes of the fluctuations of the public sector investment in fixed capital as well as stocks and their impact on the growth cycles.

EIGHT

A Comparative Dynamic Optimising Planning Model

8.1 INTRODUCTION

As is apparent, all the Indian plan models, surveyed in Chapter 2 through Chapter 6, have been formulated within the framework of the fixed plan technique (FPT). But, as mentioned earlier, the rolling plan technique (RPT) is found to be more appropriate for the Indian economy. Therefore, there arises a need to formulate comparative dynamic planning models within the framework of the rolling plan technique. Thus, the purpose of this chapter is to formulate an optimising planning model which can be operated through the fixed plan technique, the semi-rolling plan technique and the rolling plan technique so that the possibility of their comparison can be explored; and certain results and policy implications regarding the choice of planning techniques within the framework of *current-oriented, future-oriented,* and *neutral-oriented* approaches to the economy in question can be found. In this way, we bring the comparative dynamic optimisation within the scope of development planning models and thus extend the current state of planning models in this direction.

8.2 THE BASIC MODEL

A linear programming model of any size can be formulated in the following simple form:

Objective function

Maximize αX

Constraints

Subject to $MX < B$.

Non-negativity conditions

$X \geq 0$

Where the vector α, the matrix M, and the vector B are the given data, the feasible set $S = \{X/MX \leq B, X \geq O\}$ must be bounded and nonempty for the solution of the programme to yield an optimal vector X^* satisfying the condition $X^* \in S$ and $\alpha X^* \geq \alpha X$ for all $X \in S$. Then, the problem can be solved by the simplex method or its variants.

The primal form of the model described above would also have its dual form in the following way:[1]

Minimize λB

Subject to $\lambda_i M \geq \alpha$

Non-negativity condition $\lambda \geq 0$

Where the dual variables λ_i are conceptually very close to the Langragean multipliers of classical optimization theory.[2] These multipliers can be interpreted as shadow prices or scarcity indicators. In this way, linear programming planning models also deal with the price implications of alternative solutions. On the basis of this feature we may say that these models can be treated as first approximation to the computable general equilibrium models of market economies.[3]

Following the above cited model we discuss a simple unidimensional linear maximization problem over time. Since the model is unidimensional, there are no intersectoral relationships and we have the following linear programming problem which can be solved by the simplex method or its variants:

Maximize $$\sum_{t=0}^{T} \frac{C_t}{(1+\delta_c)^{t-1}} + \sum_{t=0}^{T} \frac{K_t}{(1+\delta_k)^{t-1}} \qquad (1)$$

Subject to

$$Y_t = C_t + I_t \qquad t = 1, 2, ..., T \tag{2}$$
$$Y_t = \sigma K_t \tag{3}$$
$$K_t = K_{t-1} + I_{t-1} \tag{4}$$
$$K_t \geq K_{t-1} [(1 + \eta)] \tag{5}$$
$$C_t \geq C_{t-1} [(1 + \eta)] \tag{6}$$
$$C_1 \geq \bar{C}_1 \tag{7}$$
$$O < \delta_c \leq 1 \tag{8}$$
$$O < \delta_k \leq 1 \tag{9}$$
$$K_o > O \tag{10}$$
$$C_o > O \tag{11}$$

Where

C_t is the level of consumption in period t;

K_t is the level of capital in period t;

δ_c is the discount factor for consumption;

δ_k is the discount factor for capital;
Y_t is the level of output in period t;

I_t is the investment in period t;

σ is the capital coefficient; and
η is the rate of growth of population.

The relationship (1) says that the objective function of the model or its maximand is the discounted sum of aggregate consumption (C_t) over the T years of the planning period plus the sum of the discounted values of capital stock in each year with a discount factor equal to δ_c and δ_k, respectively, such that $O < \delta_c$ and $\delta_k \leq 1$.

In this way we have combined the two types of the discount rates which have been advocated in the literature because a combination of these seems to be the best to us. The first type is the '*social rate of time preference*' which is used to assign present values to future consumption and is a normative character reflecting the society's evaluation of the relative desirability of consumption at different points in time. The second type is the '*social opportunity cost of capital*' which is a measure of the value to society of the next best alternative use to which funds employed in the public projects might alternatively be diverted.[4] We assume that the discount rate remains constant over the planning period so that the '*regret problem*' of Strotz (1956) can be avoided.[5]

Applied planning models cannot accommodate an infinite horizon because of computational reasons and changing technological coefficients and/or world prices. Therefore, our model covers a limited number of T years. This may mean that there is no explicit analysis of what is to happen after the terminal year of the plan. The post-terminal period is linked to the period covered by the planning model through the amount of productive capacity generated by the investments undertaken. The terminal capacity we leave for future years at the end of the plan period will constrain what can be done after year T. To ensure an adequate terminal capital stock to be bequeathed to future generations, we require a certain minimum average annual growth in the base year capital stock. This would guarantee that the economy-wide capital stock will grow on an average at least at the rate η : where η is either the population growth rate or some other politically determined parameter. Investment will have to be sufficient to allow such growth, and the interests of future generations will be taken into account, with potential welfare in post-terminal years depending on the magnitude of the targeted growth rate.

Now what is the justification of our objective function? We know that development planning always has many different relevant economic and social objectives.[6] These are often conflicting with each other to varying degrees. A greater achievement with respect to one objective often means a lesser achievement with respect to another, so that compromises are necessary. For example, to desire a higher growth rate of national income, it would be necessary to accept a lower rate of improvement in the average standard of living. Making compromises among conflicting objectives require political value judgements to choose and to justify an objective function. The justification of our objective function lies in the fact that a social welfare function, as Arrow (1964) sees it, has to be regarded, essentially, as a problem of aggregating individual preferences into one consistent ordering of alternative social states. Thus, if the preference function of the planner who is supposed to act on behalf of the nation has any claim to being regarded as an idealization of a social welfare function, it must at least be made sure that the postulates defining such a function bear some relationship to individual welfare. Now what constitutes the eligible set of individuals whose preferences are to count for aggregation purposes? In the theory of planning over time, the interests of the unborn generations are to be taken into account in some essential way. How shall we apply in a meaningful way any set of aggregation postulates to include the unborn, unless we introduce a method of proxy voting? This would either lead us to support an authoritarian position or we would have to postulate that an individual would not discriminate between his interest and the interests of his heirs in any way. The imagination of the Planning Agency may have to be considerably stretched in order to accommodate such a requirement. In a democratic set up of society it may be considered axiomatic that a democratic government reflects only the current preference, i.e., the preferences of the individuals who are presently members of the body politic. With this interpretation of democratic government the question of proxy voting on behalf of the unborn generations would arise to formulate a social preference. Otherwise, what would prevent current members of the society from consuming all the national product? The answer would seem to lie in the educated self-concern of the present generation for the future. And that is why we selected to maximize the discounted sum of aggregate consumption over T years plus the sum of discounted values of capital stock in each year.[7] In this way, our approach may be considered to support the view that intergenerational equity is compatible with efficient allocation of resources. Solow (1974) has interpreted intergenerational equity to mean equal consumption per capita at each date. If we find a path (given arbitrary initial conditions) which is equitable in this sense, and is also intertemporally efficient, then there is no conflict between equity and efficiency. Furthermore, such a path has an additional feature, namely, it is "maximin" -- the rule of distributive justice, proposed by Rawls (1971)[8].

Thus, in other words, a simpler justification which explains the nature and composition of our objective function is that in any economy choices must be made between provision for the present (consumption) and provision for the future (capital accumulation). While more consumption is preferable to less at any moment of time, more consumption means less capital accumulation -- and the smaller the future potential consumption. Therefore, a choice must be made between alternative consumption policies. At one extreme is the policy of consuming as much as possible today even though the potential for future consumption is jeopardized: "Live today, for tomorrow we die". At the other extreme is the Stalinist policy of consuming as little as possible today so as to increase capital and the potential for future consumption. This is to say that if the per capita terminal year capital (K_t) in the economy remains equal to the initial year per capita capital (K_o) then the economy is said to be *neutral-oriented.* Similarly, if $K_t > K_o$ then the economy is said to be *future-oriented.* On the other hand, if $K_t < K_o$ then the economy is said to be *current-oriented.* In this sense, we have focussed our attention only to the neutral-oriented and future-oriented aspects of development planning process through the help of our objective function and through the constraint in equation(5).

Thus, it is the explicit or implicit weight accorded to terminal-year capital stock that determines, jointly with the discount rates applied to consumption and to capital stock, the balance between consumption and investment during the plan period. The above discussion also explains the fundamental considerations which are to be taken into account while determining the value of the discount factors for consumption and for capital stock. These may remain equal to each other or may differ from each other depending upon the choice of the planner regarding the state of intergenerational equity and efficient allocation of resources which is a problem of long-standing interest in intertemporal welfare economics.

Equation (2) says that output is equal to consumption plus investment. Equation (3) says that output is produced by a fixed coefficient production function. We use the equalities in (3) since, in a one-sector model, there is no reason to assume that we shall operate with excess capacity. Equation (4) is merely definitional. To ensure a rising pattern of capital and consumption over time, we include 'monotonicity' constraints in equations (5) and (6). These inequalities require that capital and consumption in any one period must be at least as much as capital and consumption in the previous period augmented by a growth factor $(1+\eta)$, where η is either the population growth rate or some other politically determined parameter so that a gradualist consumption policy is followed. It is because of the fact that in a democratic society -- with a parliament voting taxes, investment expenditures, and pricing policies of public sector enterprises--it would require an extraordinary political consensus to enforce an initial drop in consumption, even if that drop is shown to emerge as the optimal solution under a Ramsey (1928) long-run welfare function. In order to avoid the possibility that the consumption monotonicity constraint holds in an unrealistic manner, a lower bound is set to consumption in the first year by assuming that $C_1 \geq \bar{C}_1$, where $\bar{C}_1$ is a political parameter, indicating the subsistence level of consumption, as is shown in equation (7). The purpose of equations (10) and (11) is to show that the initial period capital and consumption are positive.

8.3 THE FIXED PLAN TECHNIQUE (FPT)

If we adopt the fixed plan technique so that the economy chooses to pursue the initially fixed path for a planning horizon of T periods, the corresponding path of the discounted sum of aggregate consumption over T period plus the sum of discounted values of capital stock in each period would come out as a result of the solution of the basic model developed above.

Let the corresponding optimum paths of the values of consumption and the capital stock in the above problem be:

$C_o, C_1, C_2, \ldots, C_t$; and

$K_o, K_1, K_2, \ldots, K_t$
Let us define

$C_o, C_1, \ldots, C_t$ by vector $\bar{C}_t$; and

$K_o, K_1, \ldots, K_t$ by vector $\bar{K}_t$.

8.4 THE ROLLING PLAN TECHNIQUE (RPT)

If we adopt the rolling plan technique so that the economy

chooses to pursue the optimum path for a planning horizon of T periods but after each period it redefines the horizon so that it always remains constant, i.e., equal to T periods, and thus makes use of the initially fixed optimum path for one period only. The corresponding optimum paths of the discounted values of the original time profile of aggregate consumption in each period and the sum of discounted values of capital stock in each period would come out as a result of the solution of the basic model developed above with a sliding horizon of one period. In this way, our basic model takes the form of a comparative dynamic model by nature.

The concept of comparative dynamics is closely related to that of comparative statics. The main difference lies in the fact that comparative dynamics is concerned with the effects of changes in parameters etc. on the whole motion over time of a dynamic model. According to Samuelson (1947), the changes which are the concern of comparative dynamics can be any one of the followings:

1. Changes in initial conditions;

2. Changes in exogenous forces (as, e.g., in autonomous investment); and

3. Changes in internal parameters (as, e.g., in the propensity to save).

The basic method of comparative dynamics can be summarized in the following way: We have a set of functional equations whose solution gives the time path of the economic system. In this solution initial conditions, exogenous elements and internal parameters also appear. Differentiating totally the solution functions (or the functional equations themselves) with respect to the argument representing the element whose shift we are interested in, we try to determine the effect of this shift.[9]

The central notion of comparative dynamics is that we change something (just what need not concern us at the moment), and we investigate the effect of this change on the whole motion or behaviour over time of the economic system under investigation. Thus, the problem may be set out as follows:

Maximize, $$\sum_{t=0}^{T} \frac{C_t}{(1+\delta_c)^{t-1}} + \sum_{t=0}^{T} \frac{K_t}{(1+\delta_k)^{t-1}}$$

Subject to the equations (2) to (11).

Let the corresponding optimum paths be

$C_o, C^*_1, C^*_2, ..., C^*_t$; and

$K_o, K^*, K^*_1, ..., K^*_t$.

Hence, the corresponding optimum discounted sums of aggregate consumption and capital stock after one period come out to be C^*_1, and K^*_1, respectively. It may be noted here that C^*_1 and K^*_1 would be identical to C_1 and K_1, for in the initial period the optimisation problem under fixed plan technique and rolling plan technique is identical.

Since we are following the rolling plan technique, consumption and capital stock after two periods would be worked out by the solution of the basic model, extended for one period, i.e., the welfare function transforms into

Maximize $$\sum_{t=1}^{T+1} \frac{C_t}{(1+\delta_c)^{t-1}} + \sum_{t=1}^{T+1} \frac{K_t}{(1+\delta_k)^{t-1}}$$

Subject to the equations (2) to (11).

Let the corresponding optimum paths be

$C^{**}_1, C^{**}_2, ..., C^*_{T+1}$; and

$K^{**}_1, K^{**}_2, ..., K^{**}_{T+1}$.

Hence, the corresponding optimum paths of the discounted values of the original time profile of aggregate consumption in each period and the sum of discounted values of capital stock in each period after two periods come out to be

C^{**}_2 and K^{**}_2, respectively.[10]

Similarly, we shall keep on sliding the plan horizon by one period, i.e., the vector of the objective function comes out to be

$$\text{Maximize} \quad \sum_{t=2}^{T+2} \frac{C_t}{(1+\delta_c)^{t-1}} + \sum_{t=2}^{T+2} \frac{K_t}{(1+\delta_k)^{t-1}}$$

$$\text{Maximize} \quad \sum_{t=3}^{T+3} \frac{C_t}{(1+\delta_c)^{t-1}} + \sum_{t=3}^{T+3} \frac{K_t}{(1+\delta_k)^{t-1}}$$

$$\vdots$$

$$\text{Maximize} \quad \sum_{t=T}^{T+T} \frac{C_t}{(1+\delta_c)^{t-1}} + \sum_{t=T}^{T+T} \frac{K_t}{(1+\delta_k)^{t-1}}$$

Let the corresponding optimum paths of the discounted values of the original time profile of aggregate consumption in each period and the sum of discounted values of capital stock in each period in the above problem be:

C^{***}_3, C^{****}_4, C^{*****}_5, and

K^{***}_3, K^{****}_4, K^{*****}_5, after periods 3,4,5, respectively.

Hence, if we adopt the rolling plan technique, the corresponding optimum paths of the discounted values of the original time profile of aggregate consumption in each period and the sum of discounted values of capital stock in each period come out to be

C_o, C^{*}_1, C^{**}_2, C^{***}_3,....,$C^{***\cdots}_T$; and

K_o, K^{*}_1, K^{**}_2, K^{***}_3,....,$K^{***\cdots}_T$

Let us define

C_o, C^{*}_1, C^{**}_2, C^{***}_3,..., $C^{***\cdots}_T$ by vector $\bar{C}^{*}_T$ and

K_o, K^{*}_1, K^{**}_2, K^{***}_3,..., $K^{***\cdots}_T$ by vector $\bar{K}^{*}_T$

Another significant use of a comparative dynamic planning model is that of its being more useful and reasonable to approach the terminal conditions problem. In this type of models we explicitly recognize and admit that the future is essentially open-ended and hard to predict, and that our confidence in the guidelines generated by the model diminishes as the planning horizon extends into the future. Since in this type of a model we are always in a position to ignore periods close to the terminal year, we can reduce the necessarily arbitrary influence of the terminal conditions on the solution path. Such rolling plan approach constitutes the most reasonable though time consuming solution to the terminal conditions problem. In this way, we can formulate a planning model of any size for an open economy which can endogenously generate the optimal production and trade patterns corresponding to the exogenous information we are projecting, but we always stand ready to revise this information and do not trust the model's solution too far into an uncertain future. Significantly, as pointed out by Dervis, Melo and Robinson (1982), this approach is a good and robust prescription that holds not only for linear programming models, but for all planning models and, indeed, for rational behaviour in general.

8.5 RESULTS

Now corresponding to the fixed plan technique and the rolling plan technique we get two vectors $\bar{C}_T$ and $\bar{C}^*_T$ of the discounted sums of aggregate consumption and two vectors $\bar{K}_T$ and $\bar{K}^*_T$ of the sums of discounted values of capital stocks. Hence, to find out the superiority of one technique over the other, we are to compare the vectors $\bar{C}_T$ and $\bar{C}^*_T$ and/or $\bar{K}_T$ and $\bar{K}^*_T$ as per our social objective by taking an appropriate norm of a vector for converting the vector of flows into a scalar.

If we are interested in the post-plan growth potentiality of the economy under the above planning techniques, then we compare $||\bar{K}_T||$ and $||\bar{K}^*_T||$. By comparing these two vectors, we can make out the following three alternate possible propositions:

Proposition I

If at the end of the same planning period, say T, $||\bar{K}_T||$ =

$||\bar{K}^*_t||$ or $\bar{K}_t = \bar{K}^*_t$ then in the post-plan period there is no difference between the efficiency of the fixed plan technique and the rolling plan technique. We shall keep on enjoying the same levels of consumption and investment potentiality under both the planning techniques.

Proposition II

If at the end of the same planning period, say T, $||\bar{K}_T|| < ||K^*_T||$ or $K_t < \bar{K}^*_t$ then in the post-plan period the rolling plan technique is superior to the fixed plan technique and we shall keep on enjoying higher and higher levels of both the consumption and the investment under the rolling plan technique.[11]

Proposition III

If at the end of the same planning period, say T, $||\bar{K}_T|| > ||\bar{K}^*_T||$ or $K_t > \bar{K}^*_t$ then in the post-plan period the fixed plan technique is superior to the rolling plan technique. We shall keep on enjoying higher levels of both the consumption and the investment under the fixed plan technique.

Proofs of Propositions I to III

$Y_t = \sigma K_t$; and

$Y^*_t = \sigma K^*_t$.

Since $K_t \gtreqless K^*_t$

$\therefore Y_t \gtreqless Y^*_t$

$Y_t = bY_t + I_t$ where b is the marginal propensity to consume such that $O < b < 1$

$$Y^*_t = bY^*_t + I_t$$

$$\therefore C_t \gtreqless C^*_t \text{ and}$$

$$I_t \gtreqless I^*_t$$

On the other hand, if we are interested only in maximizing the consumption level during the plan period and do not worry about the growth potentiality of the economy in the post-plan period, i.e., no matter if the capital stock in the terminal period is zero, then we shall have to compare $||\bar{C}_T||$ and $||\bar{C}^*_T||$ and make out the three alternate possible propositions: $C \lesseqgtr C^*$.

8.6 POLICY IMPLICATIONS

So far we have proved the following three propositions:

$$If \quad K^*_t \gtreqless K_t \, then \, (1) I^*_t \gtreqless I_t; \text{ and } (ii) C^*_t \gtreqless C_t,$$

Here, we feel that in the rolling plan technique it is easier to bridge up the gap between K^*_t and K_t if $K^*_t < K_t$. This is because of the fact that the rolling plan technique offers the flexibility of adjusting to the changing exogenous factors from period to period. Therefore, it would be easier to invite foreign investment or to go in for foreign aid or to persuade the current population to postpone a part of their present consumption for a shorter period. We know that domestic savings do not impose a binding constraint on economic growth (i.e., domestic savings are capable of being optimally adjusted to the investment requirements) if the plan is physically, technically and organisationally feasible and makes sense on the foreign exchange side. But this approach is valid as long as no conflict appears between individual time preference of the current population and social time preference of the planning authority. However, possibilities of the conflict arise from political, sociological, behavioural, and institutional considerations imposing a definitive upper limit on the feasible rate of savings in the underdeveloped economies. Under these circumstances, the planning quantum of investment is unlikely to materialize because of infeasibilities involved in raising the domestic resources. Successful planning requires an attempt to ensure a mutual consistency between the investment plan and its sectoral allocation on the one hand, and its internal and external resource requirements on the other. Tendulkar (1971) points out that the conflict between the social and the individual preferences goes on narrowing down with higher availabilities of foreign capital inflow. Moreover, the increasing availability of foreign resources would also enable the economy to devote a continually declining proportion of gross national product to gross investment while raising the aggregate growth rate.

The importance of the implications of external resource inflow into a country are categorically reflected in the developmental philosophy of the "two-gap model" which is based on a structuralist concept of development and incorporates explicit limits on the rate of increase of domestic savings, investments, and exports. The model focusses in particular on the savings and foreign exchange constraints to development. The shortage of domestic savings limits the capital accumulation in the developing country. The shortage of foreign exchange limits the country's capacity to import.[12] If the growth in GNP depends on the importation of goods that cannot be produced at home, then the country's growth rate will be constrained by its access to foreign exchange. These two gaps--the savings gap and the foreign exchange gap--might be filled in by foreign aid. The gap between required and available savings and between required and available foreign exchange can be filled in by an inflow of foreign loans or grants from governments in the rich countries. The inflow of public foreign capital is equivalent to an inflow of savings to investment opportunities in the poor countries. By relaxing the savings and foreign exchange constraints, the inflow of foreign capital can yield an increase in national income that is several times the cost of the foreign loan.

Meier (1984) points out that "some simple calculations were used to demonstrate the need for public foreign investment. The case of India was illustrative. India's national income in 1950-51 was approximately $ 18 billion, of which about 5 per cent, or $ 90 million, was saved. This was barely enough to maintain the capital stock intact and to keep up with the annual population increase. Even a doubling of the amount of capital available from domestic sources would not provide a very rapid rate of development in India. The inflow of private foreign investment was also small. To mobilize sufficient resources to fulfil the targets of its first five-year development plan (1952-57) India had to rely on foreign aid."

The role of external resource flow in the Indian context has been analysed by Bergsman and Manne (1966) who point out that "even though faster import substitution ... in the capital goods sectors requires higher imports to be used in building up domestic capacity and, therefore, larger trade deficits in the early years. These are more than offset by the imports saved in later years. The policy implication is that a larger external resource flow in the early years decreases the total aid needed to sustain the growth targets." Similarly, Gupta (1973) also points out that the higher the level of foreign aid, the less the strain on the domestic economy in achieving certain goals, and the value of its social maximand. The larger and more favourable the supply of foreign resources, the quicker the growth of capital stock and the greater the supply of consumption goods to the society over the plan period. The productivity of foreign aid is very high in plan formulation in developing economies. Therefore, any error in forecasting the aid supply is quite likely to disrupt the entire structure of the plan. The sensitivity of plan allocation to aid changes decreases as the economy moves to a higher income and growth path.

NOTES

1. The importance of the dual form is reflected through the duality theorem which states that whenever a constraint in one of the problems is not binding, the corresponding variable in the dual problem would have a zero value. This constraint can be taken out of the problem without affecting either the value of the objective function or the optimal mix of activities.
2. See Kuhn and Tucker (1956), Karlin (1959), Gale (1960) and Hadley (1962) on the mathematical theory of constrained optimization.
3. For an excellent and detailed discussion on these lines see Dervis, Melo and Robinson (1982).
4. For a development of this approach, see Steiner (1959), Eckstein (1961), Marglin (1963), Feldstein (1964), and Prest and Turvey (1965).
5. The requirement of a process of planning over time that avoids the phenomenon of regret is that the relative rate of change in the discount

function per unit time be constant.

6. For an excellent discussion on this point, see Loucks (1975).
7. Hicks (1965) is also of the similar view.
8. Dasgupta and Mitra (1983) solve this problem of intergenerational equity with efficient allocation of resources for a general production function on capital, labour and an exhaustible resource.
9. But it must be noted that comparative dynamics, as such, does not say anything about the transition from one equilibrium growth path to another; the study of this transition belongs to stability analysis.
10. With a finite planning model there is always the disconcerting prospect that the optimal initial policy is influenced by the arbitrary length chosen for the time horizon. If the terminal date is extended beyond T periods, there is no guarantee that results would remain unchanged.
11. We should also keep in mind the multiplier-accelerator interaction as the accelerator theory of investment combined with the multiplier would generate cumulative upward movements in output.
12. This is always true in the short run whether the capital inflow is in the form of grants, hardloans, or direct private investment. However, loans and private investment naturally involve obligation in the future to amortize capital, pay interest, or repatriate profits.

NINE

A Multi-Regional Multi-Sectoral Optimising Planning Model

9.1 INTRODUCTION

Even though the idea of 'balanced regional development' has been referred to time and again, it has not been given any concrete meaning. India's being so highly uneven in economic terms makes this problem so important that it cannot be simply assumed away. Productivity of a unit of investment as well as the savings investment propensity vary from region to region.[1] Since these magnitudes also differ from sector to sector, inter-regional problems get tied up with inter-sectoral problems. Therefore, it would be desirable to discover and exploit the comparative advantages of the regions. Regional comparative advantages, in turn, are dependent upon the regional distribution of resources and upon political preferences as to the regional allocation of welfare. Unfortunately, regional planning problems within the framework of development planning models have not been discussed as such in India.[2] Therefore, in the present chapter, we make an attempt to extend the current state of Indian planning models in this direction. The importance of this derives from the fact that the planning process in India not only allocates public funds between sectors at the national level, but also between states (regions) and between important sectors and states.

Similarly, existing Indian planning models take little or no account of labour, either as a limiting factor to the growth rate or as a factor influencing the optimal sectoral composition of output and investment. In other words, these models assume that India is a completely labour surplus economy. The shadow prices generated by these models impute zero marginal productivity of labour and, therefore, equate the marginal product of capital with the marginal output-capital ratio for the economy as a whole. This practice produces a very strong bias against projects with long lives and long gestation periods because of implicit overvaluation of capital.[3]

Thus, in the present chapter, we make another extension of the current Indian planning models by making an attempt to merge economic and human resource planning through a general equilibrium approach which incorporates both into the present model. Human resources are introduced directly into the planning model through constraints on the supply and demand for various labour skills and through endogenous activities producing human capital. Labour is not treated as surplus by assumption--although the model itself might determine that there are surpluses in respect of specific skills.

The planning problem which is to be examined in this chapter within a theoretical and methodological framework may be stated in the following words:

> Find a resource allocation (economic and human) programme among 'n' sectors and between 'r' regions for the planning period 't'. The programme should lead the economy to the highest feasible, i.e., optimum, paths of the weighted and discounted sums of aggregate consumption and capital stock.

It may also be stated at the outset that this model is a synthesis and an extension of the models associated with the names of Blitzer (1970), Blitzer et al. (1969), Bruno et al. (1970), Chenery et al. (1974), Chakravarty and Lefeber (1965), Chenery and Mc Ewan (1966), Eckaus and Parikh (1965), and Manne and Weisskopf (1970). In this way, the purpose of this chapter is to develop a multi-regional, multi-sectoral model and to show the mathematical structure such a model could have.

9.2 THE BASIC MATHEMATICAL STRUCTURE OF THE MODEL

Objective Function

We have the following objective function:

Maximize

$$W = \sum_{t=1}^{T} w^r \zeta^r \left\{ \frac{C_t}{(1+\delta_c)^{t-1}} \right\}$$

$$+ \sum_{t=1}^{T} w^r \zeta^r \left\{ \frac{K_t}{(1+\delta_t)^{t-1}} \right\}, r = 1, \ldots, R \quad (1)$$

Where

ω^r is the population share of region r;

ξ^r is the weight which represents the political valuation of increments to consumption in region r;

δ_c is the discount rate of consumption such that $O \leq \delta_c \leq 1$

δ_k is the discount rate of capital such that $O \leq \delta_k \leq 1$

C_t is the level of consumption in the t-th period; and

K_t is the level of capital stock in the t-th period.

Thus, our welfare function[4] consists of the maximization of weighted and discounted sums of aggregate consumption and capital stock. The second term in equation (1) is added in order to take into account the contribution of the present generation to the welfare of the future generations. Unlike the one-dimensional case, C_t and K_t are now, respectively, merely scalar indices of consumption and capital, and not consumption and capital itself. Such scalar indices can be constructed, for example, for consumption if either consumption in any period has fixed commodity composition, or if we are given an instantaneous aggregate function involving different types of consumption goods for each region. In that case

$$C_t = V[C_1(t), C_2(t), \ldots, C_n(t)] \tag{2}$$

Where V is an aggregate function.[5]

The equation showing the composition of the wage basket for each region can be the following:

$$cC_t \leq F_t; \; C = [C_i]; \; \Sigma C_i = 1, \text{ for } t = 1,2,3,\ldots,T \tag{3}$$

Where [C] is a diagonal matrix of proportional consumption coefficients, and F_t is a column vector of sectoral output levels designed for consumption.

To make sure that consumption does not stay constant until the very end or does not fluctuate from period to period, we introduce an explicit monotonicity constraint for each region in the model such that

$$C_t \geq C_{t-1}(1 + \eta) \tag{4}$$

Where η is a predetermined parameter. In order to avoid the possibility that the consumption monotonicity constraint holds in an unrealistic manner, a lower bound is set to consumption in year 1 by assuming that $C_1 \geq \bar{C}_1$ where $\bar{C}_1$ is a political parameter indicating the subsistence level of consumption in the economy.[6]

In view of the above objective function we can now develop the model in the following way:

Production Accounting Relationships for each Region

We put the familiar sectoral supply-demand relationships in the form of following inequalities:

$$X_i(t) + M_i(t) + M^R_i(t) \geq J_i(t) + H_i(t) + N_i(t) + \theta_i(t) + F_i(t) + G_i(t) + E_i(t) + E^R_i(t) \quad \text{for } t = 1,\ldots,T \tag{5}$$

Where $X_i(t)$ = domestic production, of goods in sector i;

$M_i(t)$ = imports of goods in sector i;
$M^R_i(t)$ = imports to the region r from other regions of goods classified under sector i;

$J_i(t)$ = intermediate inputs in sector i;

$H_i(t)$ = deliveries for inventory accumulation in sector i;

$N_i(t)$ = deliveries of investment goods for new fixed capital in sector i;

$\theta_i(t)$ = deliveries of investment goods for restoring depreciated fixed capital in sector i;

$F_i(t)$ = Private consumption in sector i;

$G_i(t)$ = Government consumption of goods from sector i;

$E_i(t)$ = exports from sector i; and

$E^R_i(t)$ = exports of goods of sector i from the region r to other regions.

Each of the term in equation (5) represents a column vector of elements where i is the number of sectors. The first three terms $X_i(t)$, $M_i(t)$, and $M^R_i(t)$, are the sources of availability of the products. The last eight terms $J_i(t)$, $H_i(t)$, $N_i(t)$, $\theta_i(t)$, $F_i(t)$, $G_i(t)$, $E^R_i(t)$ and $E_i(t)$ represent use of the output of each sector. This production accounting relationship requires that the total demand for each commodity in each period does not exceed the availability of the commodity in that period.

Intermediate Products

The intermediate requirements for output in each period in each region is determined by a Leontief-type nxn matrix of input-output coefficients a(t)[7]

$$J_i(t) = a_{ij}(t)\, X_i(t), \quad \text{for } t = 1,\ldots,T \tag{6}$$

Where $a_{ij}(t)$ is the amount of good i required as an intermediate input in period 't' to produce one unit of good j. The time subscript t of the $a_{ij}(t)$ matrix indicates that it is possible to change the intermediate requirements ratio over time.

Inventory Accumulation

The inventory accumulation process is determined by a set of accelerator-type relationships by using a nxn matrix of inventory coefficients, S(t), for each region:

$$H_i(t) = S_{ij}(t)\,\{X_i(t+1) - X_i(t)\} \quad \text{for } t = 2,\ldots, T \tag{7}$$

$$H_i(1) = S_{ij}(1)\,\{X_i(2) - (I + \alpha_o)\,\overline{X_i(0)}$$

Where an element $S_{ij}(t)$ is the amount of good i required as inventory in period (t-1) to produce the unit of good j in period t; I is the identity matrix, $\underline{\alpha_o}$ is the diagonal matrix of anticipated sectoral growth rates; and $\overline{X_i(O)}$ is the pre-plan period output level.

Thus, deliveries in period t for inventory are a function of the forward difference of output $\{x_i(t+1) - X_i(t)\}$. Production for inventory in the first period $H_i(1)$ is based on the difference between output levels in the second period and output levels in the first period as anticipated in the pre-plan period. The term $S_i(1)\,(I + \alpha_o)\,\overline{X_i(O)}$ gives the total stocks of inventories at the beginning of the plan. Technical requirements only partially determine the inventory coefficients. To a considerable degree these inventory coefficients can be treated as behavioural coefficients. They also respond to both price and non-price influences. Such behavioural factors may be expected to change over time and we take into consideration this possibility in the formulation by giving a time subscript to the inventory coefficients.

Private Consumption in Each Region

For each region we have a coefficient vector $C_i(t)$ which defines the proportions of sectoral consumption in the aggregate and relates the vector $F_i(t)$ of deliveries of private consumption to aggregate consumption $C_i(t)$:

$$F_i(t) = C_i(t)\,C(t), \quad \text{for } t = 1,\ldots,T \tag{9}$$

Where $C_i(t)$ is the amount of good in one unit of aggregate consumption $C(t)$ so that $\sum_{i=1} C_i(t) = 1$.

Thus, the composition of aggregate private consumption in period t is specified by $C_i(t)$.

Government Consumption in Each Region

The following inequalities define $G_i(t)$ which is the vector of government consumption in each region in period t:

$$G_i(t) \geq G_i(t-1), \quad \text{for } t = 1,\ldots,T \tag{10}$$

The projection of government consumption may include wide variety of welfare expenditures, administrative costs, defence expenditures and other items.[8]

Foreign Trade

In optimising models aggregation introduces a problem with respect to exports and competitive imports in so far as they are endogenous. For, unless specific constraints are introduced to prevent it, in an optimal solution, either E_i or M_i or both will be zero. However, given that commodity i is an aggregate of a number of commodities, even if, from the optimality point of view, each commodity constituting the aggregate will either be exported or imported in the aggregate commodity i, both exported and imported goods may be included. Thus, the optimal solution of an aggregated model may be at variance with the truly optimal solution that would have been obtained in a more disaggregated model.[9]

Even if there are no aggregation difficulties, it may still be desirable to specify upper bounds on exports and imports of each trading sector, because it is usually unrealistic to postulate that an increasing volume of exports can be made only at decreasing unit prices, and still remain within a linear programming framework,[10] requires approximation of the marginal revenue curve (associated with a given downward sloping demand curve) by a step function.

There is yet another reason why one may wish to impose an upper bound on imports. Very often, the planning authorities have a specified target for import substitution in a given trading sector. A typical, but by no means the only, way in which this is reflected in a model is to impose a constraint stating that competitive imports should not exceed a specified proportion of total domestic availability of the commodity.

A lower bound on exports and an upper bound on imports of a sector in any given period may reflect the fact that even if optimal to do so, exports cannot be rushed down and imports cannot be pushed up beyond a certain limit because vested interests not easily dislodged develop in such activities. An upper bound on exports may also reflect the fact that, even if foreign demand were infinitely elastic, exports cannot be expanded very much in the short run because of marketing or other constraints.

Upper Bounds on Exports

Exports are constrained to grow at not more than 'b' percent per period.[11] Thus

$$E_i (t) \leq E_i (t-1) (1 + b) \tag{11}$$

$$E_{ir} (t) \leq E_{ir} (t -1) (1 + b) \tag{12}$$

Lower Bounds on Exports

Recognizing the fact that production for export markets cannot always be rapidly converted into production for domestic markets, lower bounds are placed on exports. These stipulate that exports during any time period must be at least as great as they were in the previous period. Thus:

$$E_i (t) \geq E_i (t - 1) \tag{13}$$

$E_{ir}(t) \geq E_{ir}(t-1)$ (14)

Foreign Exchange Constraints

These constraints ensure that in each time period export earnings and net foreign loans and other invisibles at least meet the cost of all imports. In other words, the total amount of imports $\sum_{i=1}^{n} M_i(t)$ in each period is limited by the availability of foreign exchange, which in turn, depends on the total amount of exports $\sum_{i=1}^{n} E_i(t)$, foreign aid from government sources, private foreign investment, and the possible recourse to the existing reserves. The latter three components, lumped together, are designated capital inflow and are specified exogenously as $\overline{A(t)}$. Thus, the foreign exchange constraints or the balance of payments constraints are given by the following equation:

$$UM(t) \leq \overline{A(t)} + UE(t), \; for \; t = 1, \ldots, T \qquad (15)$$

Where U is a unit row vector (1, 1,...,1).

Now, with a view to gradually reducing reliance on the political goodwill of donor nations, a schedule of progress towards self-reliance can be incorporated in this constraint by changing $\overline{A(t)}$ overtime such that the capital inflow is terminated by some stipulated date. Accordingly:

$$\overline{A(t)} \leq 0, \; for \; t = t - n, T \qquad (16)$$

This equation imposes the condition that capital inflow must terminate in a given period (T-n) prior to the terminal period (t). The economy must be self-sufficient for years after (T-n).

Composition of Imports for the Nation

We should divide the imports into two parts: non-competitive imports, $M_1(t)$, and competitive imports $M_2(t)$. Non-competitive imports include those goods for which no domestic capacity exists, and for which no substitution by domestic output is possible, whatever the relative prices of imports and domestic output. Few imports are strictly non-competitive in the long run for a country such as India which contains a wide variety of resources and climates. In the short run, however, there are distinct limits to some types of domestic production. Non-competitive imports are often introduced in a planning model to reflect the fact that production in any sector will often involve the use of some inputs for which there is neither current domestic production capacity nor any possibility of establishing capacity in the medium to long-term plans. Competitive imports are those imports that substitute, unit for unit, with domestic production. They are, therefore, allocated among consuming sectors, depending on the relative costs of the imports and domestic production.

The vector of non-competitive imports, $M_1(t)$, is related to output levels by fixed coefficients. The vector of competitive imports, $M_2(t)$, merely supplements the output of the corresponding domestic sectors. Total imports in each sector are the sum of the two types:

$$M_i(t) = M_i(t) + M_2(t), \quad \text{for } t = 1,\ldots,T \tag{17}$$

so that

$$M_1(t) = \sum_{r=1}^{R} M_{ir}(t)\,; \tag{18}$$

$$M_2(t) = \sum_{r=1}^{R} M_{2r}(t) \tag{19}$$

Non-Competitive Imports

We determine non-competitive imports by multiplying the diagonal matrix, $m_1(t)$, or fixed import coefficients, by the vector of domestic outputs:

$$M_i(t) = m_i(t)\,X(t)\,, \text{ for } t = 1,\ldots,T \tag{20}$$

$$M_{ir}(t) = m_{ir}(t)\,X_r(t)\,, \text{ for } r = 1,\ldots,R \tag{21}$$

$$M_1(t) = \sum_{r=1}^{R} M_{1r}(t) \tag{22}$$

Non-competitive imports, which complement domestic production, are essential and must be made if there is to be any domestic production. The requirements for such imports must be satisfied before other supplementary imports are allowed. Because of these conditions the foreign exchange available to purchase non-competitive imports can, in some circumstances, set a limit to domestic output. However, non-competitive import coefficients can be changed period by period to take into account planned programmes of import substitution.

Competitive Imports

Non-competitive imports have the effect of determining the minimum amount of imports necessary for producing domestic output, X(t). Competitive imports, $M_2(t)$, make use of whatever foreign exchange is left after satisfying non-competitive imports. While non-competitive imports are complementary to domestic production, competitive imports are substitutes. In the absence of diminishing returns, however, the model solution would tend to concentrate the use of competitive imports in only a few sectors. To the extent that diminishing returns exist, this would unduly restrict domestic capacity formation in these sectors. To avoid this possibility the maximum use of foreign exchange for competitive imports is stipulated for each sector in the following equations:

$$M_2(t) \leq M_2(t)\,[A(t) + E(t) - UM_1(t)] \qquad (23)$$

$$M_{2r}(t) \leq M_{2r}(t)\,[A_r(t) + E_r(t) - U_r M_{1r}(t)] \qquad (24)$$

$$M_2(t) = \sum_{r=1}^{R} M_{2r}(t) \qquad (25)$$

Where the vector of coefficients $m_2(t)$ is exogenously determined so that $\Sigma_i\, m_{2i}(t) > 1$. This formulation provides some scope for choice among sectors in the allocation of foreign exchange to competitive imports, but recognises limitations on such choice.[12] Further, the present formulation allows for some scope of substitution in the choice of competitive imports and of export activities.

The Capacity Constraints

The capacity constraints are formulated in the conventional manner:

$$b(t)\, x(t) \leq K(t), \quad \text{for } t = 1,...,T$$

where $b(t)$ = a diagonal matrix of capital-output ratios;

$x(t)$ = vector of sectoral outputs; and

$K(t)$ = vector of sectoral capital stocks in each sector.

This constraint ensures that output in each vector in each period does not exceed the amount producible with the fixed capital in that sector available at the beginning of that period.

Thus, for each region this constraint would be as follows:[13]

$$b_r(t)\, X_r(t) \leq K_r(t), \quad \text{for } r = 1,...,T \tag{26}$$

$$K(t) = \sum_{r=1}^{R} K_r(t); \tag{27}$$

$$b(t)\, X(t) = \sum_{r=1}^{R} b_r(t)\, X_r(t) \tag{28}$$

Investment Requirements for Each Region

The total capital in each sector in each region, represented by an element of the vector $K_r(t)$, is a composite commodity with a fixed composition. This composition is defined by a proportion matrix P, in which element p_{ij} represents that in each region the good i held as fixed capital by sector j per unit of composite fixed capital K_{rj}.

Sectoral capacities in any region may be increased in any period t by the delivery of additions to capacity Z(t). These increments of capacity, in turn, are formed by deliveries of investment goods from the sectors that produce them. The deliveries are in fixed proportions and with fixed time leads of 'h' periods prior to the completion of the addition to capacity where h=1,...,n. The amount of Z(t) that must be furnished by each sector in each period in each region is determined by the 'h' investment lag proportions matrices. The coefficients P^h_{ij} in these matrices indicate the proportions of the total increment to capacity in sector j in period t that must be supplied by sector j in period t-h.[14]

Thus the total amount of deliveries of investment goods in each period is:

$$N_{ir} = \sum p^h zr(t+h) \tag{29}$$

The constancy of the terms on the matrices P^h imply assumptions of fixed proportions of the various components of capital in finished capital of each sector and of fixed-time sequences in which these components must be provided to create the capital.[15]

Depreciated Capital for Each Region

In the present model, we assume that real depreciation depends on passage of time rather than on rate of use. Domar (1957) has already emphasized that the replacement of worn-out equipment is substantially less than the conventional allowance for depreciation in a growing economy. Therefore, one should define net investment as gross investment less replacement so that part of net investment is covered by the excess of depreciation allowances over actual replacement. In this pattern capital can produce services at a constant rate over a lifetime independent of the rate of use of the capital. At the end of this lifetime, all the productive capabilities of the capital disappear. The capital originating in sector i that wears out in sector j is $D_{ij}(t)$. The total depreciated capital in each sector in each period is than $D_j = \Sigma D_{ij}(t)$, and for all sectors in all regions:

$$D_r(t) = \overline{D_r(t)} \tag{30}$$

Depreciated Capacity for Each Region

Different lifetimes for different components of capital imply that plan and equipment depreciate in an 'unbalanced' manner. This, in turn, provides the opportunity for restoring capacity by an unbalanced production of capital of the plant or equipment. Since the components of capital stock in each sector were out at different rates, the capacity immobilized by the depreciation composition matrix d^* is defined with element $D_{ij} = D_{ij}/D_j$. Then, if $D_j(t)$ is multiplied by d^*_{ij}/P_{ij} the amount of component $D_{ij}(t)$ in sector j can be computed. The actual amount of capacity lost through depreciation in sector j is the largest loss due to the wearing out of any component and is determined by the maximum of $(d^*_{1j}/P_{ij}, d^*_{2j}/P_{2j},...,d^*_{nj}/P_{nj})\ D_j$. Therefore, the diagonal matrix 'd' can be formed whose element $d_{ij} = \text{Max}\ (d^*_{1j}/P_{1j}, d^*_{2j}/P_{2j},...,d^*_{nj}/P_{nj})$. The capacity lost through depreciation in each sector is, therefore,

$$V_r(t) = [d]\ D_r(t). \qquad (31)$$

Restoration Requirements for Each Region

It is upto the optimizing mechanism to determine $R^*(t)$, the amount of capacity lost through depreciation that will be restored. The deliveries, $\theta(t)$, from each-sector for capacity restoration are assumed, like new capital formation, to require upto h periods. So the deliveries for the purpose in any one period look h periods ahead:

$$\theta_r(t) = r^{*h}[d]^{-1}\ R^*_r\ (t + h) \qquad (32)$$

Where r^{*h} is restoration lag proportions matrices similar to p^h. The coefficients r^{*h}_{ij} indicate the proportions of the total capital replacement $r^*_j(t)/d_{ij}$ to restore capacity $R^*_j(t)$ that must be supplied by sector i in periods h.

Capital Accounting Relationships for Each Region

We define the capital accounting relationships in each region as follows:

$$K_r(t) \leq K_r\ (t\text{-}1) + Z_r(t) + R^*_r\ (t) - V_r(t),$$
$$\text{for } t = 1,...,T+(h\text{-}1). \qquad (33)$$

This merely states that $K_r(t)$ cannot be greater than the capital available in the preceding period, plus the new completed additions to capacity $Z_r(t)$, plus that part of depreciated capacity that is restored, $R^*_r(t)$, minus the capacity depreciating in period t, $V_r(t)$. Since both the restored capacity $R^*(t)$, and new capacity, $Z_r(t)$, can be zero, decumulation of capital to the extent of V(t) is possible. Therefore, to make sure that per capita capital stock does not decrease over the planning period, we introduce the following constraint:

$$K_r(t) \geq K_r(t-1)(1+\eta_r) \qquad (34)$$

Where η_r is the rate of growth of population in region r.

Restoration Ceilings for Each Region

We assume in this model that if capacity is to be restored when any component of capital depreciates, the restoration may take place in any period subsequent to its depreciation so that

$$\sum_{t=1}^{T} R^*_n(t) \leq \sum_{t=1}^{T} V_r(t), \; for \; t = 1, \ldots, (t+h)$$

Labour Constraint for Each Region

We assume labour to be classified by 'S' skill categories. The total demand for labour of each type is determined as the sum of the labour required by each sector. As in an input-output model, the increase in the demand for labour by a sector is assumed to be proportionate to the growth of its output.[16] This assumption implies that the demand for labour in the s-th skill category, L^D_s, is:

$$L^D_s = \sum_i^n e_{si}\overline{X_i(t)} + \sum_i^n e'_{si}\Delta X_i + \sum_i^I P_{s,j} ED_j(t)$$

Where e_{si} is the labour input coefficient of type S needed per unit of output of commodity i in the base year and $\overline{X}_i(t)$ is the initial level of production. In this formulation the incremental labour coefficients e'_{si} represent the increase in labour demand for each type of labour resulting from an increase in output in each sector, Δx_i, over the plan period.[17] P_{sj} is the requirement (in man years) of labour of skill levels S, per unit of human capital formation activity j; and $ED_j(t)$ is the level of education activity j during the time period t.

This formulation permits the elasticity of employment with respect to output to be greater or less than unity, according to whether the marginal labour coefficient is greater or less than the average. In addition, employment elasticities can differ by type of labour as estimated from available time series.

Although it is realistic to assume an elastic supply of unskilled labour at fairly constant real wages in India as also in many other developing countries, this is unlikely to be true for many higher skill categories. It is thus necessary in an overall planning model to predict the skill composition of the labour force. This gives an estimate of labour supply by category, L_{st}, for each year. The total supply of labour of types in each period t must be greater than or equal to the demand determined by equation (36). The imposition of constraints of this sort is readily handled in a linear programming framework. In practice, however, planners usually make trial adjustments in the vector of final demands to achieve a feasible solution or investigate the possibilities of substituting less skilled labour in some of the sectors using the scarce category.[18]

The imbalance between the skill composition of the labour force and the skill composition required by existing levels of production has been stressed as one important aspect of the unemployment problem.[19] In many countries the existence of an excess of qualified workers require them either to accept employment normally requiring lower qualifications or to remain unemployed until more satisfactory opportunities arise. This queuing phenomenon explains the growing unemployment of young educated workers, particularly in urban areas.[20]

It may also be pointed out that labour constraints are introduced in the model because of the fact that in the absence of these constraints, a planning model will substantially aggregate the marginal productivity of physical capital and of foreign aid.[21] And once labour is introduced, labour input coefficients must be estimated for each sector of the economy. If skills are disaggregated into two or more classes, it becomes essential to allow for capital-labour substitution, education and human capital formation. These trade offs are not easy to quantify. If, however, these options are omitted in a dynamic model, there will inevitably be artificial bottlenecks and instabilities in the shadow prices. Also, it would be impossible to examine any of the interesting human resource problems without disaggregating the labour supply in some meaningful way. This is obvious. However, how much to disaggregate the labour force is not an easy question to answer. Not only do the data problems become more severe at higher levels of disaggregation, but the size of the model itself becomes too unwieldy.

Labour Supply for Each Region

There are three sources for meeting the demand for labour: there are exogenous supplies of manpower for each skill level during each time period; the human capital formation activities both add to these available supplies and deplete them through training for higher skills; and labour downgrading activities provide some scope for skill substitution. Thus the equation of labour supply would be:

$$L_s = \overline{L_s(t)} + \sum_{t=1}^{T-1} \left(ED_{s,\tau} - ED_{s-1,\tau} \right) + LD_{s-1,\tau} - LD_{s,\tau}$$

This equation says that the total labour supply would be the summation of exogenous supply of labour at time t; net additions and losses from training activities in prior periods; and net gains from downgrading.

Equilibrium in the labour market requires that supply equals demand for labour in each category.

Education Capacity Constraints for Each Region

Education activities $E^d_j(t)$ are limited in the following way:

$$E^d_j(t) \leq q_j K_e(t-1) + q_j Z_r(t) + q_j P^*_r(t) - q_j V_r(t) \quad \text{for } t = 1,\ldots, T + h \qquad (38)$$

where $K_e(t)$ is the vector of capital stocks in j education sector/activities. Since the education activities, $ED_j(t)$, are to be measured in monetary units, student investment ratios, q_j, may be used to properly convert the units of measurement.

Employment Constraint for Each Region

We may also introduce the skill-wise employment constraint in the model so that unemployment is not allowed to increase.

$$N_r(t) \geq \beta_{s,r} \{L_s(t) - L_s(t-1)\} + D_r(t) + V_r(t) \tag{39}$$

where $N_r(t)$ is the level of investment in region r; and $\beta_{s,r}$ is the skill-wise net investment required per engaged person in each region.[22]

9.3 CONCLUSION

The present study lacks empiricism. Application of a planning model, inspite of problems of data availability and processing, is no doubt a stimulating exercise and offers an opportunity for realistically evaluating the usefulness of a model and revealing the structural problems of an economy. But, in case of massive data and computational requirements,nothing seems to cut ice until a strong base in terms of both time and resource is guaranteed.[23] But the present study is one such case in which the gap between a theoretical generalised study and its operational counterpart in a multi-sectoral and multi-regional framework is still unbridgeable.

NOTES

1. Depressed regions have some common characteristics: Levels of poverty and unemployment are high, frequently both in absolute terms and relative to the remainder of the country. Sectoral composition of output differs from the national economy and is associated, as both cause and effect, with the lower levels of per capita income. The growth rate of income is lower than the rest of the economy. Production tends to specialize on sectors facing a low rate of growth in demand. There is a resistance to institutional change. Neoclassical theory, with its assumption of factor and product mobility and substitutability, does not encompass the problems of unevenness of development among regions which arise from the immobility of factors. In this situation, the mobility of labour manifested in migration out of depressed regions may actually accentuate regional disparities due to the fact that it is often the young and the skilled people who move. Planning models do not

provide an appropriate tool for the analysis of institutional rigidities, although application of their results may require changes in the institutions. However, they can throw light on the constraints to regional development on both the supply side and the demand side.

2. Interestingly, economists have given much greater attention to such problems in other countries, see, for example, Chenery (1962) who evaluates both the regions for different income growth rate among regions and the broad outlines of alternative development programmes in Italy. A substantial extension of Chenery's approach has been implemented by Mac Ewan (1971) in the case of Pakistan. Norton (1971) has also developed a model for Korea, the structural characteristics of which are similar to Mac Ewan's model. These studies arrive at broadly similar conclusions: that structural shifts in sectoral production patterns are required to reduce regional income disparities; that such shifts are not costly in terms of national consumption foregone; and that government intervention is required to bring about these changes. But these studies do not analyse the inter-regional income distribution nor do they consider the level of productive employment. See, also Khan (1967), Kaser (1968) and Korean Development Association (1967).
3. See, Harberger (1967).
4. One can easily conceive of maximising many other social preference functions, other than the present one, which will yield quite different social optima from the particular optimum we are exploring here. Most of the development planning models have their maximand as the maximisation of aggregate consumption. But it would be wrong to base the strategy for economic planning for a country like India with a massive and growing volume of unemployment, a difficult foreign exchange situation, and with regional imbalances exclusively on an approach based purely on the maximisation of aggregate consumption.
5. That the consumption level in any period has a fixed commodity composition is, of course, a restrictive assumption. But it is a better assumption than the assumption of a linear valuation function involving all separate commodities separately. Non-linearities raise issues that are not particularly easy to handle computationally for large disaggregated models, although if the aggregator function is additively separable, they should not cause much difficulty.
6. Consumption can further be divided into three classes, i.e., consumption of the rich, middle, and poor people.
7. More detailed discussion of input-output planning models and of alternative formulations of the basic relations are given in Chenery and Clark (1959), Blitzer et al. (1975), Dahiya (1982) and Dervis et al. (1982).
8. Government consumption is not independent of the level and growth rate of output either on the demand or supply side. The area of education provides a good example of the inter-dependence of private output and government consumption.
9. A similar problem arises when aggregation is made with respect to seasons of a year or regions within a country. It may be optimal for a country to import a commodity in one season and to export it in another, given high storage costs. It may be optimal in one region to export a commodity but in another region to import it, if internal transport costs are sufficiently high. Thus, aggregation will result in distortions of trade flows. To minimize these aggregation biases, adhoc constraints are often introduced, placing bounds on the imports and exports of each trading sector. However, it is difficult to avoid arbitrariness in the specification of such bounds.

10. Of course, one could abandon linear programming in favour of non-linear programming and avoid piece-wise linear approximations. For some early exercises in non-linear programming, see Chenery and Krestschmer (1956) and Chenery and Uzawa (1958).
11. Since, except in extreme cases, exports depend on domestic prices which, in turn, depend on the amount and composition of productive resources, and on comparative advantage, our treatment of exports is not fully satisfactory. Though the separate projection of exports is not a grave deficiency for short-period plans, it is more serious shortcoming in models with a long planning horizon, since the model solution itself should reflect changing comparative advantage. Yet to determine comparative advantage, an analysis of world economy would be required. If a demand schedule for exports is estimated exogenously, then the choice between export promotion or import substitution can be made within the model solution. A higher degree of sectoral disaggregation is desirable for this purpose.
12. The treatment of competitive and non-competitive imports recognises the technical, political, and administrative obstacles to changes in the pattern of use of foreign exchange from time to time. Bottlenecks, due to indivisibilities in production and lack of specific material resources and of technical skills, do exist and must be introduced in the model. Though they may be absolute in the short run, they are often subject to substantial modification within several years. It would be more valid to formulate a model so that the creation of domestic capacity for all imported goods would be determined by the optimizing mechanism with constraints that perhaps reflect increasing costs but are less completely rigid than in the present framework. While this is less important for short-run than for long-run models, it does indicate a possible direction for the extension of analysis.
13. Unlike the present case, a different 'b' matrix with each specific vintage of capital may also be introduced.
14. The matrices p^h have a simple relationship to p, p_{ij} being equal to $\sum P^h_{ij}$.
15. Such fixidity is again not an accurate description of reality. The fixed-proportions assumption is an aspect of the assumption of given technology. If the choice of technology is to be made by the model solution, a set of alternative P must be stipulated with respect to the fixed sequences assumption. Since the output of each sector is homogenous, it would be possible as an alternative procedure to make capital-in-process non-specific and to indicate only the total contribution of each capital goods sector to output. This would allow investment goods to be produced in advance of the actual increment in capacity whenever the model decided it was most convenient. The later formulation would provide for flexibility in the sequence of capital formation, making it possible for the model to stretch out the lags beyond the specific minimum lags if it would be preferable to do so. This, in turn, would undoubtedly somewhat improve the overall performance of the model provided there is a more careful accounting to the production of capital-goods by each sector, their movement into use or into an inventory of "unfinished capacity" and their withdrawal from that inventory. That would, in turn, increase the number of restraints. If the model were given additional freedom in scheduling investment, it would use it, if at all, by totally interrupting investment in some year. Since the costs of such a complete interruption are not easily accounted for in a linear framework and, in reality, the output of each sector is not completely homogenous, we chose not to provide the model with the freedom to reschedule the investment sequence.

16. On this assumption, see, Tinbergen and Bos (1964).
17. Manpower projections based on equation (36) assume that whatever changes have taken place in labour requirements in the past as a result of substitution among skill categories and productivity increases will continue in the future. Since the available data rarely permit a separation to be made between substitution and technological change, employment elasticities less than one are commonly attributed to the latter factor, and future substitution possibilities are ignored. While this assumption may be valid when relative prices of different types of labour are fairly constant, it is likely to overstate the requirements for types of labour for which relative wages rise more in the future than in the past.
18. For evidence on the elasticity of substitution among different types of skilled labour, see Psacharapolous and Hinchliffe (1972), Vashist (1979), Bowles (1969) and Dougherty (1972). Unfortunately their conclusions as to high substitution are based on cross-sector data of relative wage structures and provide little evidence on substitution possibilities over a relevant plan period of five years or so.
19. See ILO (1971, 1972) reports on Sri Lanka and Kenya.
20. In terms of income distribution, it would be desirable to carry forward the projections of labour force supply and demand into projections of wage structure. One would than have the basis for estimating the major components of income from work in a form which could be linked to the size distribution of income. This, together with income from assets and with estimates of demand and functions, would close the production-income-demand-production loop. Such models are still at the experimental stage.
21. See, Harberger (1967).
22. The total employment can also be determined by multiplying the sectoral outputs by the corresponding labour output ratios:

$$l_t X_t = L_t$$

where l_t is a row vector (lxn) of sectoral labour output ratios and L_t denotes total employment in period t.

We can express additional employment as

$$\Delta L = \Delta l X_t + l_t \Delta X_t + \Delta l . \Delta X$$

Where $\Delta l X_t$ represents the effect of a change in productivity, i.e., the productivity effect;

$l_t \Delta X_t$ represents a change in sectoral output, i.e., the output effect;

$\Delta l_t . \Delta X_t$ represents the combined effect of changes in both labour productivity and sectoral output. We think that the output effect is likely to be favourable, but the productivity effect would tend to dampen the increase in employment.

24. A good description of the formidable job of application can be seen from the writings of Taylor, Eckaus and Parikh: "It may take a five men team of good quality a year to get enough data together for a good linear programming model, to have the data inserted into the computer programme package for solution, and verified there. During this process and in deriving solutions thereafter, much computer time may be required. All of this takes monetary and human resources". (Taylor, 1975, p. 83). "Realistically speaking a dynamic Linear programming exercise might tie-up several Ph.D. economists and appropriate assistants for a year or two, and $ 5000 or $

10,000 of support costs before it is completed." (Taylor, 1975, p. 95). "The development of the models and computations... required, over a period of 3 years, 150 hours of computer time on an IBM 7094" (Eckaus and Parikh 1968, p. 15).

TEN

Conclusion

In this concluding chapter we summarise the main points of this study, indicate certain promising directions for future research, and sum up with a note on recent advancements in the field of planning theories and techniques.

10.1 SUMMARY

1. From methodological point of view, development planning models can be broadly classified into seven categories according to the:

i. sectoral treatment, i.e., the number of input-output sectors;

ii. temporal treatment, i.e., the time horizon and the number of time periods;

iii. solution or computational techniques, i.e., consistency or optimization type;

iv. treatment of constraints on growth process, i.e., purely-trade-limited growth process (open-loop) or trade-and-savings-limited growth process (closed-loop);

v. substitution possibilities;

vi. objective function; and

vii. accounting techniques, i.e., input-output, semi-input-output, social accounting matrix and material balances approach.

On the basis of this classification we can formulate the following table to point out some of the characteristics of Indian planning models:

Table 10.1. Some Characteristics of Indian Planning Models

Reference	Objective Function	Open-loop or Closed-loop	Solution Technique	Problem Size			
				No. of time periods	Length of planning horizon(Yrs.)	No. of input - output sectors	No. of labour skill classes
Ali (1979)	Maximization of consumption	Open	Fiasco-Mc-Cormics sequential unconstrained minimization technique	1	1	12	0
Bergsman and Manne (1966)	No explicit objective function	Open	Consistency model, dynamic input-output interpolation technique	5	10	30	0
Chakravarti and Lefeber (1965)	Maximisation of discounted sum of consumption	Open	Linear Programming	5	5	11	0
Eckaus and Parikh (1968)	Maximization of discounted consumption, subject to consumption growth constraints	Open	Linear Programming	10	30	11	0
Frisch (1960)	Maximization of consumption of home produced goods	Open	Linear Programming	1	-	26	0

Gupta (1973)	Maximization of discounted consumption	Open	Linear Programming	10	10	4	2
Manne and Rudra (1965)	No explicit objective function	Open	Consistency model, static input-output	1	10	30	0
Manne and Weisskopf (1970)	Maximization of consumption subject to gradualist constraints	Open	Preliminary data processing to reduce number of rows and columns in the linear programming matrix	4	8	30	0
Planning Commission (1986)	No explicit objective function	Open	Consistency model	1	5	50	0
Planning Commission (1981)	No explicit Objective function	Open	Consistency model	2	(5,10)	89	0
Planning Commission (1973)	No explicit objective function	Open	Consistency model, Gauss-Siedel method	1	5	66	0
Sandee (1960)	Maximization of consumption	Open	Linear Programming	1	10	13	0
Srinivasan et al. (1965)	No explicit objective function	Open	Gauss-Siedel model, static input-output	1	(5,15)	30	0
Tendulkar (1971)	Maximization of target year aggregate consumption	Open and closed	Linear Programming	1	15	32	0
Weisskopf (1967)	Minimization of weighted sum of the domestic and foreign primary resource costs	Open	Linear Programming	1	10	150	0

Thus, from methodological point of view, Indian planning models offer a progression from the most aggregative forms of planning to the highly disaggregative; from various feasibility and consistency analysis to optimising approach; and from comparative static approach to intertemporal analysis. With all these developments, the methodology of these models has been evolving itself, on all counts, to higher levels of methodological sophistication both in the conceptual and the operational analysis. These models have also made attempts to clarify the basic nature of economy-wide development planning models, their relationship to theoretical reasoning and their usefulness in generating a dialogue between the model builders, the theorists and the policy makers. The applications of these models focus on an analysis of the interrelationships between government policy and trade, growth and income-distribution in Indian economy.

2. The development planning models used in consecutive official five-year plans in India are continuously updated and amended to suit the changing socio-economic conditions, availability of new data and to take advantage of the improving methodology of the model building. These models have passed through the following three stages:[1]

i. The First and Second Five-Year Plan models concentrated mainly on the growth potentialities of the economy, determined by the economy's savings potential and the incremental-capital-output ratio. These aggregative models belonged to the Harrod-Domar and Feldman-Mahalanobis family. They had no foreign trade sector. Their demand and supply equations were also the same.

ii. The input-output models of different variants, basically belonging to the Leontief group, came into increasing use in the Third Five-Year Plan and continued until the formulation of the Fifth Five-Year Plan. These models focussed on the need for establishing intersectoral consistencies in building the production targets. These targets mainly remained neglected in the sense that no sectoral supply constraints were formulated in these models, although in a limited and indirect way they were checked for a few specific sectors only by the use of material balances techniques. These input-output models were increasingly articulated during the Fourth and Fifth Five-Year Plans by making them 'closed', i.e., by endogenising imports and consumption in the final demand vector, respectively.

iii. The Sixth and the Seventh Five-Year Plan models integrated both the Harrod-Domar and the input-output approaches of the earlier plan models in a demand-supply frame. For this purpose an investment planning model was developed and integrated to the existing input-output system. By this, the demand-supply balances for all sectors are checked over time. Furthermore, the problems of balancing the demand and supply are tackled not only in the commodity and services market but also in the markets dealing with primary inputs like labour and capital and the other important non-renewable resources of the country.

3. The 'material balance approach' has become an essential part of Indian planning literature.[2] This technique, widely regarded as forerunner of the input-output technique, is simply a list of supplies and demands for the product in which the total supply should equal the total demand. The supply and demand sides of the balance are each broken down into the components most relevant for the product being balanced. This technique helps us to assess the capacity and output to be generated in a specific sector belonging either to a commodity or a service at a very disaggregated level, sometimes even at the level of individual projects, and the likely absorption of the commodity in the economy in terms of major consuming units for any projected year. Since all these estimates are done in physical units, the sector composition needs to be very homogenous. This is one of the limitations of this approach. Since the late 1950s this technique has been criticized on several other grounds, the most notable of these being (i) its incomplete coverage, (ii) the difficulty of revising plans once they have been balanced, (iii) difficulties of correcting initially unbalanced plans, and (iv) the tendency of this technique to treat final demand as a residual or balancing item rather than as a starting point of plan formulation. Input-output technique overcomes some of these problems in a simple and elegant fashion.

The material balance technique has been extensively used in India since the Third Five-Year Plan. But its role has been limited to that of supplementing input-output technique. This technique has helped in assessing the feasibility of production targets, stipulated mainly from the demand side by the input-output model which was used exclusively until the Fifth Five-Year Plan. But the Sixth and the Seventh Five-Year Plan models developed separate investment planning sub-models for giving a general coverage for assessing the supply constraints in all sectors. The advantages of supplementing input-output models by material balance approach, as pointed out by the Planning Commission (1981, Chapter 7), are:

i. In the input-output accounting, in however great detail we go, it is very difficult to reach at a commodity or project level, whereas there are many occasions where the planners need information on this micro level.

ii. The need for commodity level exercise increases as the number of commodities comprising a sector increases. Even in case of single commodity sector, the commodity level studies of material balances serve as an important cross-check for the results given by the input-output model. This is so because of the following two reasons:

   a. No commodity is strictly homogenous and differences amongst various grades of a commodity have to be taken into consideration, particularly if the unit prices differ significantly; and

   b. the input-output model has to rely on certain assumptions and procedures to conform to certain macro economic aggregates in making sectoral allocations.

iii. Capacity constraints in both the consuming sectors of the commodity as also for the commodity in question can be readily built into the projection process.[3]

iv. There is flexibility to subdivide/increase the number of consuming sectors depending upon technological considerations.

v. At the commodity levels the information on end-use-wise consumption pattern becomes available much earlier than at the sector level. Material balances can, therefore, be based on more recent accurate information for the base year.

vi. Material balances are constructed largely in physical units rather than in monetary values. Operational decision on capacity, production, trade and stocks of commodities are mostly taken in terms of physical units data. Loss of precision associated with the use of average prices in arriving at physical magnitudes can be easily avoided if the exercise is done directly in physical units.

4. Since the Fifth Five-Year Plan the Indian plan models have formally incorporated a number of sub-models explicitly into the national model. These sub-models were constructed (i) to go into details of certain phenomena that are complementary to the core input-output model; and (ii) to pay the attention which is technically necessary but which is not at present integrated in the main input-output model. Some of these models are precursive to the main model, while certain others are recursive. The main role of these sub-models has been to estimate the supply potentialities of the different sectors vis-a-vis (i) the investment allocation made in the different plans; (ii) the rate of completion of the existing projects and programmes; and (iii) the utilisation of the capacity available in the course of the implementation of the plan.

5. The basic development philosophy of the Indian Plan models has aimed at the following:

1. Changing income distribution in the economy to reach a certain distribution reflecting equity.

2. Capturing the demand pattern of the society as revealed through market mechanism giving full respect to consumer sovereignty.

3. Supplementing this demand pattern with the requirement pattern of the poor whose demands do not get reflected via the market mechanism.

4. Making plan decisions regarding guaranteeing a production

structure in conformity with (2) and (3) above and at the same time making optimum use of available factor endowment, and technology for maximising growth.

5. Devising economic policies in order to influence the whole gamut of production, distribution and consumption of the economy including choice of technology, the need for self-reliance and social justice and faster development of the country.

6. In this study, we have also discussed the problem of choice of planning techniques in the planning process, i.e., the fixed plan technique, the semi-rolling plan technique and the rolling plan technique. We found that, given the prerequisites, the rolling plan technique is more appropriate to Indian economy where agriculture, depending on nature's unforeseen changes; is the dominant sector of the economy in almost every aspect; foreign economic relations are crucial; and domestic activities are not fully controlled by the state. The essential prerequisites for the successful and efficient working of this technique are that of a good monitoring mechanism, an efficient administrative apparatus and an adequately prepared institutional framework.

7. The present study has also pointed out that all the Indian planning models are formulated within the framework of the fixed plan technique. These models are either static or 'comparative static' or dynamic by nature. Therefore, we make an obvious extension of the current state of plan models by formulating a 'comparative dynamic' optimising planning model within the framework of the rolling plan technique. The advantage of this type of planning model is that we can deal with changes in the initial conditions, and/or changes in the exogenous forces, and/or changes in the internal parameters. Further, we develop a method to compare the relative efficiency of the various planning techniques and point out the policy implications of these techniques within the framework of a current-oriented, future-oriented, and neutral-oriented approaches to the economy in question.

8. We have made another extension in the current state of Indian planning models by formulating a multi-regional and multi-sectoral

optimising model which can be operated within the framework of the fixed plan technique or the semi-rolling plan technique or the rolling plan technique. In this model we have also made an attempt to merge economic and human resource planning through a general equilibrium approach which incorporates both into the present model. Human resources are introduced directly into the planning model through constraints on the supply of and demand for various labour skills and through endogenous activities for the creation of human capital. Labour is no longer treated as surplus by assumption.

The significance of our extension lies in the fact that in India the most acute socio-economic and political problems which affect hundreds of millions of people are mass poverty, unemployment and under-employment. But all the planning models developed in the Indian context neither fully take into account the problems posed by such disguised and open unemployment nor deal significantly either with the idea of urgent labour-absorbing public works or with any other economic policy directly aimed at attacking mass poverty and unemployment.[4] These models take little or no account of labour either as a limiting factor in the economic growth rate or as a factor influencing the optimal sectoral composition of output and investment. The only way unemployment is reflected in these models is through the assumption that labour is free.[5] This enables the planners to focus attention on scarce resources such as capital and foreign exchange. But in the absence of labour constraints, a planning model substantially exaggerates the marginal productivity of physical capital and of foreign aid.[6] As a consequence, the planning models which have been developed so far are essentially aimed to solve the conventional neoclassical problem of resource allocation rather than to make a full analysis of the abundance of one important factor of production--labour, (skilled, semi-skilled and unskilled). The clear implication of these models is that full employment can be reached only over a relatively long period of time. Now, an important question arises: How would the unemployment problem be handled in the intervening period? This would raise the considerable problems of distributive justice and economic efficiency as, given suitable organizational efforts, unemployed labour may be put to creating extra social overhead capital. This would largely involve redistribution of aggregate consumption.

But our model would allow for alternative techniques of production and identify the labour-intensive activities and sectors. It also identifies different skill classes of labour instead of identifying all labour as homogenous. An explicit introduction of investment in human capital would also enable us to recognise health and education as productive activities. Education is a human right and as such it is a political as well as a social goal for any government. It also helps improving productivity and thus can contribute to the acceleration of economic development. Having less inequality in the educational level of a population would probably also contribute to lessen economic inequality and hence lead to more social and political stability. However, investment in education implies a changing composition in labour supply unless this supply can find a corresponding labour demand, investment in education can lead to as many new problems as those it is supposed to solve. In fact, in India the economy has not generated the needed amount and composition of labour demand to absorb the supply generated by the educational system and population growth. Although fundamental, because it involves more than only economic equalibria, the problem has not received the attention it deserves in Indian planning models which hardly mention education. But our model takes into account this aspect of development planning.

Since all the Indian planning models have ignored the crucial question of balanced regional development, another significance of our extension lies in the fact that it focusses on regional planning problem also. India's being so highly uneven in economic terms makes this problem so important that it cannot be simply assumed away. Productivity of a unit of investment as well as the savings investment propensity vary from region to region. Since these magnitudes also differ from sector to sector, inter-regional problems get tied up with inter-sectoral problems. To give any precise meaning to the policy of balanced regional development under these circumstances, we explicitly introduce the sectoral and regional problems in our model. It would also enable us to discover and exploit the comparative advantages of the regions, which, in-turn, are dependent upon the regional distribution of resources and upon political preferences as to the regional allocation of welfare.

10.2 SUGGESTIONS FOR IMPROVEMENTS

The most important lesson to be learnt from this exercise is that we must first consider what are the central planning issues in India and then we must go ahead with more experiments with similar or better models by introducing the following essential elements of structural reality in the context of Indian economy as reflected from the present study. In the earlier chapters we have discussed some of these essential elements such as the formulation of comparative dynamic type of planning models, the need to merge economic and human resource planning through a general equilibrium approach, the significance of incorporating the objective of balanced regional development, and the importance of incorporating closed-loop variants in planning models.[7]

Since the objectives of development plans in India encompasses not only economic goals but socio-economic and political aspirations also, any realistic model for development would need formalisation of the socio-economic and political factors, whether in cardinal or ordinal forms. But despite the elaborate model structure of the Seventh Five-Year Plan, it has not been possible to capture the full realities of planned development mainly due to the non-inclusion of several institutional and non-economic forces relevant to development process. Therefore, there is much room for further improvements both by adopting quantifications and formal modelling and by extending the coverage to include additional non-economic variables. There are thus several social and cultural factors which affect a large number of pure economic relationships. For example, factor productivity of many economic activities is significantly influenced by the quality of human resources used as inputs in the production process ("disembodied progress"). Again the quality of human resources is affected by health, education, nutrition, housing and environment, work incentives and opportunities for participation. But the provision of health, education etc. itself depends largely on the level of income and rate of investment in the economy. Understanding of all these complex relationships and their incorporation into the plan model, to cover many economic and socio-cultural variables, can alone ensure a truly integrated development plan.

In the light of all these observations, we make the following suggestions for further improvements in the area of plan modelling:

Income Distribution[8] and Rural Development

Growth with social justice has been a major issue in discussion related to planning in India. So far only a few studies have been conducted in India to work out the implications for planning of ensuring a minimum level of living. These studies are mainly conducted by the Planning Commission (1962, 1973, 1981, 1986) and Srinivasan et al. (1965). Besides their redistributive planning aspects, these studies have drawn pointed attention to the problem of absolute poverty, quantified its magnitude on the basis of the minimum normative level and argued in favour of redistribution for the removal of poverty.[9] From the methodological point of view, the models employed in these studies are essentially similar in structure and belong to a comparative-static open-loop framework within a modified open input-output system. By construction, these models specify growth and redistribution as independent social objectives, and hence are unappropriate for examining the inter-connections between these two social objectives.[10] In addition, the assumptions implied by the open-loop framework are also implausible for planning in a mixed economy under a federal democratic socio-political environment.[11] Similarly, the input-output accounting system on which these models are based neither gives prominence nor accommodates the functional and institutional distribution of income which are integrally connected to individual living standards and other development policy objectives.

Another significant issue of concern is that the Indian economy can be characterized as having both the regional dualism between rural and urban areas; and the technological dualism between modern, capital-intensive technologies and forms of organisation on the one hand, and the traditional, labour-intensive on the other hand. We can further notice a dual-dual structure of the Indian economy where a large sub-sector of agriculture consists of commercial, often export-oriented, crops produced with mechanised techniques. The demographic pressures on scarce land resources and a relatively high proportion of population in rural areas are the causes of widespread and persistent poverty. Therefore, attempts should be made at modelling rural development within a general consistency or optimising, multisectoral framework to analyse the effects of alternative agricultural development strategies--i.e., unimodel strategy; bimodel or dual strategy; and 'industrialisation first' strategy--on income distribution.[12]

The Accounting Framework

The accounting framework which has been repeatedly used in Indian planning models is that of input-output system which neither gives prominence nor accommodates the functional and institutional distribution of income which are integrally connected to individual living standards and other development policy objectives. The 'system of national accounts' (SNA)[14] and the social accounting matrix (SAM) have not been taken as a basis for any modelling exercise. The SAM can be termed as an extended version of the SNA.

The 'social accounting matrix' identifies the distribution of income between different factors and socio-economic groups.[15] This particular form of economic accounting can be naturally viewed as an extension of the input-output system to deal with the distributional issues. As an accounting framework the elements of a SAM record transactions in current prices. By convention, each element is to be read as an expenditure for the column in which it is located and as a receipt of its row. Thus, SAMs are essentially single entry book-keeping. Since each account has both receipts and expenditures, the number of rows and columns of a SAM are equal. Moreover, since accounting consistency requires that receipts and expenditures are equal to total, it follows that the vectors of row and column totals of a SAM are equal. Hence, a SAM is a square matrix of transaction, T, such that

$$T_i \equiv t \equiv T_i$$

Where t is the vector of row totals, i is the summation vector (all elements unity) and T_i is, therefore, the row vector of column totals.

As a framework for numbers, derivation of the SAM corresponding to a model yields a consistent data base as a starting point. As a framework for model algebra it does more than this since the model outputs must generate new SAMs. In this sense SAMs capture the accounting constraints or identities. Hence, they are useful both for initial caliberation and for ensuring subsequent consistency. Beyond this, SAMs define the taxonomies within a model and hence the crucial questions concerning levels and type of disaggregation.

In the following figure, as shown by Sarkar and Taylor (1982), we present schematically how a typical SAM is organised.[16] SAM will typically have an equal number of rows and columns. Loosely speaking, one can consider entries in the rows as "deliveries" of income flows to different recipients, and entries in the column as income claims. The totals in corresponding rows and columns are equal. These totals may be called, again rather loosely, gross production. Some of the principal blocks are labelled in the schematic.

Block I is the interindustry matrix. Block 2 has value added to households, government and public sector production. The household value added can be disaggregated to several income classes. To permit the study of the distributional impact of various policies, knowledge of the sectoral origin of income flows to classes of income recipients arranged by income level can be very useful. Such disaggregations are emphasized in most SAMs.

Just as Block 2 in the schematic shows income flows to households resulting from production and other economic activities, Block 3 gives incomes corresponding to government production activity, and Block 4 captures taxes, subsidies and transfers. In addition, payments for intermediate inputs are also accounted here. Private, public and foreign savings flows are summarised in Block 5. These sum to total investment in Block 7. Intermediate and final demands on the part of households and government appear in Block 6. It must be noted here that column sums for expenditure (including saving) of economic agents in Blocks 5 and 6 must just balance incomes from the sums of rows in Blocks 2 and 3. Exports and investment as contributors to final demands are accounted for in the enteries in Blocks 7 and 8. Row and Column totals--"gross production"--are summarized in Blocks 9 and 10.

In this way, there are two fundamental ingredients of a SAM. The first is that of the factors of production consisting primarily of the labour and capital which are used in the process of production and receive income from it. The second is that of institutions, foremost among them being households (which we may wish to study in different categories) which supply labour and capital. Other institutions are firms or corporations which provide capital; and government which levies taxes in addition to the supply of capital.

The account for the 'rest of the world' is also necessary because an economy has many transactions with the rest of the World. The "surplus or deficit" is a direct consequence of this; and the current transactions are normally not equal and must be balanced by borrowing or landing or use of reserves. See Table 10.3 also.

Thus, the core of a SAM is the circular process of demand, production and income with a duality in the circular process: Factors of production receive money from production; institutions from factors of production; and production from institutions. On the other way round, the supply of goods and services: factors of production to the production process; production to institutions; and institutions to factors of production. This is shown in the following figure:

The operational usefulness of a SAM can be shown by pointing out the following major advantages of this accounting system:[17]

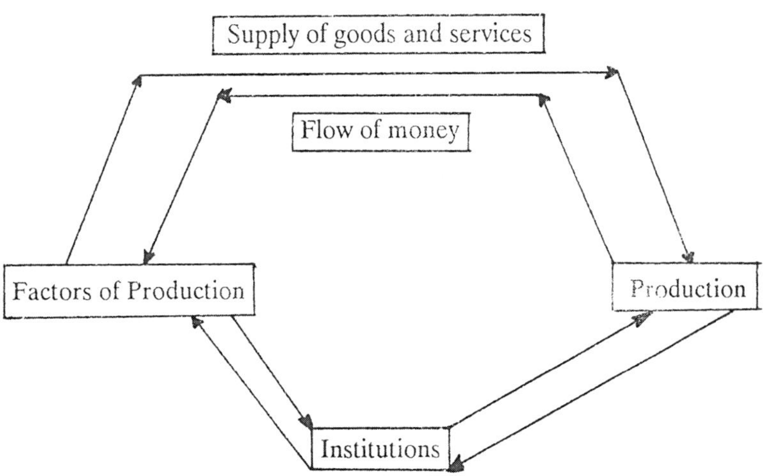

Table 10.2: Schematic for a Social Accounting Matrix

SECTOR DELI-VERING \ SECTOR RECEIVING						
		COLUMNS				
		INPUT-OUTPUT TABLE 1	INTER-HOUSE-GOVT. DEMANDS 6	EXPORTS 8	INVESTMENTS	TOTALS-GROSS PRODUCTION 9
	ROWS	VALUE ADDED				
		HOUSE-GOVERNMENT 2				
		GOVERNMENT ACTIVITIES 3				
		IMPORTS-TARIFFS-TAXES 4				
			SAVINGS 5			
	TOTALS - GROSS PRODUCTION 10					

Table 10.3: Schematic Social Accounting Matrix

			1	2	3	4	5	6	7	8
			EXPENDITURES							
			Factors	Indirect Taxes	Institutions Current Accounts	Communities	Activities	Consolidated Institutions Capital Account	Rest of World	Total Incomes
1.	Receipts	Factors				value added to factors	Payment of	income from rest of world	Net, factor Incomes	Factor
2.		Indirect taxes				Indirect tax payments				Indirect Taxes
3.		Institutions Current Accounts	Allocation of factor incomes to institutions	Indirect Taxes	Current transfers between institutions				Net non-factor income from rest of World	Incomes of Institutions
4.		Commodities			Consumption expenditures	Commodity-Commodity transactions	Purchase of interme-diate inputs	Investment expenditure	Exports	Commodity Demands
5.		Activities				Domestic Commodity Supplies				Total Revenue
6.		Consolidated Institutions Capital Account			Savings				Balance of payments current deficit	Total savings
7.		Rest of World				Imports				Imports
8.		Total Expenditure	Factor Incomes	Indirect Taxes	Incomes of Institutions	Commodity Supplies	Total Costs	Total Investment	Imports	

i. It provides a systematic and consistent way of identifying the initial conditions which exist in an economy. Obviously, it gives an appropriate and thorough specification upon which the development strategy can be built. Different initial conditions will require different packages of policy measures even where the objective function is similar.

ii. The SAMs also suggest the kind of data needed for the formulation of development policy and the form in which this information might be presented. Hence, the complete classification scheme, underlying the various sub-systems or blocks of the SAM, provides necessary guidelines to statistical organisations regarding the specific type of information that policy makers seek. In turn, the guidelines may be of great assistance to statistical organisations in the process of designing surveys and censuses and in gathering and tabulating other types of information. Thus, it is clearly a step forward in the upgrading of statistics.

iii. The SAM approach to development planning is free from a narrow specification of the objective function. It is quite flexible, and capable of modelling very different initial conditions as well as makes it possible to trace through the system the effects of different sets of policy without having to specify the preference function ex ante.

iv. We can bring into the framework of a SAM not only the various transactions accounts but also the financial counterpart of these real transactions and the flow of capital funds into investment. In some ways, this is one of the most intriguing uses of a SAM, as it brings together two related aspects of development, the real and the financial. The parsimonious use of financial data and the neglect of its relationship with the real economy have often been noted.

v. A SAM is more economical in that it has only half as many enteries as a series of double-entry accounts; and the interconnections between accounts are obvious.

vi. It is an integrated description of macroeconomic structure, although the extent of its information context clearly depends upon the range and net work of classifications that can be achieved which in turn will largely depend on the detail and quality of available data. Nevertheless, the SAM is seen as a way of tracking past performance and giving factual answers to fundamental questions about the inter-relationship between the distribution of income and the structure of production.

vii. A SAM is a very good way of representing the necessary accounting identities with the additional feature that through its presentation of the accounts it assists in identifying the agents and the variables which are of particular interest. Even the most sophisticated multisectoral consistency models have either explicitly incorporated or at least alluded to the desirability of incorporating a SAM as a framework to their data base.[18]

viii. In the context of development planning models, one can distinguish five different distributions that might be of interest to policy makers, the distribution to: (1) factors of production, (2) institutions, (3) socio-economic groups, (4) individuals and (5) households. A SAM provides an invaluable statistical framework for the analysis of the mappings between the different kinds of distributions one may want to consider.

ix. The multiplier analysis of a SAM shows how changes in one or more elements of a SAM generate changes elsewhere in the matrix.[19]

The above discussion clearly suggests that continuous attempts must be made to formulate SAMs for the Indian economy at different points of time. So far perhaps the only attempt in this direction is made by Sarkar and Rao (1981).

Computable General Equilibrium Models

The input-output accounting system has been the basis for all the Indian plan models.[20] The essential assumptions of input-output accounts are that each sector produces only one output and that inputs are required in fixed proportions to output in each sector, i.e., constant returns to scale in production. For Indian type economy the input-output model contains no policy variables.[21] Even the simple material balances system is a powerful tool for policy analy is because it embodies the requirement for economy-wide consistency of sectoral production plans.[22]

The major problem in using simple input-output models to analyse development in a mixed market economy is that the models do not contain the incentive instruments that are the major policy tools of planning in such economies. Policies such as indirect taxes, subsidies, exchange-rate manipulations, and direct controls over some prices all affect the economy through their effects on prices and costs in various markets. Thus, these models cannot directly capture many of the policy links that are of primary concern to policy makers.

Significantly all these issues are taken care of in 'Computable General Equilibrium' (CGE) models. Moreover, migration models of Harris-Todaro (1970) type have also been included in CGE models and have empirically turned out to be very important.[23] The essential features of these models are that they solve for prices endogenously in both factor and product markets; incorporate income distribution, monetary phenomena, inflation, and foreign trade; and allow for varying principles of market clearing and institutional behaviour.[24] Therefore, attempts should be made to formulate CGE models for Indian Economy.[25]

Monetary Modelling

Virtually every planning model built to date has been designed to investigate how quantities are affected by policy inventions. Both in normative models and in positive planning models, the emphasis is on real quantities : physical output, final demands, trade, investment, and employment. With the exception of a few macro models, prices, wages and money in planning models are "veils" and are not included in any endogenous interactive feedback mechanisms. Input-output and linear programming models have never tried to incorporate money in any way.

We should make attempts for the realistic incorporation of

monetary effects into empirical general equilibrium models.[26] In most theoretical general-equilibrium models, money is "neutral" in the sense that changes in the average price level do not affect real variables such as employment and output. We should make efforts to extend and improve the incorporation of non-neutral monetary effects into both theoretical and empirical general-equilibrium models.

We can add a macro-monetary super structure that interacts with the multisector general equilibrium models. For example, monetary behaviour equations can be attached to the model to capture the demand for and supply of financial assets and the interaction between money and the real sphere of the economy. Significantly, such an approach, in which the price level is determined endogenously, would extend the field of application of CGE models from the analysis of problems of industrial strategy, protection, and trade policy to problems of inflation, 'Keynesian' imbalances between aggregate supply and demand, and short-run stabilization policy.

Foreign Trade Sector

There are certain very crucial problems associated with the planning of the foreign trade sector which are not yet reflected in any Indian planning model[27]:

i. A planning model should distinguish at least two types of foreign exchange, i.e, tied versus free exchange. This would mean separate estimation of the relevant unit price or transactions in each type of exchange with respect to exports and imports. In fact, we should recognize more than two types of foreign exchange.[28]

ii. The planning models do not recognize adequately the investment in marketing and concentrates only on the investment needed to create export or import substituting production.[29]

iii. The planning models assume a single known 'world' price for each tradeable good and, thus, neglect the important feature of uncertainty.

iv. The factor of planning technological change and transfer through foreign trade has not yet been incorporated into a quantitative model though it has been already recognized as important.[30]

v. We should also introduce separate trading activities (with corresponding upper and lower bounds) for trade with each major block of countries and should introduce corresponding balance of payments constraints into a planning model.[31] Planning models have paid no attention to the repayment liabilities as well as to the varying internal composition of foreign aid as it is made available from time to time.

vi. There has been a debate on the possible links between trade policy and technical progress. On the one hand, economists argue that protection of industry is a precondition for rapid industrialization and that technical progress depends directly on the growth of industry through the spread of industrial techniques and industrial attitudes. On the other hand, it is argued that protection stifles competitive innovation, prevents the introduction of new products and methods and reduces contact with the world market and hence slows down the pace of technical progress in an economy. But so far we have not been able to incorporate these considerations formally in a multi-sector planning model.

vii. Planning models should also relax the assumptions of fixed import coefficients; and that exports are either stagnant or determined by factors beyond our control.

viii. It is unrealistic to assume in an empirical application to a developing economy that domestically produced goods and imported goods under the same sectoral classification are essentially the 'same' especially at the level of aggregation found in planning models. Differences in product quality reflect the imperfect transmission of technological knowledge of different labour skills in developed and developing countries.[32] Therefore, planning models should also specify that imported and domestically produced goods are imperfect substitutes. Such models can incorporate assumptions ranging from complete in-substitutability (for example, neoclassical trade theory models) by varying the parameters specifying the elasticity of substitution in use for different sectors.[33]

ix. Because of the widespread use of tarriff protection and price subsidies to influence resource allocation and industrialization, it is of great practical interest to be able to analyse the implications of alternative tarriff and subsidy policies in a trade-oriented planning model.

x. The planning models should be developed to focus on the impact of alternative trade strategies on industrialization and income distribution; and mainly on the alleviation of poverty.[34]

xi. The semi-input-output method may also be empirically applied to Indian data.[35] This method is primarily concerned with the choice of sectors to be developed and the selection of projects on the basis of a country's comparative advantages. Thus, it makes a systematic treatment of efficiency in production and foreign trade which derives from a country's comparative advantages. It makes a distinction between international and national sectors, a distinction based on the tradeability of the commodities produced, and is similar to Little and Mirrlees' (1974) distinction between tradeable and non-tradeable goods.[36]

xii. Changing comparative advantage position with respect to different commodities should also be reflected adequately in the structure of planning models.

Substitution Possibilities

Planning models have tended to exclude substitution possibilities other than through international trade. But now it is evident from econometric studies that there are substantial substitution possibilities between capital and labour in most types of production and that price elasticities of demand for commodities are significantly different from zero. Since computational methods for solving planning models that incorporate production functions and demand functions are now available, there is no reason to continue to ignore these possibilities in economy-wide planning models.[37] Theoretically, planning models without any substitution possibilities may give rise to some serious difficulties and unrealistic results. Programming models without substitution have a relative insensitivity of the primal and a high sensitivity of the dual variables.[38] By including elements of substitution greater flexibility of planning models can be achieved through the avoidance of temporary bottlenecks, better utilisation of scarce resources, and more meaningful dual variables. A planning model when put to empirical use must reflect the following three types of actual substitution possibilities of a developing economy:[39]

i. Inter-temporal substitution or substitution between present and future consumption;[40]

ii. direct factor substitution (primary and intermediate) in the production process;[41] and

iii. indirect substitution or substitution between commodities through varying the composition of international trade and other final demand in a development planning model.[42]

Non-linearity and Cardinal Utility

Development planning models in India have been making the assumption of linearity.[43] The thorough going linearity in the models result in a 'flip-flop' or 'bang-bang' behaviour in consumption and investment levels which is awkward for realistic planning. If we correct this 'flip-flop' behaviour through the imposition of additional constraints then the constraints become more important than the optimization procedure and hence the problem is not really solved. Thus, another improvement in such models would be to relax the assumption of linearity.[44]

Though the idea of cardinal utility (which provides a straightforward way to retain the principle of optimality and yet to evaluate trade-offs between growth and equity) has been introduced into aggregative models of a labour surplus economy by Newbery (1972) and Stern (1972) yet these cardinal interpersonal comparisons have not been introduced into any multi-sectoral planning model in India.[45]

Data Base

In Indian economy, it is apparent that human capital development; qualitative improvements of goods and services; maintenance of old social overheads; conservation of the non-reproducible environment etc. have very deficient statistical accounting. Thus, they are either completely ignored or barely treated in compiling national income accounts. Accordingly, they are also neglected in planning models. Further refinement of interindustry planning models can be possible and useful if a strong and satisfactory informational basis for planning models is made; and the problems of institutional and implementational bottlenecks are quantified.

We should also keep in mind that the Leontief assumption of constant returns to scale with fixed technological coefficients is inapplicable to traditional Indian agriculture as it is undergoing some structural alteration and also as the land is scarce. Hence, the use of Leontief matrices may introduce considerable error in estimating investment requirements for the economy as a whole and for agriculture in particular. Moreover, since many of the policy conclusions are highly sensitive to the production and composition of agriculture sector, this sector should be treated in a more realistic sense by disaggregating it within the framework of planning models.[46]

Prices

Attempts should be made to open real planning models to financial influences. As pointed out earlier, these models should include monetary elements, and particularly inflation's variable speed and complex effects on economic behaviour through its alterations of expectations. These models should encompass the private sector and also weave into it price control as one of the major policy objectives to control inflation. It should be realised that the control of inflation effectively involves the overall supply and demand management. This involves two aspects: first, the quantification of the various factors, and second, advance action on the basis of the forecasts. This, therefore, necessitates the inclusion of the private sector in planning and also the preparation of a short-term plan model.

Since the set of relative prices of factors of production and of consumer goods, respectively, affect the demand for and use of these factors and goods, planning models should incorporate responses to changing incentives that correspond to changes in relative prices.

Economies of Scale

The efficiency of market mechanism as an instrument for investment allocation is being repeatedly questioned in the development literature. Such questions are given rise by the interdependencies between sectors that are not reflected in the structure of existing prices. Planning models have been formulated to provide an alternative source of the information necessary, but incompletely extant in the market, for making investment decisions. To date Indian planning models have incorporated a limited set of interdependencies between sectors--those arising from input-output relations, competition for scarce resources, and changes in relative factor scarcities over time.

Economies of scale in interdependent sectors constitute empirically important case in which market signals are inefficient instruments of investment planning. Therefore, plan models should be extended to include external economies and diseconomies.[47]

10.3 SUMMING UP

Three lines of research captured attention among model building development economists during the recent years. One was organization and analysis of national accounts data in terms of a social accounting matrix (SAM). The second was construction of elaborate computable general equilibrium (CGE) models based on the data as summarized in a SAM. And the third was the realisation that most of the economic content of the CGE models could be captured by simple-one-or-two-sector analogs based squarely on the general economic structure originally described by Kalecki and Keynes.[48] In so far as these pioneers had something to say about how the market-related part of poor mixed economies operates, the new planning approach promises to be more practical than its predecessors. Previous work concentrated on neoclassically "optimal" resource allocation, successfully evading all considerations of economic conflict and dissonance in poor regions of the world. Aside from directly useful exercises such as computation of investment project criteria and similar tasks, the earlier generation of models (dating from roughly 1950 to 1975) was sufficiently Pangleesian to be almost completely ignored.

A whole family of CGE models appeared during the late 1970s, attempting to 'explain' patterns of income distribution and sectoral outputs in the short-run. The models usually took as given a description of the economy such as contained in a SAM and asked how the enteries of the matrix would change in response to shifts in exogenous variables and policy moves. Though in practice they have many sectors and income classes, the essentials of these models can usually be described in terms of one or two sectors, two or three groups of income recipients and a generally Keynesien or Kaleckian economic environment.[49]

NOTES

1. For a detailed and excellent discussion on these points, see Planning Commission (1981).
2. Since the start of centralized planning in the Soviet Union, all European communist countries have applied the material balances technique to the formulation of their plans. For a detailed analysis on the operation of this technique, see Ellman (1969), Kornai (1959, 1969), Manove (1971), Manove and Weitzman (1978), Montias (1959) and Nove (1970). For the basic theory of input-output technique, see Chenery and Clark (1959), Dorfman et. al. (1958) and Leontief (1941, 1966). On the comparison of these techniques see Hare (1981).
3. Capacity constraints assume greater importance when planning horizon is less than the gestation period of the projects which produce the commodity.
4. It may be pointed out here that Mahalanobis (1953) considered the employment problem in an explicit way but his analysis was based on overlying drastic simplifications. Gupta (1973) classified labour into two skill classes. There have been several other studies on this problem which are essentially theoretical in nature. For example, Sen (1968) raises important questions relating to the real cost of labour, which ultimately reduces to the question of savings constraint on development path. Mathur (1965) and Srinivasan (1962) discuss problems of choice of techniques in its dynamic aspect with the objective of minimizing the time to reach full employment. Dixit (1968) and Dasgupta (1968) also find out the optimal time paths of accumulation and employment in a labour-surplus economy. See, also, Lefeber (1968) and Lewis (1954).
5. Of course, the procedure to justify the neglect of labour as a factor of production on the ground of its being a free factor is internally consistent when it is assumed that domestic savings levels are perfectly adjustable. But even in that case the problem of deriving the implied time path for employment remains to be much ignored.

6. See Harberger (1[illegible]7).
7. The only plan model with a closed-loop variant in the Indian context is by Tendulkar (1971). Other closed-loop models are formulated by Blitzer (1982) for Turkey; Adelman (1966) for Argentina; Celasum (1972) for Turkey; Martens and Pindyck (1975) for Tunisia; and Murakami et al. (1970) for Japan.
8. Cline (1975) conducts an excellent survey of the literature on income distribution and development. He examines the relevance of general distribution theories to developing economies and describes recent theoretical and empirical work on the relationship between development and income distribution as well as the literature in the relatively less explored area of how policy instruments can be applied to increase equity within developing economies. In a recent thought provoking paper Tinbergen (1986) discusses the essential features of the concepts of development and income distribution, the impact of income distribution and development on each other, the combined process of development and income distribution, the aims and means of socio-economic policies, and planning as a preparation of policies. See Robinson (1976b) also on income distribution and the social welfare function.
9. Berry (1981) has also conducted a study to investigate the impact of expenditure redistribution on factor requirements within the framework of a 33-sector dynamic input-output model in which investment is in part endogenously determined. His analysis shows that even 'radical' distributions of private consumption expenditure would have no significant impact on the level of employment, or indirectly through increasing labour requirements or reducing scarce resource requirements. See Sinha et al. (1978), Stewart (1978) and Mohammad (1981) also
In the Indian case, Gaiha (1980) points out that redistribution of purchasing power produces the largest increase in employment with a given fixed investment; and that redistribution by itself is not capable of overcoming the foreign exchange constraint.
10. In recent years, a number of studies have been undertaken in which hypothetical income distributions have been used to analyse the effects of income redistribution on economic growth. The models of this set have combined savings and consumption functions according to income groups, input-output relationships, and factor coefficients to determine these effects. Some such models are those of Cline (1972), Morley and Smith (1973), Pyatt et al. (1972), Paukert (1974), Planning Commission (1973, 1981, 1986) and Mohammad (1981).
11. For a detailed discussion on this aspect, see Tendulkar (1974).
12. Dutta (1978) shows the changes in the incidence of poverty and relative inequality in India during 1960-61 to 1973-74 for both the rural and urban sectors and points out the intersectoral disparities. In order to measure the incidence of poverty over time, he uses two different measures of the extent of poverty. The first measure is the percentage of people below a fixed poverty line, which is defined in terms of real per capita consumption. The second measure is Sen's poverty index, which is sensitive not only to the percentage of people in poverty but also to the gaps in the incomes of the poor, and which gives more weight per unit of lower incomes. He measures the relative inequality by the concentration ratio or Gini Coefficient. He establishes the proposition that the rural sector deserves more attention vis-a-vis the urban sector. He shows that the rural sector is relatively more impoverished and there is a declining trend in the average per capita consumption expen-

diture of the rural community as a whole. Other eminent economists such as Bardhan (1973) and Dandekar and Rath (1971), have propounded the thesis that agricultural growth in India has been accompanied by an increase in rural poverty, thus implicitly arguing for a radical change in the institutional structure. But Ahluwalia (1976), Dutta (1980), and Lal (1976) are of the opposite view. Dutta shows that the pattern of distribution has remained almost unchanged from the 1960s onwards.

13. Adelman and Robinson (1978) pay explicit attention to such links.
14. See United Nations (1968).
15. Since the early 1970s there has been considerable interest and momentum in the design, construction and uses of SAMs in developing countries. A number of SAMS have been constructed so far. Significant contributions in this field are made by Pyatt and Thorbecke (1976), Pyatt and Round (1977), Pyatt and Roe (1977), Taylor (1979), Grais (1982), Hayden and Round (1982), Sarkar and Rao (1981), King (1981) and Eckaus et al. (1981, 1979). They demonstrate aspects of the design, construction and practical applications of SAMs as appropriate frameworks for presenting macro-economic data in order to monitor objectives of economic development more effectively.
16. SAMs may be constructed in different ways with different accounts for different purposes.
17. These advantages have been pointed out in the literature on SAMs, especially by Pyatt and Thorbecke (1976), King (1981) and Hayden and Round (1982).
18. See, for example, Adelman and Robinson (1978), Taylor (1979), Dervis et al. (1982), de Melo (1979), Dervis and Robinson (1978), and Grais (1981).
19. See Round (1982) on this aspect of SAMs. On the feasibility to use the SAM approach to analyse income distribution using multipliers analogous to those from an input-output model, see Cline (1972), Weisskoff (1972) and Pyatt and Round (1979).
20. Saluja (1980) gives a detailed account of historical developments of input output tables for India. This is an excellent work giving details about the concepts and methodology of construction of input-output tables and the applications of the technique.
21. The input-output model is suitable for a command economy where sectoral outputs are set by the Government.
22. Of course, there are a number of extensions of the simple input-output model, without moving to dynamic models, that exploit its consistency properties and make it a useful tool for policy analysis. For example, one can use the inverse to calculate 'multipliers' that give the impact on endogenous variables of shifts in exogenous elements of final demand. This type of 'identity based' planning is clearly useful because it forces policy makers to work within the context of a consistent system, even if there is not much of the behavioural content.
23. For example, see Ahmed (1974), de Melo and Dervis (1977) and Adelman and Robinson (1978 a).
24. See Adelman and Robinson (1978). Gruver (1986) conducts an excellent survey of CGE models. Dervis et al. (1982, Chapter X) illustrate how a CGE model can be used as a tool to help us understand past developments.
25. The only very simple CGE model for India is formulated by Sarkar and Rao (1981).
26. Adelman and Robinson (1978a) have made an attempt in this direction.

27. For an excellent survey on foreign trade sector in planning models, see Srinivasan (1975).
28. See Bhagwati and Eckaus (1970) on cost of aid tying.
29. In the Indian context, Ahmad (1968) has shown that during 1951-52 to 1965-66 import substitution contributed a large proportion of the growth of output. Moreover, the capital-intensive industries contributed the major portion of this import substitution. Some of the important studies on import substitution in the Indian context are those of Desai (1969, 1972), Bhagwati and Wibulswadi (1972), Bhagwati and Desai (1970), Hazari (1967), Reddaway (1962) and Bhagwati and Srinivasan (1975). At this point it is pertinent to point out that many economists have emphasized that countries adopting import substituting industrialization policies have experienced a worsening of the factor-price distortions and a reduction in the labour absorption. These countries indirectly redistribute incomes in favour of the manufacturing sectors and against the generally poorer agricultural sector. On these lines, see Lewis (1973), Krueger (1972), and Little et al. (1970).
30. See Vernon (1970).
31. Kornai (1969) has moved a step forward in this direction by introducing two separate balance of payments constraints accounting for Hungary's trade with Eastern and Western blocks.
32. This view of imperfect substitutability between domestic and imported goods amounts to introducing the possibility of two-way trade. Michalopoulos (1975) gives an empirical support to this possibility of substitution in the case of capital goods. See Armington (1969a) for the presentation of a theory of demand for products distinguished by place of production.
33. See Armington (1969a) who indicates the quantitative importance of the elasticity of substitution in computing the effects of price changes on the pattern of foreign trade.
34. Mohammad (1981) makes an assessment of two types of trade policies--import substitution and export diversification--in achieving economic growth and income inequality in the Indian context. He provides a link between growth and equality through employment. This is a closed static consistency input-output model based on the methodology due to Pyatt et al. (1972) and Paukert et al. (1974). Mohammad also discusses the effect of redistribution on trade and growth. He concludes that export promotion is favourable to the generation of higher levels of employment and income, while import substitution seems to be much less favourable to the growth of employment, gross domestic product and income. For a comprehensive survey of trends in India's exports, see Nayyar (1976). Robinson and de Melo (1976) make an excellent theoretical study on industrialisation and income distribution. They also experiment with policy subsidies through their endogenous solution of wages and prices.
35. The semi-input-output method has been described and presented in a number of places, see, for example, Tinbergen (1966a. 1966b. 1967), Pronk and Schreuel (1969), Carillo-Arronto (1968). Netherlands economic Institute (1970) and Kuyvenhoven (1978).
36. For discussion on tradeable and non-tradeable goods, see Hinshaw (1975) and Oppenheimer (1974, 1975).
37. For an exploration of these problems, see Chenery and Raduchel (1971).
38. See Manne (1974) on this point.
39. See Tinbergen and Bos (1962) and Chenery and Raduchel (1971).
40. Intertemporal substitution has been the subject of a vast literature on

Ramsey-type optimal savings models and turnpike theory. See, for example, Chakravarty (1969), Manne (1974) and Taylor (1975) who discuss applications of dynamic planning models incorporating inter-temporal substitution.

41. Elaborating Chenery and Raduchel (1971), Duloy and Hazell (1975) distinguish two kinds of factor substitution: (a) substitution in factor supply; and (b) substitution in the technology set. Also see, Mc Kinnon (1964), Blitzer (1975) and Leontief (1966).
42. Weisskopf (1971) and Clark (1970), among others, examine import substitution strategies on the basis of a comparison of foreign and domestic resource cost of potential imports.
43. Ginsburgh and Waelbroeck (1989) point out that the two main weaknesses of linear models are due to their 'strong' linearity and the assumption of given world prices both of which contribute to generate solutions of extreme (inter) national specialisation. They suggest that the first weakness can be avoided by using linear approximations on non-linear functions. To deal with the second problem, these models should have a structure inspired by international trade theory, which analyses policies of one country in terms of a 'two country model' leading to a general equilibrium system describing relations between the country and an explicitly defined 'rest of the world'.
44. The main theoretical innovations with respect to the substitution of non-linear functions for the linear relations commonly used in input-output analysis and linear programming are made by Kendrick and Taylor (1971), Chenery and Raduchel (1971), Taylor (1971) and Westphal (1971). A number of linear programming models incorporate non-linear functions by using piece-wise linear approximation. See, for example, Mac Ewan (1971), Bergendorff et al. (1973) and Markowitz and Manne (1957). On the application of optimal control theory to the construction and solution of non-linear dynamic planning models, see Stoleru (1965), Kendrick and Taylor (1969, 1970), Martens and Pindyck (1975), Taylor (1971), and Pindyck (1973). In the Indian case, see Ali (1979) who formulates a static non-linear programming model. Nachane (1986) conducts an excellent survey of control theory based planning models.
45. Chakravarty (1969) has extensively studied the properties of an isoelastic cardinal utility function in an open-loop framework of a labour surplus economy. He assumes a constant marginal productivity of capital over an infinite planning horizon. Most of his analysis is based upon continuous time parameters and utility integrals rather than sums.
46. Chakravarty (1977) suggests the decomposition procedure for this purpose which is not optimal in a basic theoretical sense. He suggests that agricultural planning should be treated as a separate subject and agriculture be treated as an exogenous sector in a multisector planning model. Minhas (1968) also suggests a procedure for agricultural planning.
47. Westphal (1971) makes such an attempt in his study of Korea.
48. On CGE models see Lysy and Taylor (1980), Adelman and Robinson (1978), de Melo et al. (1978) and Taylor (1979).
49. For detailed discussion on this aspect, see the pioneer work of Taylor (1979).

References

Abramovitz, M., et al., eds. (1959), *The Allocation of Economics Resources*, Stanford University Press, Stanford.

Acharya, S.N. and B.R. Hazari (1971), "Linkages and Imports: A Comparative Study of India and Pakistan," *Journal of Development Studies*, Vol. 8, No. 1.

Adelman I., ed. (1969), *Practical Approaches to Development Planning: The case of Korea*, Johns Hopkins Press, Maryland.

Adelman, I.; D.C. Cole; R. Norton and L.K. Jung (1969), "The Korean Sectoral Model," in I. Adelman, ed., op. cit.

Adelman, I.; M. Hopkins; S. Robinson; G.R. Rodgers, and R. Wery (1979), "A Comparison of Two Models for Income Distribution Planning," *Journal of Policy Modeling*, Vol. I, pp. 37-83.

Adelman, I. and C.T. Morris (1973), *Economic Growth and Social Equity in Developing Countries*, Stanford University Press, Stanford.

Adelman, I., and S. Robinson (1978a), *Income Distribution Policies in Developing Countries*, Stanford University Press, Stanford.

Adelman, I. (1966), "A Linear Programming Model of Educational Planning: A Case Study of Argentina," in I. Adelman & E. Thorbecke (eds.), op.cit.

Adelman, I. and Chenery, H.B. (1966), "Foreign Aid and Economic Development: The Case of Greece, "*Review of Economics & Statistics*, February, pp. 1-19.

Adelman, I. and S. Robinson (1978b), "Income Distribution, Import Substitution, and Growth Strategies in Developing Countries," in Richard Day and A. Cigno, *Modelling Economic Change: The Recursive Programme Approach*, North-Holland, New York.

Adelman, I. and F.T. Sparrow (1966), "Experiments with Linear and Piece-wise Linear Dynamic Programming Models" in I. Adelman and E. Thorbecke, eds., op. cit.

Adelman, I., and E. Thorbecke, eds. (1966), *The Theory and Design of Development*, Johns Hopkins Press, Baltimore.

Aggarwala, R. (1971), *An Econometric Model of India*, Frank Cass, London.

Ahluwalia, I.J. (1979), *Behaviour of Prices and Outputs in India: A Macroeconomic Approach*, Macmillan, Delhi.

Ahluwalia, M.S. (1976), "Inequality, Poverty, and Development," *Journal of Development Economics*, Vol. 3, September, pp. 307-42.

Ahluwalia, M.S.; N.G. Carter and H.B. Chenery (1979), "Growth and Poverty in Developing Countries", World Bank Staff Working Paper No. 309 (revised), Washington D.C.

Ahluwalia, M.S., and H.B. Chenery (1974), "Model of Distribution and Growth, "in H.B. Chenery et al., eds., *Redistribution with Growth*, Oxford University Press, London.

Ahmad, J. (1968), "Importt-substitution and structural change in Indian manufacturing industry," *Journal of Development Studies.*

Ahmed, F. (1974), "Migration and Employment in a Multi-Sector Model: An application to Bangladesh," Unpublished Ph.D. Dissertation, Princeton, University, Princeton.

Ahluwalia, M.S., and F. Lysy (1979), "Welfare Effects of Demand Management Policies: Impact Multipliers Under Alternative Model Structures," *Journal of Policy Modeling*, Vol. I, No. 3, pp. 317-43.

Alagh, Y.K. (1983), "Agricultural Development Planning and Policies in the ESCAP Region," *Experiences in Agricultural Development Planning in Selected Countries of Asia*, ESCAP, Bangkok.

Alagh, Y.K.; S.P. Kasyap and G.V.S.N. Murthy (1984), "Policy Modelling for Planning in India", in S.I. Cohen, P.A. Cornelisse, R. Teckens and E. Thorbecke (eds.), *The Modelling of Socio-Economic Process,* Gower, Aldershot, pp. 58-87.

Alagh, Y.K. and K.C. Mujumdar (1982), "Input-output Model Used for 1978-1983 Draft Plan–A Brief Outline", in S. Bhagwan Dahiya (ed.), op. cit.

Ali, I. (1982), "A Generalization of the Model of Trade: Distinction Between Domestically Produced and Imported Goods," in S. Bhagwan Dahiya (ed.), op. cit.

Ali, I. (1979), "The Domestic and Imported Goods Dichotomy in a Model of Trade", *The Indian Economic Review*, October, Vol. 14, No. 2, pp. 127-146.

Almon, C. (1963), "Consistent Forecasting in a Dynamic Multi-Sector Model," *The Review of Economics and Statistics*, Vol. 45, pp. 148-162.

Altimir, O. (1979), "Income Distribution and Poverty Profiles," World Bank, Washington, D.C., March.

Armington, P. (1969a), "A Theory of Demand for Products Distinguished by Place of Production," *IMF Staff Papers,* Vol. 16, pp.

159-178.

Armington, P. (1969b), "The Geographic Pattern of Trade and the Effects of Price Changes," *I.M.F. Staff Papers,* Vol. 16, pp. 179-201.

Arndt, H.W. (1955), "External Economies in Economic Growth", *Economic Record,* Vol. 31, November, pp. 92-214.

Arrow, K.J. (1951). "Alternative proof of the substitution theorem for Leontief Models in the general case," Chapter IX, in T.C. Koopmans (ed.) *Activity Analysis of Production and Allocation,* John Wiley & Sons, New York.

Arrow K.J. (1954), "Import Substitution in Leontief Models," *Econometrica,* Vol. 22, October, pp. 481-92.

Arrow K.J. (1962), "The Economic Implications of Learning by Doing," *Review of Economic Studies,* June, Vol. 29, pp. 155-173.

Arrow, K.J. (1964), *Social Choice and Individual Values,* Willey, New York.

Arrow, K.J. and F. Hahn (1971), *General Competitive Analysis,* Holden-Day, San-Francisco.

Arrow, K.J.; L. Hurwicz; and H. Uzawa, eds. (1958), *Studies in Linear and Non-Linear Programming,* Stanford University Press, Stanford.

Arrow, K.J. S. Karlin and P. Suppes, eds. (1960), *Mathematical Methods in the Social Sciences,* Stanford University Press, Stanford.

Arrow, K.J. and M. Kurz (1970), *Public Investment, The Rate of Return and Optimal Fiscal Policy,* Johns Hopkins Press, Baltimore.

Arthur, W.B. and G. Mc. Nicoll (1975), "Large-Scale Simulation Models in Population and Development: What Use of Planners",

Population and Development Review, Vol. No. 2, pp. 251-66.

Atkinson, A.B. (1969), "Import Strategy and Growth Under Conditions of Stagnant Export Earnings, *Oxford Economic Papers,* Vol. 21, No. 3.

Bacha, E., and Lance Taylor (1971), "Foreign Exchange Shadow Prices: A Critical Review of Current Theories", *Quarterly Journal of Economics,* Vol. 90, May, pp. 197-218.

Bacha, E. and Lance Taylor, (1976), "The Unequalizing Spiral: a First Growth Model for Belinda," *Quarterly Journal of Economics,* Vol. 90, May, pp. 197-218.

Bacharach, M. (1970), *Biproportional Matrices and Input-output Change,* Cambridge University Press, Cambridge.

Balassa, B. (1980), "The Process of Industrial Development and Alternative Development Strategies," World Bank Staff Working Paper No. 438, The World Bank, Washington, D.C.

Ballentine, J. and R. Soligo (1974), "Consumption and earnings pattern and income distribution," Mimeo., Programme of Development Studies, Rice University, Houston.

Balassa, B. et al. (1980), *Development Strategies in Semi-Industrial Countries,* Johns Hopkins Press, Baltimore.

Banerjee, N. (1977), "Exports and Indian Economy," *Economic and Political Weekly,* Vol. 12, No. 16, April.

Bardhan, P.K. (1971), "Uncertainty, Resource Allocation, and Factor Shares in a Two-Sector Model," Working Paper No. 79, Department of Economics, M.I.T.

Bardhan, P.K. (1973), "Planning Models and Income Distribution with Special Reference to India," Mimeographed, Indian Statistical Institute.

Bardhan, P.K. (1974), "The Pattern of Income Distribution in India," in P. Bardhan and T.N. Srinivasan, eds., *Poverty and Income Distribution in India,* Statistical Publishing Society, Calcutta.

Bardhan, P. (1977), *Wages and Unemployment in a Poor Agrarian Economy: A Theoretical and Empirical Analysis,* The World Bank, Washington, D.C.

Barna, T. (1954), *The Structural Interdependence of the Economy,* John Wiley and Sons.

Barna, T. (1963), *Structural Interdependence and Economic Development*, St. Martin's Press.

Bator, F.M. (1958), "The Anatomy of Market Failure," *Quarterly Journal of Economics,* Vol. 72, August, pp. 351-79.

Batra, R.N. (1974), "Resource Allocation in a general equilibrium model of production under uncertainty," *Journal of Economic Theory*, 8, pp. 50-63.

Batra, R.N. (1975), "Production uncertainty and the Hecksher-Ohlin Theorem," *Review of Economic Studies*, pp. 259-268.

Benard J. and J. Versluis (1974), *Employment Planning and Optimal Allocation of Physical and Human Resources,* ILO, Geneva.

Bergendorff, H.; C.R. Blitzer and H.K. Kim (1973) "Applications of Control Theory to Leontief-Type Planning model," Mimeographed, IBRD.

Bergendorff, H. and P.B. Clark (1973), "Chile: An Experimental Model For Testing Consumption Redistribution," Mimeographed, IBRD.

Bergendorff, H.; P.B. Clark and L. Taylor (1973), "Welfare Gains" from Optimization in Dynamic Planning Models," *Economics of Planning,* Vol. 13, No. 1-2, 1973, pp. 75-90.

Bergsman, J. and A.S. Manne (1965), "An Almost Consistent Intertemporal Model for India's IV and V Plans," *Economic Weekly,* 20 November, pp. 1733-1741.

Bergsman, J. and A.S. Manne (1966), "An almost Consistent Intertemporal Model for India's Fourth and Fifth Plans," in I. Adelman and E. Thorbecke (eds.), op. cit.

Berry, Roger (1981), "Redistribution, Demand Structure and Factor Requirements: The Case of India," *World Development,* Vol. 9, No. 7, July, pp. 621-35.

Bhaduri, A. (1982), *Existing State of Macroeconometric Modelling in India,* Mimeographed, ESCAP, Bangkok.

Bhagwati, J.N. (1962), "On How to Decide What to Import and What to Produce", *Oxford Economic Papers,* Vol. 14, No. 2.

Bhagwati, J.N. (1971), "The Generalized Theory of Distortions and Welfare," in Bhagwati et al., op. cit.

Bhagwati, J.N. (1978), *Foreign Trade Regimes and Economic Development: Anatomy and Consequences of Exchange Control Regimes,* Ballinger, Cambridge, Mass.

Bhagwati, J.N. and S. Chakravarty (1969), "Contribution to Indian Economy Analysis: A Survey," *American Economic Review,* Supplement, September, pp. 1-73.

Bhagwati, Jagdish N. Desai, P. (1970), *India: Planning For Industrialization,* Oxford University Press, London.

Bhagwati, J.N. and R.S. Eckaus, eds. (1970), *Foreign Aid: Selected Readings,* Penguin Books, Harmondsworth.

Bhagwati, J.N. and E. Grinols (1975), "Foreign Capital Dependence, Destabilisation and Feasibility of Transition to Socialism," *Journal of Development Economics,* Vol. 2, pp. 85-98.

Bhagwati, J.N.; R.W. Jones; R.A. Mundell and J. Venek, eds. (1971), *Trade Balance of Payments and Growth,* North-Holland, Amsterdam.

Bhagwati, J.N. and T.N. Srinivasan (1974), "On Reanalyzing the Harris-Todaro Model: Policy Rankings in the Case of Sector-Specific Wages", *American Economic Review,* Vol. 64, pp. 502-08.

Bhagwati, J.N. and T.N. Srinivasan (1975), *Foreign Trade Regimes and Economic Development: India,* NBER, New York.

Bhagwati, J.N. and T.N. Srinivasan (1978), "Shadow Prices for Project Selection in the Presence of Distortions: Effective Rates of Protection and Domestic Resource Costs," *Journal of Political Economy,* Vol. 86, No. 1, pp. 97-116.

Bhagwati, J.N. and C. Wibulswadi (1972), "A Statistical Analysis of Shifts in the Import Structures in LDC's," *Bulletin of Oxford University Institute of Statistics,* May.

Bhattacharya, B.B. (1975), *Short-Term Income Determination,* Macmillan, Delhi.

Bhattacharya, B.B. (1982), *The Government Budget, Inflation and Growth in India.* Mimeo, Institute of Economic Growth, Delhi.

Bhattacharya, B.B. (Forthcoming), *Public Expenditure, Inflation and Growth: A Macroeconomic Analysis for India,* Oxford University Press, New Delhi.

Bisschop, J. and A. Meeraus (1980), "Toward Successful Modeling Applications in Strategic Planning Environment," Mimeographed, The World Bank, Washington, D.C.

Blinder, A. (1975), *Towards an Economic Theory of Income Distribution,* M.I.T. Press, Cambridge, Mass.

Blitzer, C.R. (1975), Employment and Human Capital Formation," in C.R. Blitzer; P. Clark and L. Taylor, eds., op. cit.

Blitzer, C.R. (1982), "A Perspective Planning Model for Turkey: 1969-1984', in S. Bhagwan Dahiya, ed., op. cit.

Blitzer, C.R.; P. Clark, and L. Taylor (1975), *Economy-Wide Models and Development Planning*, Oxford University Press, London.

Blitzer, C.R.; H. Cetin and A.S. Manne (1969), "A Dynamic Five Sector Model for Turkey, 1967-82," Memorandom No. 70, Research Centre in Economic Growth, Stanford University, April. Reprinted in S.B. Dahiya, (ed.), 1982, op.cit.

Bowles, S. (1969), *Planning Educational Systems for Economic Growth,* Harvard University Press, Cambridge, Massachusetts.

Bodkin, Ronald G. (1976), "A Large-Scale Input-Output Econometric Model of Canadian Economy", in Keran R. Polenske and J.V. Skolka (eds.), *Advances in Inputs-Output Analysis*, Ballinger, Cambridge, Mass.

Brada, J.C. (1971), "Taut planning and the Allocation of investment in a stochastic economy," *Economic of Planning*, 11, pp. 81-94.

Brada, J.C. (1973), "Uncertainty, the Structure of Production and the Pattern of Trade of Centrally Planned Economies," *Economics of Planning*, 13, pp. 175-185.

Brahmananda, P.R. (1978), *Planning For a Futureless Economy,* Himalaya Publishing House, Bombay.

Brahmananda, P.R. and C.N. Vakil (1956), *Planning for an Expanding Economy*, Vora & Co., Bombay.

Brainard, W.C. and Cooper, R.N. (1968), "*Uncertainty and diversification in International Trade*," Food Research Institute Studies in Agricultural Economics, Trade, and Development, 8, pp. 257-285.

Brody, A. (1970), *Proportions, Prices and Planning,* North-Holland, Amsterdam.

Brown, A. and A. Deaton, (1972), "Surveys in Applied Economics: Models of Consumer Behaviour", *Economic Journal*, Vol. 82, pp. 1145-1236.

Bruno, M. (1966), "A Programming Model for Israel," in I. Adelman and E. Thorbecke, eds., op. cit.

Bruno, M. (1967), "Optimal Patterns of Trade and Development," *Review of Economic and Statistics,* Vol. 49, November, pp. 545-54.

Bruno, M. (1971), "Optimal Patterns of Trade and Development," in H.B. Chenery, ed., *Studies in Development Planning,* Harvard University Press, Cambridge, Mass.

Bruno, M. (1974), "Structural Change and the Dynamics of the Real Exchange Rate," Mimeographed, Hebrew University and Falk Institute.

Bruno, M. (1975), "Planning Models, Shadow Prices, and Project Evaluation," in C.R. Blitzer et al. (eds.), op. cit.

Bruno, M. (1979), "Income Distribution and the Neoclassical Paradigm: Introduction to a Symposium," *Journal of Development Economics,* Vol. 6, pp. 3-10.

Bruno, M.; C. Daugherty; and M. Fraenkel (1970), "Dynamic Input-Output, Trade and Development," in A.P. Carter and A. Brody (eds.), op. cit.

Bruton, H.J. (1969), "The Two Gap Approach to Aid and Development: Comment," *American Economic Review,* Vol. 59, June, pp. 439-46.

Bruton, H.J. (1970), "The Import Substitution Strategy of Economic Development," *Pakistan Development Review,* Vol. 10 (Summer), pp. 123-46.

Bulmer-Thomas, V., (1978), "Trade, Structure and Linkages in Costa Rica," *Journal of Development Economics*.

Bulmer-Thomas, V. (1982), *Input-Output Analysis in Developing Countries: Sources, Methods and Applications,* John Wiley & Sons, New York.

Bodkin, R.G.; L.R. Klein and K. Marwah (1982), "Macro-Econometric Modelling: A Schematic History and a View of Its Possible Approach," Unpublished Manuscript, May.

Carrillo-Arronte, R. (1968), *An Empirical Test on Interregional Planning: A Linear Programming Model For Mexico,* Rotterdam University Press, Rotterdam.

Carter, A. and A. Brody, eds. (1970), *Contribution to Input-Output Analysis,* North-Holland, Amsterdam.

Carter, N.G. (1967), "A New Look at the Sandee Model," in K. Shell (ed.), op. cit.

Cass, D. (1965), "Optimum Growth in Aggregated Model of Capital Accumulation," *Review of Economic Studies,* Vol. 32.

Celasum, M. (1972), "Perspectives of Economic Growth in Turkey (1972-1977), Experiments With Three Aggregative Models," Middle East Technical University, Ankara.

Celasum, M. (1978), "A Computable General Equilibrium Model for the Analysis of Structural Transformation and Relative Price Changes," *METU Studies in Development,* No. 20, pp. 1-24.

Chakrabarty, S.K. (1977), *Price Behaviour in India,* Macmillan, Delhi.

Chakraborty, D. and T.T. Rao (1981), "Aggregation Problem in Input-Output Analysis: A Survey," *Artha Vijnana,* Sept-Dec., Vol. 33, No. 3 & 4, pp. 326-45.

Chakravarty, S. (1962), "Optimum Savings With a Finite Planning Horizon," *International Economic Review,* September, pp. 338-355.

Chakravarty, S., (1964a) "An Appraisal of Alternative Planning Models," in P.N. Rosenstein-Rodan, (ed.) op. cit.

Chakravarty, S. (1964b), "The Use of Shadow Prices in Programme Evaluation," in P.N. Rosenstein-Rodan, (ed.) op. cit.

Chakravarty, S. (1968), *The Logic of Investment Planning,* North-Holland, Amsterdam.

Chakravarty, S. (1969), *Capital and Development Planning,* M.I.T. Press, Cambridge, Mass.

Chakravarty, S. (1973), "Theory of Development Planning-An Appraisal" in H.C. Bos; H. Linneman and P.de Wolff, eds. *Economic Structure and Development,* North-Holland, Amsterdam.

Chakravarty, S. (1977), "Planning Techniques in India," in *Survey of Research in Economics,* Vol. 1, Allied Publishers, Bombay.

Chakravarty, S. (1980), "Relevance of Growth Models to Development Planning," *Pakistan Development Review,* Vol. 19, No. 2, pp. 101-112.

Chakravarty, S. and R.S. Eckaus (1964a), "Choice Elements in Intertemporal Planning," in P.N. Rosenstein-Rodan (ed.), op. cit.

Chakravarty, S. and R.S. Eckaus (1964b), "An Approach to a Multi-Sectoral Intertemporal Planning Model," in P.N. Rosenstein-Rodan (ed.), op. cit.

Chakravarty, S. and L. Lefeber (1965), "An Optimising Planning Model," *The Economic Weekly,* February, pp. 237-252.

Champernowne, D. (1974), "A Comparison of Measures of Inequality of Income Distribution," *Economic Journal,* Vol. 84, pp. 787-816.

Chenery, H.B. (1954), "Applications of Inter-industry Analysis to Problems of Economic Development," in T. Barna (ed.), op. cit.

Chenery, H.B. (1959), "The Interdependence of Investment Decisions," in M. Abramovitz et. al. eds., op. cit.

Chenery, H.B. (1961), "Comparative Advantage and Development Policy." *American Economic Review,* March, pp. 18-51.

Chenery, H.B. (1962), "Development Policies for Southern Italy," *Quarterly Journal of Economics*, November, 515-547.

Chenery, H.B. (1963), "The Use of Inter-Industry Analysis in Development Programming," in T. Barna (ed.) op. cit.

Chenery, H.B. (1969), "The Two-Gap Approach to Aid and Development: A Reply to Bruton," *American Economic Review,* June, pp. 44-49.

Chenery, H.B., ed. (1971), *Studies in Development Planning,* Harvard University Press, Cambridge, Mass.

Chenery, H.B. (1973), "Alternative Strategies for Development." World Bank Staff Working Papers No. 165, October, Washington, D.C.

Chenery, H.B. (1975), "The Structuralist Approach to Development Policy", *Papers and Proceedings of the American Economic Association,* 65 (May): 310-16.

Chenery, H.B. (1979),. "*Structural Change and Development Policy,*" Oxford University Press, London.

Chenery, H.B.,; Ahluwalia, M.S.; Bell, C.L.G.; Duloy, J.H. and Jolly, R. (1974), *Redistribution with Growth,* Oxford University Press, London.

Chenery, H.B. and Bruno, M. (1962), "Development Alternatives in an Open Economy: The Case of Israel, "*Economic Journal,* March, pp. 79-103.

Chenery, H.B. and Carter, N.G. (1973), "Foreign Assistance and Development Performance," *American Economic Review,* May, pp. 459-68.

Chenery, H.B. and Carter, N.G. (1976), "Internal and External Aspects of Development Plans and Performance in Aid-receiving Countries," in *Methods of Long-terms Planning and Forecasting,* ed., T.S. Khachaturov, Macmillan, London.

Chenery, H.B. and Clark, P.G. (1959), *Interindustry Economics,* John Wiley and Sons, New York.

Chenery, H.B. and Kretschmer, K. (1956), "Resource Allocation for Economic Development," *Econometrica,* October, pp. 365-99.

Chenery, H.B., and Mac Ewan, A. (1966), "Optimal Patterns of Growth and Aid: The Case of Pakistan," in I. Adelman and E. Thorbecke, eds., op. cit.

Chenery, H.B., and Raduchel, W.J. (1971), "Substitution in Planning Models," in H.B. Chenery, ed., op. cit.

Chenery, H.B. and A.M. Strout (1966), "Foreign Assistance and Economic Development," *American Economic Review,* September, pp. 679-733.

Chenery, H.B. and Syrquin, M. (1975), *Patterns of Development, 1950-1970,* Oxford University Press, London.

Chenery, H.B. and Uzawa, H. (1958), "Non-Linear Programming in Economic Development," in K.J. Arrow, L. Hurwicz, and H. Uzawa, eds., op. cit.

Chenery, H.B., and Westphal, L.E. (1969), "Economies of Scale and Investment over Time." in *Public Economics,* ed., J. Margolis, St. Martin's Press, New York.

Cheng, L. (1980), *The Market Failures Approach to International Trade and Specialization* Ph. D. Thesis, Department of Economics, University of California, Berkely.

Chitre, V.S. (1982), "Growth Cycles in the Indian Economy," *Artha Vijnana,* December, 34, No. 4, pp. 293-450.

Choudhary, N.K. (1963), *An Econometric Model of India, 1930-35* Ph. D. Dissertation, (Unpublished), University of Wisconsin.

Choudhary, N.K.; Desai, M.; Gupta, D. B.; Krishnamurty, K.; Krishna, K.L., and Nagar, A.L. (1974), *Towards an Econometric Model of the Indian Economy,* in 3 volumes, Mimeographed, Report submitted to the ICSSR, Delhi.

Clark, Colin (1940), *The Conditions of Economic Progress*, Mcmillan, London.

Clark, P.B. (1970), *Planning Import Substitution*, North-Holland, Amsterdam.

Clark, P.B. and L. Taylor, (1971), "Dynamic Input-Output Planning with Optimal End Conditions: The Case of Chile," *Economics of Planning,* pp. 10-30.

Cline, William R. (1972), *Potential Effects of Income Redistribution of Economic Growth-Latin American Cases,* Praeger, New York.

Cline, William R. (1975), "Distribution and Developement: A Survey of Literature", *Journal of Development Economics*, December.

Cooper, Charles (1983), "Extensions of the Raj-Sen Model of Economic Growth," *Oxford Economic Papers,* Vol. 35, No. 2, July, pp. 170-185.

Corden, W.M. (1974), *Trade Policy and Economic Welfare,* Oxford University Press, London.

Cornelisse, P.A. and C.B. Tilanus (1965), "The Semi-Input-Output Method: with an Application to Turkistan Data," *De Economist.* 114, No. 9/10, Sept-Oct, pp. 521-33.

Cornelisse, P.A. and Versluis, J. (1969), "The Semi-Input-Output Method Under Upper Bounds," in H.C. Bos (ed.) *Towards*

Balanced International Growth, North-Holland, Amsterdam.

Cremer, J. (1989), "How Should You Do Sensitivity Analysis"? in S. Bhagwan Dahiya, ed., *Theoretical Foundations of Development Planning.*

Dahiya, S. Bhagwan (1977), "The Technique of the Rolling Plan" *Kurukshetra University Research Journal*, Vol. 11, pp. 3-16.

Dahiya, S. Bhagwan (1978), "A Comparative Dynamic Optimising Planning Model," *Kurukshetra University Research Journal*, Vol. 12, pp. 20-31.

Dahiya, S. Bhagwan, ed. (1982a), *Development Planning Models* (Two Volumes), Inter-India, New Delhi.

Dahiya, S. Bhagwan (1982b), "Development Planning Models in India: A Survey," in S. Bhagwan Dahiya, ed., op. cit., Vol. 1.

Dahiya, S. Bhagwan (1982c), "Economy-Wide Multi-Sectoral Models for Development Planning: a Survey," in S. Bhagwan Dahiya, ed., op. cit., Vol. II.

Dahiya, S. Bhagwan (1983), "A Multi-Sectoral, Multi-Regional Optimising Planning Model for India: Theoretical Structure," *Kautilaya.*

Dahiya, S. Bhagwan (1986a), "Some Reflections on the Methodological Evolution of Development Planning Models," *International Journal of Development Planning Literature,* January-March, pp. 71-83.

Dahiya, S. Bhagwan (1986b), "The Choice of Planning Techniques in the Planning Process," *International Journal of Development Planning Literature,* April-June, pp. 181-195.

Dahiya, S. Bhagwan (1986c), "Development Planning Models in India: Some Observations", *International Journal of Development Planning Literature,* October-December, pp. 454-464.

Dahiya, S. Bhagwan (1986d), "Planning Techniques for Social Justice: The Discussant's View", *The World Economic Congress,* New Delhi, December, 1986.

Dahiya, S. Bhagwan (1987a), "Macro-Statistical Models, and Development Policy," *Asian Economic Review,* Vol. 29, No. 1, April, pp. 1-21.

Dahiya, S. Bhagwan (1987b), "On the Evolution of Development Planning", in Giancarlo Gandolfo and Ferrruccio Marzano, eds., *Keynesian Theory, Planning Models and Quantitative Economics,* Dott. A Giuffre Editore, Milano, pp. 161-223.

Dahiya, S. Bhagwan (1988), "Evolution of Development Planning in India", *Asian Economic Review,* Vol. 30, No. 1, April.

Dahiya, S. Bhagwan, ed. (1989), *Theoretical Foundations of Development Planning,* Concept Publishing Co., New Delhi.

Dahiya, S. Bhagwan and Singer, H.W. (1986), "The Roots of Industrialisation Strategy in India: 1949-56", *Asian Journal of Economics and Social Studies.*

Dandekar, V.M. and Rath, N.R. (1971), "Poverty in India, *Economic and Political Weekly,* January 2 & 9, pp. 25-48 & 106-146.

Das, R.K. (1974), *Optimal Investment Planning,* Rotterdam University Press, Rotterdam.

Das, S.K. (1977), "Uncertainty and the Heckscher-Ohlin Theorem: A Comment," *Review of Economic Studies,* 44, pp. 189-190.

Dasgupta, D. (1978), "Catenary Turnpikes and Rolling Plans: Synthesis and Extensions," *Indian Economic Journal,* April-June, Vol. 25, pp. 1-18.

Dasgupta, P.S. (1968), "Unemployment and Optimal Growth," *Economic and Political Weekly,* 21 September.

Day, R.H. (197), "Adaptive Processes and Economic Theory", in R.H. Day and T. Groves, (eds.), *Adaptive Economic Models*, Academic Press, New York.

Day, R. and A. Cigno (1978), *Modelling Economic Change: The Recursive Programming Approach,* North-Holland, New York.

Day, R.H. & P.E. Kennedy (1970), "Recursive Economic Systems: An existence Analysis," *Econometrica*, 38, September, pp. 666-681.

Dervis, K. (1975), "Substitution, Employment, and Intertemporal Equilibrium in a Non-Linear Multi-Sector Planning Model for Turkey," *European Economic Review,* Vol. 6, pp. 77-96.

Davis, K. and S. Robinson, (1978), "The Foreign Exchange Gap, Growth and Industrial Strategy in Turkey: 1973-83". World Bank Staff Working Paper No. 306, Washington, D.C.

Dervis, K.; J. de Melo and S. Robinson (1981), "A General Equilibrium Analysis of Foreign Exchange Shortages in a Developing Economy," *Economic Journal,* December, pp. 891-906.

Davis, Kamal; Jaime de Melo; and Sherman Robinson (1982), *General Equilibrium Models for Development Policy*, Cambridge University Press, Cambridge.

Desai, Maghanand J. (1973), "Macro-economic Models for India: A Survey," *Sankhya,* Series B, June.

Desai, P. (1969), "Alternative Measures of Import Substitution," *Oxford Economic Papers,* Vol. 21, No. 3, pp. 344-59.

Desai, P. (1972), *Import Substitution in the Indian Economy,* Hindustan Publishing Co.

Diamand, M. (1978), "Towards a Change in the Economic Paradigm Through the Experience of Developing Countries", *Journal of Development Economics,* Vol. 5, pp. 19-53.

Diaz-Alejandro, C. (1975), "Trade Policies and Economic Development," in *International Trade and Finance,* ed., P.B. Kenen, Cambridge University Press, New York.

Diaz-Alejandro, C. et al. (1979), "Exchange Rate Policy in Semi-industrialized Countries: A Symposium," *Journal of Development Economics,* Vol. 6, No. 4, pp. 459-548.

Dixit, A.K. (1968), "Optimal Development in the Labour-Surplus Economy," *Review of Economic Studies,* January.

Dixon, P.B. (1975), *The Theory of Joint Maximization,* North-Holland, Amsterdam.

Dixon, P.B.; B. Parmenter; G. Ryland, and J. Sutton (1977), *Orani, A General Equilibrium Model of the Australian Economy,* Vol. 2, Government Publishing Service, Canberra.

Dobb, M. (1960), *An Essay on Economic Growth and Planning,* Routledge and Paul, London.

Domar, E. (1957), *Essays in the Theory of Economic Growth,* Oxford University Press, New York.

Dorfman, R. (1969), "An Economic Interpretation of Optimal Control Theory", *American Economic Review,* pp. 817-831.

Dorfman, R.; P.A. Samuelson, and R.M. Solow (1958), *Linear Programming and Economic Analysis,* McGraw-Hill, New York.

Dougherty, C.R.S. (1972), "Substitution and the Structure of the Labour Force," *Economic Journal,* March, pp. 170-182.

Duloy, J.H. and P.B.R. Hazell (1975), "Substitution and Non-linearities in Planning Models," in C.R. Blitzer et al., eds., op. cit.

Dutta, Bhaskar (1980), "Intersectoral Disparities and Income Distribution in India: 1960-61 to 1973-74," *Indian Economic Review,* Vol. 15, No. 2, pp. 119-38.

Dutta, Manoranjan (1964), "A Prototype Model of India's Foreign Sector," *International Economic Review.*

Easley, D. and D.F. Spulber (1981), "Stochastic Equilibrium and Optimality with Rolling Plans," *International Economic Review,* Vol. 22, No. 1, February, pp. 79-103.

Eckaus, R.S. (1967), "Planning in India," in Max Millikan (ed.) *National Economic Planning,* Scientific Book Agency, Calcutta.

Eckaus, R.S. (1973), "Absorptive Capacity as a Constraint Due to Maturation Process," in J.N. Bhagwati and R.S. Eckaus (eds.), *Development and Planning,* M.I.T. Press, Cambridge.

Eckaus, R.S. and L. Lefeber, (1962), "Capital Formation: A Theoretical and Empirical Analysis," *Review of Economics and Statistics,* May.

Eckaus, R.S.; F.D. McCarthy, and M. Mohieldin (1979), "Multisector General Equilibrium Models for Egypt," M.I.T., Department of Economics, Working Paper No. 233, Cambridge Mass.

Eckaus, R.S.; D. Mc Carthty; and A. Mohie-Eldin (1981), "A Social Accounting Matrix for Egypt, 1976", *Journal of Development Economics,* October, No. 2, pp. 183-203.

Eckaus,R. and Parikh, K. (1968), *Planning for Growth: Multisectoral Intertemporal Models Applied to India,* M.I.T. Press, Cambridge, Mass.

Eckstein, O. (1957), "Investment Criteria for Economic Development and the Theory of Intertemporal Welfare Economics" *Quarterly Journal of Economics,* February, pp. 56-85.

Eckstein, O. (1961), "A Survey of the Theory of Public Expenditure Criteria," in J.M. Buchanan (ed.), *Public Finance: Needs, Sources and Utilization,* Princeton University Press, Princeton.

Edelman, J.A.; and Chenery, H.B. (1977), "Aid and Income Distribution," in J. Bhagwati, ed., *The New International*

Economic Order: The North - South, Debate, M.I.T. Press, Cambridge, Mass.

Ehrenpreis, D. (1977), "Some Models in Indian Development Planning," *Swedish Journal of Economics,* December, Vol. 72, pp. 301-319.

Ellman, M.J. (1968), "The Use of Input-output in Regional Economic Planning: The Soviet Experience," *Economic Journal,* December, pp. 855-867.

Ellman, M.J. (1969), "The Consistency of Soviet Plans," *Scottish Journal of Political Economy,* February, pp. 50-74.

Evans, H.D. (1972), *A General Equilibrium Analysis of Protection: The Effects of Protection in Australia,* North-Holland, Amsterdam.

Fane, G. (1971), "Import Substitution and Export Expansion: Their Measurement and an Example of Their Application," *Pakistan Development Review,* Vol. II, No. 1, pp. 1-17.

Fane, G. (1973), "Consistent Measures of Import Substitution," *Oxford Economic Papers,* Vol. 25, No. 2, pp. 251-61.

Fei, J.C.H. and Ranis, G. (1964), *Development of the Labour Surplus Economy,* Homewood, III: Irwin.

Fei, J. and G. Ranis (1974), "Income Inequality by Additive Components," Discussion Paper 207, Economic Growth Center, Yale University, New Haven.

Fei, J. and G. Ranis (1975), "A Model of Growth and Employment in the Open Dualistic Economy: The Case of Korea and Taiwan," *Journal of Development Studies,* January, pp. 32-63.

Fei, J.; Ranis, G., and Kuo, S.W.Y. (1979), *Growth with Equality: The Taiwan Case,* Oxford University Press, New York.

Feldstein, M.S. (1964), "Net Social Benefit Calculation and the Public Investment Decision", *Oxford Economic Papers.*

Feltenstein, A. (1980), "A General Equilibrium Approach to the Analysis of Trade Restrictions with an Application to Argentina," *IMF Staff Papers,* Vol. 27, No. 4, pp. 749-84.

Findlay, R. (1970), "Factor Proportions and Comparative Advantage in the Long Run." *Journal of Political Economy,* February, pp. 27-34.

Findlay, R. (1971), "The Foreign Exchange Gap and Growth in Developing Economies, in *Trade, Balance of Payments, and Growth,* ed., J. Bhagwati et al., North-Holland, Amsterdam..

Findlay, R.E. (1973), *International Trade and Development Theory,* Columbia University Press, New York.

Fleming, M. (1955), "External Economies and the Doctrine of Balanced Growth," *Economic Journal,* June, pp. 241-56.

Fox, K.A.; J.K. Sengupta, and E. Thorbecke (1966), *The Theory of Quantitative Economic Policy,* North-Holland, Amsterdam.

Frank,C.R, Jr. and R. Webb, eds., (1977), *Income Distribution Policy Alternatives in Developing Countries,* Brookings Institution, Washington, D.C.

Frank, C.R., Jr.; K.S. Kim, and L. Westphal (1975), *Foreign Trade Regimes and Economic Development: South Korea,* National Bureau of Economic Research, New York.

Frisch, R. (1960), *Planning for India,* Asia Publishing House, Delhi.

Furtado, C. (1964), *Development and Underdevelopment,* University of California Press, Berkeley.

Gaiha, R. (1977), *A Model of Manpower Planning for India,* Unpublished Doctoral Thesis, University of Manchester.

Gaiha, R. (1980), "Choice of Strategy in a Labour Abundant Developing Economy-An Empirical Analysis," *Economics of Planning,* Vol. 16, No. 2, pp. 68-86.

Gale, D. (1960), *The Theory of Linear Economic Models*, McGraw-Hill, New York.

Galenson, W., and Leibenstein, H. (1955), "Investment Criteria, Productivity and Economic Development", *Quarterly Journal of Economics,* August, pp. 343-70.

Gandolfo, G. (1981), *Qualitative Analysis and Econometric Estimation of Continuous Time Dynamic Models*, North-Holland, Amsterdam.

Gandolfo, G. (1986), "Recent Trends in Macro-Econometric Model Building for Policy Planning," *International Journal of Development Planning Literature,* April-June, No. 2, pp. 167-179.

Georgescu-Roegen, N. (1951), "Some Properties of a Generalized Leontief Model," Chapter X in T.C. Koopmans (ed.), *Activity Analysis of Production and Allocation*, John Wiley & Sons, New York.

Gersovitz, M. (1982), "The Estimation of the Two-Gap Models," *Journal of International Economics,* pp. 111-24.

Ghosh, A. (1959), "A Note on Multisector Growth Models," *Arthaniti,* November, pp. 14-18.

Ghosh, A. (1966), "Mathematical Models in Research Related to Planning in India: A Review," *Economics of Planning,* pp. 154-178.

Ghosh, A. (1981), "Input-Output Models for Planning in a Mixed Economy-A New Approach," *Artha Vijnana,* Sept-Dec., Vol. 33, pp. 326-45.

Ghosh, A.K. (1979), *Prices & Economic Fluctuations in India, 1861-1947*, S. Chand & Co., New Delhi.

Ghosh, D.; Lahiri, A.K.; Madhur, S. and Roy, P.L. (1983), *A Model for India: Summary of Specifications and Estimated Results,* Mimeographed, Delhi.

Ginsburg, V. and J. Waelbroeck (1978), "Computational Experience with a Large General Equilibrium Model," in J. Los., ed., op. cit.

Ginsburg, V. and J. Waelbhroeck (1980), *Activity Analysis and General Equilibrium Modeling,* North-Holland, Amsterdam.

Ginsburg, V. and J. Waelbroeck (1983), "Planning Models and General Equilibrium Activity Analysis,", in H. Scarf and J. Shoven, eds., op. cit.

Ginsburg, V. and J. Waelbroeck (1989), "On the Design of Linear Programming Models for Open Economies," in S. Bhagwan Dahiya, ed., op. cit.

Goldman, S.M. (1968), "Optimal Growth and Continual Planning Revision," *Review of Economic Studies,* April, Vol. 35, pp. 145-54.

Goldman, S.M. (1969), "Sequential Planning and Continual Planning Revision," *Journal of Political Economy,* July/August, Vol. 77, pp. 653-664.

Goodwin, R.M. (1948), "Secular and Cyclical Aspects of the Multiplier and the Accelerator," *in Income, Employment & Public Policy: Easays in Honor of A.H. Hansen*, Northen, New York.

Goodwin, R.M. (1961), "The Optimal Growth Plan for an Under-Developed Economy," *Economic Journal,* December, 756-74.

Goreux, M.I. (1977), *Interdependence Planning: Multilevel Programming Studies of the Ivory Coast,* Johns Hopkins Press, Baltimore, Md.

Goreux, I.M. and A.S. Manne, eds. (1973), *Multi-level Planning: Case Studies in Mexico,* North-Holland, Amsterdam.

Grais, Wafik (1982), "The Supply and Demand of LFabour by Level of Education," in S.B. Dahiya (ed.), op. cit.

Griffin, K.B. and Enos, J.L. (1970), *"Foreign Assistance: Objectives* and Consequences," *Economic Development and Cultural Change,* April, pp 313-27.

Griffin, K.B., and Khan, A. (1978), "Poverty in the Third World: Ugly Facts and Fancy Models," *World Development,* March, pp. 295-304.

Grubel, H.G. and P.J. Lloyd (1975), *Intra-Industry Trade: The Theory and Measurement of International Trade in Differentiated Products,* Macmillan and Halsted, London.

Gruver, Gene W. (1986), "Computable General Equilibrium Models: an overview of applications to development," *International Journal of Development Planning Literature,* January-March, pp. 85-104.

Gupta, D.K. and Y.P. Venieris, (1981), "Introducing New Dimensions in Macro Models: The Socio Political and Institutional Environments," *Economic Development and Cultural Change,* Vol. 30, No. 1, October, pp. 31-58.

Gupta, G.S. (1973), "A Monetary Policy Model for India," *Sankhya,* Series B.

Gupta, S. (1977), "A Model for Income Distribution, Employment, and Growth", World Bank Occasional Staff Papers, No. 24, Johns Hopkins Press, Baltimore.

Gupta, S.P. (1973), *Planning Models in India with Projections to 1975,* Vikas, Delhi.

Gupta S.P. (1986), "Planning Strategies and Techniques in India," in *Planning Integrated Development: Methods Used in Asia,* UNESCO, Paris.

Habr, J. (1966), "A Contribution to the Theory of Sliding Plans," in *Problems of Economic Dynamics and Planning,* Pergamon Press, Oxford & London.

Hadley, G. (1962), *Linear Programming,* Addison-Wesley, Reading, Mass.

Hahn, F.H. (1960), "Equilibrium Dynamics in Heterogeneous Capital Models," *Quarterly Journal of Economics,* Vol. 80, pp. 633-46.

Hansen, B. (1967a), *Long and Short-term Planning in Underdeveloped Countries,* North-Holland, Amsterdam.

Hansen, B. (1967b) *Lectures in Economic Theory Part II Theory of Economic Policy and Planning,* Student LItteratur, Lund.

Harberger, A. (1967), "Techniques of Project Appraisal," in M. Millikan (ed.) *National Economic Planning,* Scientific Book Agency, Calcutta.

Harberger, A.C. (1971), "Three Basic Postulates for Applied Welfare Economics: An Interpretative Essay," *Journal of Economic Literature,* No. 3, pp. 785-97.

Harcourt, G. (1972), *Some Cambridge Controversies in the Theory of Capital,* Cambridge University Press, Cambridge.

Hare, Paul G. (1981), "Aggregative Planning by Means of Input - Output and Material Balances System," *Journal of Comparative Economics*, pp. 272-91.

Harris, J. and M. Todaro (1970), "Migration, Unemployment and Development: A Two-Sector Analysis," *American Economic Review,* pp. 126-42.

Harrod, R. (1939), "An Essay in Dynamic Theory," *Economic Journal,* March, pp. 14-33.

Hawrylyshyn, O.; A. Martens; R.S. Pindyck and M. Hamza (1976), *Planning for Economic Development,* Praeger Publishers, Inc.,

New York.

Hayden, C. and J.I. Round (1982), "Developments in Social Accounting Methods as Applied to the Analysis of Income Distribution and Employment Issues," *World Development,* June, pp. 451-465.

Hazari, B.R. (1967), "The Import intensity of Consumption in India," *Indian Economic Review,* October.

Hazari, B.R. and J. Krishnamurty (1970), "Employment Implications of India's Industrialization: Analysis in an Input-Output Framework," *Review of Economics and Statistics,* Vol. 52, No. 2.

Heal, G. (1973), *The Theory of Economic Planning,* North-Holland, Amsterdam.

Helpman, E. and Razin, A. (1978), *A Theory of International Trade Under Uncertainty*, Academic Press, New York.

Hicks, J. (1965), *Capital and Growth,* Oxford University Press, London.

Hinshaw, R. (1975), "Non-Traded Goods and the Balance of Payments: Further Reflections," *Journal of Economic Literature,* June, Vol. 13, No. 2, pp. 475-479.

Hirshman, A.O. (1958), *The Strategy of Economic Development,* Yale University Press, New Haven.

Inagaki, M. (1970), *Optimal Economic Growth: Shifting Finite Versus Infinite Time Horizon*, North-Holland, Amsterdam.

International Labour Organisation (1971), *Matching Employment Opportunities and Expectations: A Programme of Action for Ceylen*, Geneva.

International Labour Organisation (1972), *Employment, Incomes and Equality: A Strategy for Increasing Productive Employment in Kenya*, Geneva.

Intriligator, M.D., ed. (1971), *Frontiers of Quantitative Economics,* North-Holland, Amsterdam.

Intriligator, M.D. (1978), *Econometric Models. Techniques and Applications,* Prentice-Hall, Inc.

Intriligator, M.D. and E. Sheshinski (1981), *Toward a Theory of Planning,* Unpublished Manuscript.

Jabara, C.L. and Thompson, R.L. (1980), "Agricultural comparative advantage under international price uncertainty: the case of Senegal," *American Journal of Agricultural Economics.*

Jain, S. (1975), *Size Distribution of Income: A Compilation of Data,* Mimeographed, The World Bank, Washington, D.C.

Johansen, L. (1975), *A Multi-Sectoral Study of Economic Growth,* North-Holland, Amsterdam, 2nd Enlarged edition.

Johansen, L. (1977), *Lectures on Macroeconomic Planning,* Vol. 2, North-Holland, Amsterdam.

Johansen, Leif (1982), *Econometric Models and Economic Planning and Policy: Some Trends and Problems,* Institute of Economics, University of Oslo.

Johansen, L.; H. Alstadtheim, and A. Langsether (1968), "Explorations in Long Term Projections for the Norwegian Economy", *Economics of Planning,* Vol. 8, No. 1-2, pp. 70-117.

Jorgenson, D. (1963), "Capital Theory and Investment Behaviour", *American Economic Review,* Vol. 53, pp. 247-59.

Joregensen, D.W. (1966), "Testing Alternative Theories of the Development of a Dual Economy," in I. Adelman and E. Thorbecke, eds., op. cit.

Kaldor, N. (1966), "Alternative Theories of Distribution," *Review of Economic Studies,* Vol. 23, pp. 83-100.

Kalecki, Michael (1971), *Selected Essays on the Dynamics of the Capitalist Economy, 1930-1970,* cambridge University Press, Cambridge.

Karlin, S. (1959), *Mathematical Methods and Theories in Games, Programming and Economics*, Addison-Wesley, Reading, Mass.

Kaser, M.D. (ed.), (1968), *Economic Development for Eastern Europe*, Macmillan, London.

ten Kate, A. (1972), "The Semi-Input-Output Method with Endogenous Capital Formation: A Reconsideration," Discussion Paper No. 15, Netherlands School of Economics, Rotterdam.

Keesing, D. (1967), "Outward-looking Policies and Economic Development," *Economic Journal,* June, pp. 303-20.

Kehee, T.J. (1980), "An Index Theorem for General Equilibrium Models with Production," *Econometrica,* Vol. 48, pp. 1211-32.

Keller, W.J. (1980), *Tax Incidence: A General Equilibrium Approach,* North-Holland, Amsterdam.

Kelley, A.; J. Williamson, and R. Cheetham (1972), *Dualistic Economic Development: Theory and History,* University of Chicago Press, Chicago.

Kemp, M.C. (1976), *Distribution, Welfare, Uncertainty: three topics in the theory of international trade*, North-Holland, New York.

Kendrick, D. (1972), "On the Leontief Dynamic Inverse," *Quarterly Journal of Economics,* Vol. 86, pp. 693-696.

Kendrick, D.A. and L. Taylor (1969), "A Dynamic Non-Linear Planning Model for Korea," in Adelman, ed., op. cit.

Kendrick, D.A. and L. Taylor (1970), "Numerical Solution of Non-linear Planning Models," *Econometrica,* May, Vol. 38, pp. 453-467.

Kendrick, D.A. and L. Taylor (1971), "Numerical Methods and Non-Linear Optimizing Models for Economic Planning," in H.B. Chenery (ed.), op. cit.

Keynes, John Maynard, (1936), *The General Theory of Employment Interest and Money*, Harcourt Brace & Co., New York.

Khan, A.R. (1967), "A Multi-Sectoral Programming Model for Regional Planning in Pakistan," *Pakistan Development Review,* Spring, pp. 29-65.

Khan, M.S. (1970), *Planning and Economic Development in India,* Asia Publishing House, Bombay.

Kim, K.S. (1969), "Capital Imports, External Debts, and Growth in the Mahalanobis Model," *Indian Economic Journal,* Vol. 16, pp. 488-91.

Kim, K.S. (1989), "Optimum Investment Planning Under the Minimum Time Objective in an Open Economy," in S. Bhagwan Dahiya (ed.) op. cit.

King, A. (1989), "The Fel'dman-Domar-Mahalanobis Development Models", in S. Bhagwan Dahiya, ed., op. cit.

King, B. (1981), "What Is a SAM? A Layman's Guide to Social Accounting Matrices," World Bank Staff Working Paper No. 463, Washington, D.C.

Klein, L. R. (1969), "Scope and Limitations of Macroeconometric Model Building," unpublished manuscript, May.

Klein, L.R. (1981), *Econometric Models as Guides for Decision Making,* The Free Press, New York.

Kmenta, J., and J.B. Ramsey, eds., (1981), *Large Scale Econometric Models-Theory and Practice,* North-Holland, Amsterdam.

Komiya, R. (1959), "A Note on Professor Mahalanobis's Model of Indian Economic Planning," *Review of Economics and Statistics,*

February, pp. 29-36.

Koopmans, T.C. (1950), "Utility Analysis of Decisions Affecting Future Well-Being," *Econometrica,* Vol. 18, April.

Koopmans, T.C. (1951), "Alterjnative Proof of the substitution Theorem for Leontief Models in the case of the three industries," Chapter 8 in T.C. Koopmans, (ed.) *Activity Analysis of Production & Allocation*, John Wiley & Sons, New York.

Koopmans, T.C. (1967), "Objectives, Constraints, and Outcomes in Optimal Growth Models," Econometrica, pp. 1-15.

Korean Development Association (1967), *A Study of Regional Planning by Using Regional Input-Output Model,* Seoul.

Kornia, J. (1967), *Mathematical Plänning of Structural Decisions*, North-Holland, amsterdam.

Kornai, J. (1969), "Multi-level Programming: A First Report on the Model and on the Experimental Computations," *European Economic Review,* Vol. I, pp. 134-191.

Kornai, J. (1972), *Rush Versus Harmonic Growth,* North-Holland, Amsterdam.

Kornai, J. (1975), "Models and Policy: The Dialogue Between Model Builder and Planner," in C.R. Blitzer et al. (eds.) op. cit.

Krishna, Raj (1982), "Research Requirements of Economic Planning in India," in *Relevance in Social Science Research* (ed.), Institute of Economic Growth, Allied, New Delhi, pp. 287-99.

Krishnamurty, K. (1964), *An Econometric Model of India, 1948-61,* Ph.D. Dissertation (Unpublished), University of Pennsylvania.

Krishnamurty, K. (1984), "Inflation and Growth: A Model for India," *Indian Economic review,* Vol. 19. No. 1, January-June.

Krishnamurty, K. and V. Pandit (1984), "Macroeconometric Modelling of the Indian Economy: an Overview," *Indian Economic Review*, Vol. 19 No. 1, January-June.

Krishnamurty, K; Saibaba, P. and Kazmi, N.A. (1984), "Inflation and Growth: A Model for India," *Indian Economic Review.*

Krishnan, T.N. (1973), "The Fifth Five Year Plan Model: A Comment," *Economic and Political Weekly,* Vol. 8, August, pp. 1445-1456.

Krueger, A. (1972), *Exchange Control, Liberalization and Development: Turkey,* Columbia University Press, Mimeographed.

Kubo, Y.; J. Lewis; J. de Melo and S. Robinson (1983), "Multisector Models and the Analysis of Alternative Development Strategies," World Bank Staff Working Paper, Washington, D.C.

Kumar, D. (1974), "Changes in Income Distribution and Poverty in India: A Review of the Literature," *World Development,* Vol. 2, No. 1.

Krueger, A. (1979), "Interactions Between Inflation and Trade Regime Objectives in Stabilization Programs," Mimeographed, Univesity of Minnesota, Minneapolies.

Kuhn, H.W. and A.W. Tucker (1956), "Linear Inequalities and Related Systems," *Annals of Mathematics Studies*, Vol. 38, Princeton University Press, Princeton, N.J.

Kuyvenhoven, A. (1978), *Planning with the Semi-Input-Output Method with Empirical Applications to Nigeria,* Martinus Nijhoff, Leiden.

Kuznets, S. (1955), "Economic Growth and Income Inequality," *American Economic Review,* March, pp. 1-28.

Kuznets, S. (1966), *Modern Economic Growth,* Yale University Press, New Haven.

Kuznets, S. (1971), *Economic Growth of Nations*, Harvard University Press, Cambridge, Mass.

Lage, G. (1970), "A Linear Programming Analysis of Tariff Protection," *Western Economic Journal,* Vol. 8, No. 2, pp. 167-185.

Lal, D. (1976), "Distribution and Development: A Review Article," *World Development*, Sept., pp. 725-738.

Lal, Deepak (1980), *Prices for Planning: Towards the Reform of Indian Planning,* Heinemann, London.

Leela, R. and N. Somasekhara (1972), "Predictions of Mahalanobis and Performance of Plans: A Juxtaposition," *Indian Economic Journal*, October-December, Vol. 20, pp. 174-189.

Lefeber, L. (1964), "A Simple Optimizing Planning Model," in P.N. Rosenstein-Rodan, ed., op. cit.

Lefeber, L. (1966), "Comment on Bergsman-Manne Model," in I. Adelman and E. Thorbecke, eds., op. cit.

Lefeber, L. (1968), "Planning in a Surplus Labour Economy", *American Economic Review,* June, Vol. 88, pp. 343-373.

Leibenstein, H. (1978), *General X - Efficiency Theory and Economic Development,* Oxford University Press, London.

Lele, Uma and John W. Mellor (1981), "Technological Change, Distributive Bias and Labour Transfer in a Two-Sector Economy," *Oxford Economic Papers,* November, pp. 426-41.

Leontief, W.W. (1941, 1951), *The Structure of American Economy*, Oxford University Press.

Leontief, W.W. (1966), *Input-Output Economics,* Oxford University Press, New York.

Leontief, W.W. (1971), "Theoretical Assumptions and Non-Observed Facts," *American Economic Review,* Vol. 61, No. 1, pp. 1-7.

Lewis, J. Parry (1962), "The Conditions for Constant Growth in the Model of Raj and Sen," *Oxford Economic Papers*, No.2.

Lewis, R.S. (1973), "Agricultural Taxation and Intersectoral Resource Transfers," *Food Research Institute Studies,* Vol. 12, No. 2.

Lewis, W.A. (1955), *The Theory of Economic Growth,* Allen and Unwin, London.

Lewis, W.A. (1954), "Economic Development with Unlimited Supplies of Labour," *The Manchester School of Economics and Social Studies,* Vol. 20, May, pp. 139-191.

Lewis, W.A. (1966), *Development Planning,* George Allen and Unwin, London.

Lewis, W.A. (1972), "Reflections of Unlimited Labour," in *International Economics and Economic Development,* ed., L.E. DiMarco, Academic Press, New York.

Lewis, W.A. (1980), "The Slowing Down of the Engine of Growth," *American Economic Review,* Vol. 70, No. 4, pp. 535-64.

Lipton, M. (1962), "Balanced and Unbalanced Growth in Underdeveloped Countries," *Economic Journal,* September, pp. 641-57.

Little, I.M.D. (1960), "The Strategy of Indian Development," *National Institute of Economic Review,* No. 9, May 20-29.

Little, I.M.D. (1961), "The Real Cost of Labour and the Choice Between Consumption and Investment," *Quarterly Journal of Economics.*

Little, I.M.D. and Mirrlees, J.A. (1974). *Project Appraisal and Planning for Developing Countries,* Heinemann, London.

Little, I.M.D.; Scitovsky, T; and Scott, M. (1970), *Industry and Trade in Some Developing Countries: A Comparative Study*, Oxford University Press. London.

Lluch, C. (1973), "The Extended Linear Expenditure System," *European Economic Review,* Vol. 4, pp. 21-32.

Lluch, C. (1979), "Models of Employment and Income Distribution," *Journal of Development Economics,* Vol. 6, No. 1, pp 31-47.

Los. J. ed. (1978), *Computing Equlibria: How and Why,* North-Holland, Amsterdam.

Loucks, D.P. (1975), "Planning for Multiple Goals," in C.R. Blitzer et al. (eds.), op. cit.

Luenberger, D.G. (1972), "Mathematical Programming and Control Theory: Trends of Interplay," in A.M. Geoffrion (ed.) *Perspectives on Optimization*, Addison-Wesley, Reading, Mass.

Lysy, F. and L. Taylor (1980), "A Computable General Equilibrium Model for the Functional Distribution of Income: Experiments for Brazil, 1959-71," in L. Taylor et. al. op. cit.

Mac Evan, A. (1971), *Development Alternatives in Pakistan,* Harvard University Press, Cambridge, Mass.

Mahalanobis, P.C. (1955), "The Approach of Operational Research to Planning in India," *Sankhya,* December, pp. 3-131.

Mahalanobis, P.C. (1961), *Talks on Planning,* Asia Publishing House, Delhi.

Majumdar, K.C. and M.K. Panda (1982), "A Comparative Study of Sixth and Fifth Plan Models," *Economic and Political Weekly,* August 28, pp. 415-22.

Malinvaud, E. (1977), *The Theory of Unemployment Reconsidered*, Oxford University Press, London.

Malinvaud, E. (1981), "Econometrics Faced With the Needs of Macro-Economic Policy," *Econometrica*, Vol. 49, No. 6, pp. 1363-75.

Mammen, T. (1973), "Indian Money Market: An Econometric Study," *International Economic Review*.

Manove, M. (1971), "A Model of Soviet-type Economic Planning," *American Economic Review*, June, pp. 390-406.

Manove, M. and M. Weitzman (1978), "Aggregation for Material Balances," *Journal of Comparative Economics*, March, pp. 1-12.

Manne, A.S. (1966), "Key Sectors in the Mexican Economy, 1962-72," in I. Adelman and E. Thorbecke, eds., op. cit.

Manne, A.S. (1961), "Capacity, expansion and probabilistic growth," *Econometrica*, 29, pp. 632-649.

Manne, A.S. (1963), "Key Sectors in the Mexican Economy," in *Studies in Process Analysis*, ed., A.S. Manne and H.M. Markowitz, John Wiley and Sons, New York.

Manne, A.S. (1970), "Sufficient Conditions for Optimality in an Infinite Horizon Development Plan," *Econometrica*, Vol. 38, January, pp. 18-38.

Manne, A.S. (1974), "Multi-Sectoral Models for Development Planning: A Survey," *Journal of Development Economics*, Vol. 1, pp. 574-95.

Manne, A.S.; H. Chao and R. Wilson (1978), " Computation of Comparative Equilibria by Sequence of Linear Programmes", Mimeographed, Stanford University, Stanford.

Manne, A.S.; S. Kim and T.F. Wilson (1980), "A Three-Region Model of Energy, International Trade and Economic Growth,"

Mimeographed, Department of Operations Research, Stanford University, Stanford.

Manne, A.S. and A. Rudra (1965), "A Consistency Model for India's Fourth Plan," *Sankhya,* Series B., Vol. 27, February, pp. 57-144.

Manne, A.S. and T.E. Weisskopf (1970), "A Dynamic Multi-Sector Model of India: 1967-75," in A.P. Carter and A. Brody, (eds.) op. cit.

Marglin, S. A. (1963), "The Opportunity Cost of Public Investment". *Quarterly Journal of Economics.*

Marglin, S.A. (1967), "The Rate of Interest and the Value of Capital With Unlimited Supplies of Labour," in K. Shell (ed.), op. cit.

Markowitz, H.M. and A.S. Manne (1957), "On the Solution of Discrete Programming problems," *Econometrica*, pp. 84-110.

Marris, R. (1970), "Can We Measure the Need for Development Assistance," *Economic Journal,* pp. 650-668.

Martens, A. and R.S. Pindyck (1975), "An Optimal Control Model for Multi-Sectoral Investment Planning in Tunisia," *Journal of Development Economics,* June, pp. 99-120.

Marwah, K. (1963), *An Econometric Model of Price Behaviour in India,* Ph.D. Dissertation, Unpublished, University of Pennsylvania.

Marwah, K. (1972), "An Econometric Model of India: Estimating Prices, their Role and Sources of Change," *Indian Economic Review.*

Mathur, G. (1965), *Planning for Steady Growth,* Basel Blackwell, Oxford.

Mathur G. (1979), "Growth models and Analysis of Development," *World Development,* October, Vol. 7, No. 10, pp. 973-83.

Mathur, P.N. (1963), "Output and Investment for Exponential Growth in Consumption-An Alternative Formulation and Derivation of Their Technological Upper Limits," *Review of Economic Studies,* pp. 73-82.

Mathur, P.N. et al. (1969), "Input-Output Flow Table (32x32) 1963 (at purchasers prices)," in P.N. Mathur and P. Venkatramaiah (eds.), *Economic Analysis in Input-Output Framework*, Input-Output Research Association, Poona.

Matthews, R.C.O., ed. (1979), *Economic Growth and Resources: Trends and Factors,* Macmillan, New York.

Mayer, W. (1976), "The Rybczynski, Stolper-Samuelson and factor price equalization theorems under price uncertainty," *American Economic Review*, 66, pp. 797-808.

Mc Kinnon, R.E. (1964), "Foreign Exchange Constraints in Economic Development and Efficient Aid Allocation," *Economic Journal,* June, pp. 388-409.

Meade, J.E. (1961), *A Neo-classical Theory of Economic Growth,* George Allen & Unwin, London.

Meerman, J. (1979), *Public Expenditure in Malaysia: Who Benefits, and Why?* Oxford University Press, London.

Mehra, S. (1966), "Surplus Labour in Indian Agriculture, *Indian Economic Review*.

Mellor, J.W. (1974), *Economics of Agricultural Development.*

Melo, J.de (1977), "Distortions in the Factor Market: Some General Equilibrium Estimates," *The Review of Economics and Statistics,* No. 4, pp. 398-405.

Melo, J.de (1978), "Estimating the Costs of Protection: A General Equilibrium Approach," *Quarterly Journal of Economics,* No. 2, pp. 209-27.

Melo, J.de (1978a), "Tariffs and Resource Allocation in a Walrasian Trade Model," *International Economic Review.*

Melo, J.de (1980), "Tariffs and Resource Allocation in Partial and in General Equilibrium," *Welwirtschaftliches Archiv,* Band 116, pp. 114-30.

Melo, J.de, and K. Dervis (1977), "Modelling the Effects of Protection in a Dynamic Framework," *Journal of Development Economics,* pp. 149-72.

Melo, J.de, and S. Robinson (1978), "Tradeability in Trade Theory," Mimeographed, The World Bank, Washington, D.C.

Melo, J.de, and S. Robinson (1980), "The Impact of Trade Policies on Income Distribution in a Planning Model for Colombia," *Journal of Policy Modeling,* pp. 81-100.

Melo, M.de (1979), "Agricultural Policies and Development: A Socio-Economic Investigation Applied to Sri Lanka," *Journal of Policy Modeling,* Vol. I, No. 2, pp. 201-16.

Mennes, L.B.M.; J. Tinbergen, and J.G. Waardenburn (1969), *The Element of Space in Development Planning,* North-Holland, Amsterdam.

Michaely, M. (1977), "Exports and Growth: An Empirical Investigation," *Journal of Development Economics,* 4, January, 49-53.

Michalopoulos, C. (1975), "Production and Substitution in Two-Gap Models," *Journal of Development Studies,* Vol. II, No. 4, pp. 343-56.

Mincer, J. (1970), "The Distribution of Labour Incomes: A Survey with Special Reference to the Human Capital Approach," *Journal of Economic Literature,* Vol. 8, No. 1, pp. 1-26.

Minhas, B.S. (1968), "Growth with Stability: A Framework for Agricultural Planning," *Economic and Political Weekly,* Special No.

Mirrlees, J.N. and N.H. Stern (1972). "Fairly Good Plans," *Journal of Economic Theory*, April, pp. 268-288.

Mishan, E.J. (1976), *Cost Benefit Analysis,* Prager, New York.

Mitra, A. (1957), "A Note on the Mahalanobis' Models," *Economic Weekly,* March 16, pp. 372-374.

Mitra, Tapan (1981), "Efficiency, Weak Value Maximality and Weak Value optimality in a Multisector Model," *Review of Economic Studies,* October, Vol. 48, No. 4, pp. 643-47.

Mohammed, S. (1977), *Trade, Growth and Income Equality: A Case Study of India,* Unpublished Ph.D. Thesis, University of Delhi.

Mohammed, S. (1981), "Trade, Growth and Income Redistribution: A Case Study of India," *Journal of Development Economics,* August, Vol. 9, No. 1, pp. 131-47.

Montias, J.M. (1959), "Planning with Material Balances in Soviet-type Economies," *American economic Review*, Dec., pp. 963-85.

Morishima, M. (1973), *Marx's Economics: A Dual Theory of Value and Growth,* Cambridge University Press, Cambridge.

Morishima, M. (1977), *Walras' Economics: A Pure Theory of Capital and Money,* Cambridge University Press, Cambridge.

Morley, S.A., and G.W. Smith (1970), "On the Measurement of Import Substitution," *American Economic Review,* No. 4, pp. 728-35.

Morley, S. and G. Smith (1973), "The Effects of Changes in the Income, Labour, Foreign Investment and Growth in Brazil", in *Authoritarian Brazil: Origins, Policies and Future,* Yale University Press, New Haven.

Morley, S. and J.G. Williamson (1973), "The Impact of Demand on Labour Absorption and the Distribution of Earnings: The Case of Brazil," Programme of Development Studies, Paper No. 39, Rice University, Houston.

Murakami, Y.; K. Tokoyama: and J. Tsukui (1970), Efficient Paths of Accumulation and the Turnpike of the Japanese Economy," in A.P. Carter and A. Brody (eds.), op.cit.

Mussa, M. (1974), "Tariffs and the Distribution of Income: The Importance of Factor Specificity, Substitutability and Intensity in the Short and Long Run," *Journal of Political Economy*, Vol. 82, No. 6, pp. 1191-1203.

Myrdal, G. (1957), *Economic Theory and Underdeveloped Regions,* Duckworth, London.

Myrdal, G. (1968), *Asian Drama: An Enquiry into the Poverty of Nations,* Pantheon, New York.

Nachane, D.M. (1986), "Control Theory and Development Planning Models - an assessment," *International Journal of Development Planning Literature*, Oct-Dec., pp. 402-432.

Nanjundayya, B. and K.C. Majumdar (1974), "Growth, Social Justice and Self-reliance: A Rejoinder," *Economics and Political Weekly,* 27, April.

National Council of Applied Economic Research, (1983), *Present Status of the COMGEMI Model: Structure and Applicability,* (Mimeo), New Delhi.

Nayyar, D. (1976), "India's Export Performance in the 70s," *Economic and Political Weekly,* Vol. XI, No. 20.

Negishi, T. (1962), "On the Stability of a Competitive Economy: A Survey Article," *Econometrica*, October, pp. 635-69.

Neisser, H. (1956), "Investment Criteria, Productivity, and Economic Development," *Quarterly Journal of Economics,* November, pp. 644-646.

Nelson, P.R. (1970), "The Effective Exchange Rate: Employment and Growth in a Foreign Exchange Constrained Economy," *Journal of Political Economy,* Vol. 78, pp. 546-564.

Nerlove, M. (1966), "A Tabular Survey of Macro-Econometric Models," *International Economic Review,* No. 2, May, pp. 127-75.

Netherlands Economic Institute (1970), *The Identification of Potential Industries in Ethiopia,* Rotterdam.

Newbery, D. (1972), "Public Policy in the Dual Economy," *Economic Journal,* June, pp. 567-590.

Norton, H. (1971), "A Linear Programming Model of Regional Investment Allocation," Ph.D. Dissertation, Johns Hopkins University.

Nova, A. (1970), *The Soviet Economy*, George Allen & Unwin, London.

Nurkse, R. (1959), *Patterns of Trade and Development,* Almquist and Wiksell, Stockholm.

Nurkse, R. (1961), "Balanced and Unbalanced Growth," in *Equilibrium and Growth in the World Economy,* ed., G. Harberler and R.M. Stern, Harvard University Press, Cambridge, Mass.

Nurkse, R. (1963), *Problems of Capital Formation in Underdeveloped Countries,* Oxford University Press, Oxford.

Oppenheimer, P.M. (1974), "Non-traded Goods and the Balance of Payments: A Historical Note," *Journal of Economic Literature,* September, pp. 862-888.

Oppenheimer, P.M. (1975), "Non-trade Goods: A Rejoinder," *Journal of Economic Literature*, June, pp. 479-480.

Pack, H. (1971), *Structural Change and Economic Policy in Israel,* Yale University Press, New Haven.

Page, John M. Jr. (1982), *Shadow Prices for Trade Strategy and Investment Planning in Egypt,* World Bank Staff Working Paper No. 521, Washington, D.C.

Pandit, V. (1973), "Income and the Price Level in India, 1950-51 to 1965-66," *Sankhya,* Series B.

Pandit, V. (1982), "Macroeconomic Structure and Policy in a Less Developed Economy", Working Paper No. 235, Delhi School of Economics, Delhi.

Pandit, V. (1984), "Macroeconomic Adjustments in a Developing Economy: A Medium Term Model of Outputs and Prices in India," *Indian Economic Review,* 1984.

Pani, P.K. (1977), *Macroeconomic Model of India,* Macmillan, Delhi.

Papenck, G.F. (1972), "The Effect of Aid and Other Resource Transfers on Savings and Growth in the Developed Countries," *Economic Journal,* September, pp. 934-50.

Papenck, G.F. (1978), "Economic Growth, Income Distribution, and the Political Process in Less Developed Countries," in *Income Distribution and Economic Inequality,* ed., Z. Griliches et al., Campus Verlag, Frankfurt.

Paukert, F. (1973), "Income Distribution at Different Levels of Development: A Survey of Evidence." *International Labour Review,* August-September, pp. 97-125.

Paukert, F.; J. Solka, and J. Maton (1974), "Redistribution of Income, Patterns of Consumption and Employment: A Case Study of the Phillipines," Working Paper, WEP, ILO, May.

Phelps, E.S., ed. (1973), *Economic Justice,* Harmondsworth, Baltimore.

Phelps, E.S. and R.A. Pollak (1968), "On Second-Best National Saving and Game Equilibrium Growth," *Review of Economic Studies,* April, pp. 180-200.

Pindyck, R.S. (1973), *Optimal Planning for Economic Stabilization,* North-Holland, Amsterdam.

Planning Commission (1952), *The First Five Year Plan,* Government of India, New Delhi.

Planning Commission (1962), *Perspectives of Development: 1961-1976: Implications of Planning for a Minimum Level of Living,* Government of India, New Delhi.

Planning Commission (1964), *Notes on Perspective of Development, India 1960-61 to 1975-76*, Government of India, New Delhi.

Planning Commisison (1973), *A Technical Note on the Approach to the Fifth Plan of India, 1974-1979,* Government of India, New Delhi.

Planning Commission (1977), *Studies on the Structure of Indian Economy and Planning for Development,* Government of India, New Delhi.

Planning Commission (1978), *The Draft Five Year Plan 1978-1983,* Government of India, New Delhi.

Planning Commission (1981), *A Technical Note on the Sixth Plan of India (1980-85)*, Government of India, New Delhi.

Planning Commission (1986), *A Technical Note on the Seventh Plan of India (1985-90),* Government of India, New Delhi.

Polenske, K.R. and J. Skollka, eds. (1976), *Advances in Input-Output Analysis,* Ballinger, Cambridge, Mass.

Pomery, J. (1979), "Uncertainty and International Trade," in R. Dornbusch and T.A. Frenkel (eds.) *International Economic Policy*, Johns Hopkins Press, Baltimore.

Porters, R.C. (1970), "Terminal Year Investment in Finite Horizon Planning Models," *Pakistan Development Review,* No. 2.

Powell, A.A. (1981), "The Major Streams of Economy-Wide Modelling: Is Rapproachment Possible?" in J. Kmenta and J.B. Ramsey, eds., op cit.

Prasad, P.R. (1966), "Sectoral Models of Growth: A Critique," *Indian Economic Review*, April, Vol. 1, pp. 103-110.

Prest, A.R. and Turvey (1965), "Cost-Benefit Analysis," *Economic Journal.*

Preston, R.S. (1972), *The Wharton Annual and Industry Forecasting Model*, University of Pennsylvania, Philadelphia.

Pronk, J.P. and R.J. Schrauel (1969), "Some Reflections on the Effectiveness of Project Versus Plan Aid," in H.C. Bos (ed.), *Towards Balanced International Growth*, North-Holland, Amsterdam.

Psacharopoulos, O., and K. Hinchliffe (1972), "Further Evidence on the Elasticity of Substitution Among Different Types of Educated Labour," *Journal of Political Economy*, Vol. 80, No. 4, pp. 786-796.

Pyatt, G. (1976), "On the Interpretation and Disaggregation of Gini Coefficients," *The Economic Journal*, Vol. 86, No. 342, pp. 243-55.

Pyatt, G.; J. Bharier; R. Lindley; R. Mabro and Sabolo (1972), *A Methodology for Development Planning Applied to Iran*, Mimeographed, ILO Mission, Warwick, February.

Pyatt, G. and A. Roe (1977), *Social Accounting for Development Planning*, Cambridge University Press.

Pyatt, G. and J. Round (1979a), "Social Accounting Matrices for Development Planning," *The Review of Income and Wealth*, Series 23, No. 4, pp. 339-64.

Pyatt, G. and J. Round (1979b), "Accounting and Fixed Price Multipliers in a Social Accounting Matrix Framework," *Economic*

Journal, Vol. 89, pp. 850-73.

Pyatt, G. and E. Thorbecke (1976), *Planning Techniques for a Better Future,* International Labour Office, Geneva.

Qayum, A. (1960), *Theory and Policy of Accounting Prices,* North-Holland, Amsterdam.

Radner, R. (1975), "Economic Planning Under Uncertainty: Recent Theoretical Development," in M. Bornstein, ed., *Economic Planning: East & West*, Ballinger, Cambridge, Mass.

Raj, K. N. (1961), "Growth Models in Indian Planning, "*Indian Economic Review*, February, pp. 242-261.

Raj, K.N. and A.K. Sen (1961), "Alternative Patterns of Growth Under Conditions of Stagnant Export Earnings," *Oxford Economic Papers,* Vol. 13, February, pp. 43-52.

Ramana, D.N. (1969), *National Accounts and Input-Output Accounts of India,* Asia Publishing House, Bombay.

Ramsey, F.P. (1928), "A Mathematical Theory of Saving," *Economic Journal,* Vol. 38, pp. 543-559.

Ranis, G. (1973), "The Exchange Constraint on Development-A Partial Solution to the Problems: Comment," *Economic Journal.*

Rao, C.H.H. (1975), *Technological Change and the Distribution of Gains in Indian Agriculture*, Macmillan, New Delhi.

Ranis, G. and Fei, J.C.H. (1961), "A Theory of Economic Development," *American Economic Review,* September, pp. 533-65.

Rao, T.D. (1982), "Distribution of Urban Income and Wealth by Size," *Artha Vijnana,* June, No. 2, pp. 134-41.

Rawls, J. (1971), *A Theory of Justice,* Harvard University Press, Cambridge, Mass.

Reddaway, W.B. (1962), *The Development of Indian Economy,* Homewood, Irwin.

Reynolds, L.G. (1969), "Economic Development with Surplus Labour: Some Complications," *Oxford Economic Papers,* March, pp. 89-103.

Reserve Bank of India (1983), *An Econometric Model of Indian Economy,* Mimeographed, Econometric Division, Bombay.

Robbins, L. (1932), *The Nature and Significance of Economic Science,* London.

Robinson, Joan (1976), "Planning Models: Two Views," *Economic and Political Weekly,* 28 February, pp. 361-63.

Robinson, S. (1972), "Sources of Growth in Less Developed Countries: A Cross-Section Study," *Quarterly Journal of Economics,* pp. 391-408.

Robinson, S. (1976a), "A Note on the U Hypothesis Relating Income Inequality and Economic Development," *American Economic Review,* pp. 437-40.

Robinson, S. (1976b), "Income Distribution Within Groups, Among Groups, and Overall: A Technique of Analysis," Discussion Paper No. 65, Research Programme in Development Studies, Princeton University, Priceton, N.J.

Robinson, S. (1976c), "Toward an Adequate Long-Run Model of Income Distribution and Economic Development," *American Economic Review,* No. 2, pp. 122-7.

Robinson, S. and K. Dervis (1977), "Income Distribution and Socioeconomic Mobility: A Framework for Analysis and Planning," *Journal of Development Studies,* No. 4, pp. 347-64.

Robinson, S. and J.de. Melo (1976), "Planning Model Featuring Trade, Intra-sector Product Differentiation and Income Distribution," Discussion Paper No. 69, Princeton University,

Princeton, N.J.

Robinson, S. and Syung-Nak Song (1972), "A Dynamic Input-Output Model of the Korean Economy," Research Programme in Economic Development, Discussion Paper No. 30, Princeton University, Princeton, N.J.

Rodgers, G.B. (1975), "Nutritionally Based Wage Determination in the Low-Income Labour Market," *Oxford Economic Papers,* No. 1, March.

Rodgers, G.B.; M. Hopkins; and R. Wery (1977), "Population, Employment and Inequality: Bachue-Philippines," International Labour Office, Geneva.

Rodgers, G.; R. Wery; and M. Hopkins (1976), "The Myth of the Cave Revisited: Are Large-Scale Behavioral Models Useful," *Population and Development Review,* Vol. 2, No. 3-4, pp. 395-411.

Rosen, G. (1962), "A Note on the Patterns of Growth with Stagnant Export Earnings," *Oxford Economic Papers,* Vol. 14, No. 2.

Rosenstein-Rodan, P.N. (ed.) (1964), *Capital Formation and Economic Development,* George Allen and Unwin, London.

Rosenzweig, M. (1978), "Rural Wages, Labour Supply and Land Reform," *American Economic Review,* December.

Roumasset, J.A. (1976), *Rice and Risk*, North-Hollant, New York.

Round, Jeffery, I. (1982), "Social Accounting Matrices and Development Planning," in S.B. Dahiya, (ed.), op.cit.

Rudra, A. (1964), "Agriculture and Industry-Relative Rates of Growth," *Economic Weekly,* November, 7.

Rudra, A. (1972), "A Model Maker's Model," *Economic and Political Weekly,* February, pp. 337-342.

Rudra, A. (1975), *Indian Plan Models,* Allied Publishers, New Delhi.

Ruffin, R.J. (1974), "Comparative advantage Under uncertainty," *Journal of International Economics*, 4, pp. 243-259.

Saito, K.W. (1977), "The Determinants of Savings Behavior: A Survey of the Evidence." Development Economics Department, Memorandum (March), World Bank, Washington, D.C.

Saluja, M.R. (1968), "Structure of Indian Economy: Inter-Industry Flows and Pattern of Final Demand," *Sankhya,* Series, B, January, 1964-65.

Saluja, M.R. (1980), *Input-Output Tables for India*, Wiley Eastern, New Delhi.

Samuelson, P.A. (1947), *Foundations of Economic Analysis,* Harvard University Press, Cambridge, Mass.

Samuelson, P.A. (1951), "Abstract of Theorem Concerning Substitutability in Open Leontief Models," in *Activity-Analysis of Production and Allocation,* ed., T.C. Koopmans, Wiley, New York.

Samuelson, P.A. (1965), "A Catenery Turnpike Theorem Involving Consumption and Golden Rule," *American Economic Review,* June, pp. 486-496.

Samuelson, P.A. (1967), "Indeterminacy of Development in a Reterogeneous Capital Model with Constant Saving Propensity," in K. Shell (ed.) op. cit.

Sandee, J. (1959), *A Long Term Planning Model for India,* U.N. Report No. TAA/IND022, United Nations, New York.

Sandee, J. (1960), *A Demonstration Planning Model for India,* Asia Publishing House, New York.

Sanderson, W.C. (1980), "Economic-Demographic Simulation Model: A Review of Their Usefulness for Policy Analysis," International Institute for Applied Systems Analysis, Laxenburg, Austria.

Sarkar, H. and S.V. Subba Rao (1981), "A Short-term Macro Forecasting Model for India-Structure and Uses," *Indian Economic Review,* Vol. 16, Nos. 1-2, pp. 55-80.

Sarkar, H. and S.V. Subba Rao (1981a), "A Social Accounting Matrix of India for 1980-81," *Margin,* Vol. 13, No. 4, pp. 27-44.

Sarkar, H. and L. Taylor (1982), "Macro Planning Models for Development: Current Issues and Perspective," in S. Bhagwan Dahiya (ed.), op. cit.

Sarris, A.H., and I. Adelman (1982), "Incorporating Uncertainty into Planning of Industrialization Strategies for Developing Countries," World Bank Staff Working Paper No. 503, Washington, D.C.

Scarf, H. and T. Hansen (1973), *The Computation of Economic Equilibria,* Yale University Press, New Haven.

Scarf, H. and J. Shoven, eds. (1983), *Applied General Equilibrium,* Oxford University Press.

Scitovsky, T. (1954), "Two Concepts of External Economies," *Journal of Political Economy,* April, pp. 143-51.

Scott, M.F.G. (1962), "Alternative Patterns of Growth - A Comment," *Oxford Economic Papers,* Vol. 14, No. 2.

Selowsky, M. (1979), *Who Benefits from Government Expenditure: A Case Study of Colombia,* Oxford University Press, London.

Sen, A.K. (1957), "Some Notes on the Choice of Capital Intensity in Development Planning." *Quarterly Journal of Economics,* November, pp. 561-84.

Sen, A.K. (1961), "On Optimising the Rate of Saving," *Economic Journal,* September, pp. 479-496.

Sen, A.K. (1968), *Choice of Techniques*, Basil Blackwell, Oxford.

Sen, A.K. (1970), "Models of Education Planning and Their Applications," *Journal of Development Planning,* Vol. 2, United Nations, New York.

Sen, A.K. (1970a), *Collective Choice and Individual Welfare,* Holden-Day, San Francisco.

Sen, A.K. (1973), *On Economic Inequality,* Norton, New York.

Sen, A.K. (1974), "Poverty, Inequality and Unemployment: Some Conceptual Issues in Measurement," in P. Bardhan and T.N. Srinivasan, eds., op. cit.

Sen, A.K. (1975), *Employment, Technology and Development,* Oxford University Press.

Sengupta, J.K. (1972), *Stochastic Programming: Methods and Applications,* North-Holland, Amsterdam.

Sengupta, J.K. and V.Y. Rao (1963), "An Application of Stochastic Linear Programming to the Indian Planning Model," *Indian Journal of Economics,* January, pp. 139-154.

Sengupta, J.K. and G. Tintner (1963), "On Some Economic Models of Development Planning, "*Economia Internazionale,* February, pp. 34-50.

Shell, K. (ed.) (1967), *Essays on the Theory of Optimal Growth,* M.I.T. Press, Cambridge, Mass.

Sims, Christopher A. (1980), "Macroeconomics and Reality," *Econometrica,* January, pp. 1-48.

Sinha, Narain (forthcoming), *Whither Indian Econometric Models-A Survey,* Mimeographed, Institute of Economic Growth, Delhi.

Sinha, Narain, (1986), *A Structural Model for Indian Economy,* R.B.S.A. Publishers, Jaipur.

Sinha, Radha; Peter Pearson; Gopal Kadekodi; and Mary Gregory, (1982), "A Model for Income Distribution and Growth in India," in D.B. Gupta, Y.C. Halan; and P.B. Desai (eds.) *Development Planning and Policy*, Wiley Eastern, New Delhi.

Sinha, R.P. et al. (1978), *Poverty, Income Distribution and Employment in India,* University of Glasgow, Mimeographed.

Skolka, J. and Garguel (1976), "Changes in Income Distribution, Employment and Structure of the Economy: A Case Study of Iran," Working Paper No. 45, September, WEP, ILO, Geneva.

Soligo, R. (1973), "Factor-Intensity of Consumption Patterns, Income Distribution and Employment Growth in Pakistan," Programme of Development Studies, Paper No. 44, Rice University, Houston.

Solow, R. (1956), "A Contribution to the Theory of Economic Growth," *Quarterly Journal of Economics,* February, Vol. 70, pp. 65-94.

Solow, R. (1970), *Growth Theory: An Exposition,* Oxford University Press, New York.

Spulber, D.F. (1986), "Economic Planning With Rolling Horizons", *International Journal of Development Planning Literature,* October-December, pp. 433-41.

Spulber, N. and R.A. Becker (1986), "Theoretical Issues in Optimal Planning," *International Journal of Development Planning Literature,* July-September, pp. 237-54.

Squire, L. and H. Van Der Tak (1975), *Economic Analysis of Projects,* Johns Hopkins Press, Baltimore, Md.

Sraffa, Piero (1960), *Production of Commodities by Means of Commodities,* Cambridge University Press, Cambridge.

Srinivasan, T.N. (1962), "Investment Criteria and Choice of Techniques of Production," *Yale University Economic Essays.*

Srinivasan, T.N. (1965), "A Critique of the Optimising Planning Model," *Economic Weekly,* February,

Srinivasan, T.N. (1975), "The Foreign Trade Sector in Planning Models," in C.R. Blitzer et al., op. cit.

Srinivasan, T.N. (1977), "Development, Poverty and Basic Needs: Some Issues", *Food Research Institute Studies,* Vol. 16, No. 2.

Srinivasan, T.N. (1981), "Malnutrition," *Journal of Development Economics,* February, Vol. 8, No. 3.

Srinivasan, T.N.; M.R. Saluja, and J.C. Sabharwal (1965), "Studies in the Structure of the Indian Economy," Discussion Paper No. 4, Indian Statistical Institute, New Delhi.

Srivastava, D.K. (1981), "Policy Simulation with a Macroeconomic Model of the Indian Economy", *Journal of Policy Modelling.*

Steiner, P.O. (1959), "Choosing Among Alternative Public Investments in the Water Resources Field," *American Economic Review.*

Stern, N.H. (1972), "Optimum Development in a Dual Economy," *Review of Economic Studies,* April.

Stewart, J.R. (1978), "Potential Effects of Income Redistribution on Economic Growth: An Expanded Estimating Procedure Applied to Mexico," *Economic Development and Cultural Change,* No. 3, April.

Stoleru, L.G. (1965), "An Optimal Policy for Economic Growth," *Econometrica,* April, pp. 321-48.

Stone, R. (1954), "Linear Expenditure System and Demand Analysis: An Application to the pattern of British Demand". *Economic Journal,* pp. 511-27.

Stone, R., and J.A.C. Brown (1962), "Output and Investment for Exponential Growth in Consumption," *Review of Economic Studies,*

No. 80, pp. 241-45.

Streeten, P. (1972), *The Frontiers of Development Studies,* Macmillan, London.

Strotz, R. (1956), "Myopia and Inconsistency in Dynamic Utility Maximization," *Review of Economic Studies*, No. 3, pp. 165-180.

Sukhatme, P.V. (1977), "Nutrition and Poverty," Ninth Lal Bahadur Shastri Memorial Lecture, Indian-Agricultural Institute, New Delhi.

Syrquin, M. (1976), "Sources of Industrial Growth and Change: An Alternative Measure," Mimeographed, The World Bank, Washington, D.C.

Syrquin, M.; L. Taylor; and L. Westphal, eds. (1983), *Economic Structure and Performance: Essays in Honour of Hollis B. Chenery,* Academic Press.

Szal, R., and S. Robinson (1977), "Measuring Income Inequality," in C.R. Frank Jr. and R. Webb, eds., op. cit.

Takayama, T. and G.C. Judge (1971), *Spatial and Temporal Price and Allocation Models,* North-Holland, Amsterdam.

Taylor, L. (1969), "Development Patterns: A Simulation Study," *Quarterly Journal of Economics,* May, pp. 220-41.

Taylor, L. (1971), "Investment Timing in Two-Gap Models," in H.B. Chenery (ed.), op. cit.

Taylor, L. (1975), "Theoretical Foundations and Technical Implications," in C.R. Blitzer et al., op. cit.

Taylor, L. (1976), "Book Keeping Function," *Economic and Political Weekly,* 28 February, pp. 361-63.

Taylor, L. (1979), *Macro Models for Developing Countries,* McGraw Hill, New York.

Taylor, L.; E. Bacha; E. Cardoso; and F. Lysy (1980), *Models of Growth and Distribution for Brazil,* Oxford University Press, London.

Taylor, L.; P. Ide; and E. Sheshinski (1971), "System Manual for a Forecasting Model of the Chilean Economy," Mimeographed, Harvard University.

Taylor, L. and F. Lysy (1979), "Vanishing Income Redistributions: Keynesian Clues About Model Surprises in the Short Run", *Journal of Development Economics,* pp. 17-30.

Tendulkar, S.D. (1971), "Interaction between Domestic and Foreign Resources in Economic Growth: Some Experiments for India," in H.B. Chenery, ed., op. cit.

Tendulkar, S.D. (1974a), "Planning for Growth, Redistribution and Self-reliance in the Fifth Five Year Plan," *Economic and Political Weekly,* January 12 and 19, pp. 27-40 and 63-80.

Tendulkar, S.D. (1974b), "Planning Models for Growth and Distribution in India: An Assessment," in T.N. Srinivasan and P.K. Bardhan (eds.), *Poverty and Income Distribution in India: an Assessment,* Statistical Publishing Society, Calcutta.

Tendulkar, Suresh D. (1977), "Planning Process, Planning Commission and Rollover Planning-Some Basic Issues," *Economic and Political Weekly*, October.

Thisen, J.K. (1983), "An Input-Output Approach for Sectoral Output and Employment Planning: Case Study of Algeria," Unpublished manuscript.

Theil, H. (1958), *Economic Forecast and Policy,* North-Holland, Amsterdam.

Theil, H. (1964), *Optimal Decision Rules for Government and Industry,* North-Holland, Amsterdam.

Tinbergen, J. (1939), *Business Cycles in the U.S.A.: 1919-32*. League of Nations, Geneva. (Agathon Press, New York, 1968 Edition).

Tinbergen, J. (1952), *On the Theory of Economic Policy*, North-Holland, Amsterdam.

Tinbergen, J. (1954), *Centralization and Decentralization in Economic Policy*, North-Holland, Amsterdam.

Tinbergen, J. (1955), "The Relevance of Theoretical Criteria in the Selection of Investment Plans," in *Investment Criteria and Economic Growth*, ed., M. Millikan, Cambridge University Press, Cambridge.

Tinbergen, J. (1956, 1964), *Economic Policy: Principles and Design*, North-Holland, Amsterdam.

Tinbergen, J. (1958), *The Design of Development*, Johns Hopkins Press, Baltimore.

Tinbergen, J. (1959a); *Selected Papers*, edited by L.H. Klassen; L.M. Koyck, and H.J. Witteveen, North-Holland, Amsterdam.

Tinbergen, J. (1959b), "On the Theory of Income Distribution," in J. Tinbergen, *Selected Papers*, op. cit.

Tinbergen, J. (1960), "Optimum Savings and Utility Maximization Over Time," *Econometrica*, April, Vol. 29, pp. 481-89.

Tinbergen, J. (1964), *Central Planning*, Yale University, New Haven.

Tinbergen, J. (1966a), *Essays in Regional and World Planning*, NCAER, New Delhi.

Tinbergen, J. (1966b), "Some Refinements of the Semi-Input-Output Method," *Pakistan Development Review*, Vol. 6, No. 2, pp. 243-247.

Tinbergen, J. (1967), *Development Planning*, Mc Graw Hill, New York.

Tinbergen, J. (1986), "Income Distribution and Development," *International Journal of Development Planning Literature*, No. 1, January-March.

Tinbergen, J. and H.C. Bos (1962), *Mathematical Models of Economic Growth,* Mc Graw Hill, New York.

Tinbergen, J. and H.C. Bos, (1964), "A Planning Model for the Educational Requirements of Economic Development," in *The Economics of Education: The Residual Factor and Economic Growth,* OECD, Paris.

Tsukui, J. (1968), "Application of a Turnpike Theorem to Planning for Efficient Accumulation: An Example for Japan," *Econometrica,* January, pp. 172-186.

Tsukui, J. and Y. Murakami (1979), *Turnpike Optimality in Input-Output System,* North-Holland, Amsterdam.

Tsuru, S. (1957), "Some Theoretical Doubts on India's Plan-frame," *Economic Weekly*, January, pp. 77-79.

Turnovsky, S.J. (1974), "Technological and Price Uncertainty in a Ricardian Model of International trade," *Review of Economic Studies*, 41, 201-217.

United Nations (1968), *A System of National Accounts,* Series F, No. 2, Rev. 3, United Nations, New York.

United Nations Statistical Office (1975), *Towards a System of Social and Demographic Statistics,* Department of Economics and Social Affairs, ST/ESA/STAT, SERF, 18, United Nations, New York.

Uzawa, H. (1964), "Optimal Growth in a Two-Sector Model of Capital Accumulation," *Review of Economic Studies,* January, 1-24.

Vaidyanathan, A. (1956), "A Survey of the Literature on Investment Criteria and Development of Underdeveloped Countries," *Indian Economic Journal,* October, 122-44.

Vashist, B.K. (1979), "A Programming Model of Educational Planning for Haryana," Unpublished Ph.D. Thesis, Kurukshetra University, Kurukshetra.

Venkatramaiah, P. et al. (1972), "Input-Output Table for India, 1963", *Artha Vijnana*.

Venkatramaiah, P.; A.R. Kulkarni and Argade (1975), "Regional Input-Output Matrices, India 1955," *Artha Vijnana*, reprint series, Gokhale Institute of Politics and Economics, Pune.

Vernon, R., ed. (1970), *The Technology Factor in International Trade*, Columbia University Press, New York.

Visaria, Pravin (1981), "Poverty and Unemployment in India: An Analysis of Recent Evidence," *World Development*, No. 3, March, pp. 277-300.

Watanabe, S. (1972), "Exports and Employment: The Case of Republic of Korea," *International Labour Review*, No. 6, December.

Watanabe, T. (1961), "A Test of the Constancy of Input-Output Coefficients among Countries," *International Economic Review*, September, pp 340-50.

Weisskoff, Richard (1972), "A Multi-Sector Simulation Model of Employment, Growth and Income Distribution in Puerto Rico: A Re-Evaluation of "Successful" Development Strategy," Mimeographed, Yale University, New Haven, Conn.

Weisskoff, T.E. (1967), "A Programming Model for Import Substitution in India," *Sankhya*, Series B, December, pp. 257-306.

Weisskopf, T.E. (1971), "Alternative Patterns of Import Substitution in India," in H.B. Chenery, ed., op. cit.

Weisskopf, T.E. (1972), "The Impact of Foreign Capital Inflow on Domestic Savings in Underdeveloped Countries." *Journal of International Economics*, February, 25-38.

Weitzman, M.L. (1971), "Shiftable Versus Non-Shiftable Capital: A Synthesis," *Econometrica,* pp. 511-530.

Westphal, L.E. (1971a), *Planning Investments with Economies of Scale,* North-Holland, Amsterdam.

Westphal, L.E. (1971b), "An Intertemporal Planning Model Featuring Economies of Scale," in H.B. Chenery, ed., op. cit.

Westphal, L.E. (1975), "Planning with Economies of Scale," in C.R. Blitzer; P.B. Clark, and L. Taylor, eds., op. cit.

Westphal, L.E. and Kim, K.S. (1977), "Industrial Policy and Development in Korea," World Bank Staff Working Papers, No. 263, Washington, D.C.

Willes, P. (1956), "Growth Versus Choice," *Economic Journal,* June, pp. 244-55.

Yaari, M. (1964), "On the Consumer's Life-time Allocation Process," *International Economic Review,* September, pp. 304-317.

Yap, L. (1975), "Internal Migration in Less Developed Countries: A Survey of the Literature," World Bank Staff Working Paper No. 215, Washington, D.C.

Index